One Woman's Spiritual Adventures

Friends in High Places

Conversations with the Dead

KATIE LETCHER LYLE

No part of this publication may be reproduced
in whole or in part, or stored in a retrieval system,
or transmitted in any form or by any means,
electronic, mechanical, photocopying, recording,
or otherwise, without written permission of the author,
except for the inclusion of brief quotations in a review.
For information regarding permission, please write to:
info@barringerpublishing.com

Copyright © 2011 Katie Letcher Lyle
All rights reserved.

Barringer Publishing, Naples, Florida
www.barringerpublishing.com
Cover, graphics, layout design by Lisa Camp
Editing by Carole Greene
Cover photography by Kekoa

ISBN: 978-0-9833088-8-1
Library of Congress Cataloging-in-Publication Data
Friends in High Places / Katie Letcher Lyle

Printed in U.S.A.

All characters appearing in this work are fictitious.
Any resemblance to real persons, living or dead, is purely coincidental.

Table of Contents

1. Visiting Ghosts 5
2. The Light of Reason 33
3. Midlife School: The Monroe Institute 56
4. Reincarnation: Joseph's Case 98
5. Spirit Retrieval, AKA Ghost Busting 103
Photos 145
6. Rockbridge Area Hospice 151
7. Imagination: The Eyes of the Soul 160
8. Weighing London Psychics 176
9. Hidden Help: My Upstairs Crew 196
10. Remote Viewing: The Proof 202
11. Way-Out Stuff: Talking to Other Species 221
12. Talking to the Dead in Church 236
13. Just Remember: A Message from the Dead 242
Final Comment 262
Endnote 264
Grateful Thanks 267
Bibliography 269
About the Author 274

Friends in High Places

1. Visiting Ghosts

Recently, I believe I experienced my first ghost. Experienced, as in "felt." I had occasion, on a Mexican dig, to spend the night in the jungle, in a hammock in a Mayan hut. Twelve other people were in the hut in hammocks, too. I awoke to experience small hands fooling with my feet. I was sure it was one of the many children who lived in the compound of four huts, five dogs, two pigs, a cow, and eighteen people that I counted. I lay there and waited a moment, puzzled, then sat up slowly so as not to alarm the child. There was absolutely nothing there. Just my backpack leaning against a table leg, everyone else asleep.

Next morning, I told the story to my Mayan guide, who absolutely believed me, and consulted with the family. They had lost two children. There was a cenote (well) nearby, and they believed that was where the ghosts of dead children dwelt. They believed one of them had visited me in the night. Even more recently (yesterday) at our local Habitat Resale Store, where I volunteer for several hours a week, a fellow volunteer, as we were chatting about this book, said that once in his long life, he too had a visitation from a ghost. Norris Aldridge was a college sophomore when he was awakened early one morning by a woman's voice demanding that he wake up. It was clear and insistent. He was extremely puzzled to find no one around who'd called him. He went on to class, and learned later that his grandmother had died at just the time a female voice called him to wake up.

Ghosts! How we love them! How we fear them, even if we don't believe in them! Ghost stories crop up *everywhere*, in all cultures. That is my first reason, right there, to consider that maybe ghosts do exist, and are real. I myself have never seen a ghost, but it's a subject that I have forever been fascinated with. And I know tons of people I trust who have seen ghosts.

I don't talk to many people about this subject (or spiritual subjects in general), as it doesn't seem a great topic for cocktail parties and dinners. I am an academic, live in a small academic town that prides itself on rational, no-nonsense thinking. But occasionally I do get into an interesting conversation on the subject of life after death. I do sometimes ask people if they've ever seen a ghost. And when I do, I am amazed at how matter-of-fact people can be on the subject, and how many people have seen ghosts, or claim to have.

You may wonder how sane I am. Some of this book may call my sanity into question. Here's who I am: a writer, actually seventy-two, though inside perhaps not yet out of my teens. I am a consumer of all esoteric literature, a mate to a man one year older than I am who has changed my life in wonderful ways. I was married forty years, the last two decades made fairly miserable because my husband fell ill with the terrible disease of alcoholism.

I had a happy childhood, and a congenial and successful career as a college English professor, a moderately successful writing career with twenty books you can still buy on Amazon, membership on many local boards, most notably our area Hospice for the last fourteen years. Except for a few Elderhostels each year that I teach at the nearby Natural Bridge

Friends in High Places

Hotel conference site, my academic career is winding down. That's okay with me; at some point we have to pass the reins to a younger, more hip, generation. I'm lucky to be healthy, and take no prescription drugs, which I think is a good sign. With dedicated and convivial women, I take aerobics three times a week, and three more days a week I walk four miles with another chatty and congenial bunch of women. Nick (my partner) and I socialize, travel as much as we can afford, and live fairly quietly. We both enjoy good food and drink. We don't see any point in getting married. On Saturdays, I take a zumba dance class.

What else do you need to know? Oh, I am the mother of a forty-year old landscaper, my good and gorgeous son, mother-in-law to his lovely wife, and the mother of a 33-year-old handicapped daughter whose gentleness and wisdom I stand in awe of, and whose life I've documented in my memoir *All Time Is Now*. Jennie has always been one of my pathways to light. I love cats and currently am slave to three. At one time in the late fifties during the period I remember was called "urban renewal," I was a folk singer in Baltimore, then Nashville. I have been a fairly frequent public speaker. I divorced my husband—in desperation—in 2002, after roughly seventeen years of despair and darkness.

In 1991 I accidentally launched myself on what has turned out to be a serious search for spiritual meaning. At over seventy, I suppose I naturally want to believe that we survive death. I thought—at the time I inadvertently stepped on a spiritual path—that I was just writing a magazine article about a curious man (Robert Monroe) whose book I'd read (and found interesting, although I concluded that he was crazy). I have to be clear: I was an atheist and, having rejected Christianity, found nothing to replace it. Religion, which offers answers for many, hasn't worked for me. Not ever, really, despite many years of being what's called a "good Episcopalian," paying attention to sermons, loving the liturgy, singing in the choir, helping with the annual bazaar, presiding over the

Katie Letcher Lyle

Young People's Group, and teaching Sunday School to the little folks. But I found little light in my church immersion. In the fifties I watched my father (then the Senior Warden) get up in the middle of a sermon, walk rapidly down the center aisle, slam the doors and leave the church forever, because he wouldn't tolerate the church's integrating. But I stayed. I loved how Robert E. Lee Memorial Episcopal Church smelled, and the way the sunlight of late morning lit up the gorgeous stained glass over the altar. I probably became a writer at least partially as a result of being weekly washed in the beautiful language of the King James Bible, and the years of learning and singing the uplifting hymns of the 1940 Episcopal hymnal. I listened carefully to the sermons. I left the church, I admit, possibly for wrong reasons, one day when I was about twenty and home from college, and there was a guest in the choir with a magnificent voice. Her name was Dolores Jones, and I later learned that she was a famous opera singer from Baltimore. But as I left the choir room after changing out of my black robe and white surplice into my Sunday clothes, one of the old church stalwarts stopped me on the sidewalk of the church, and said, "My goodness, but you certainly did look white sitting up there in the choir next to that Nigger." I recall actually gasping. Though I do not count myself a great liberal, that was the excuse I needed to leave, for she epitomized the mean and spiritually unenlightened people that church seemed full of—and my father had not been the only one who left over integration. But if that sent me running, how deep was my so-called Christian faith? Like an oil-slick on deep water, as it turned out.

Later I tried to join the Catholics in college—thinking they were the real, original Christians and thus more seriously Christian, than others—but I was politely refused. If I couldn't accept the virgin birth and Jesus literally rising from the dead, I was obviously not someone they wanted to deal with. Attracted to a gorgeous young (and unmarried!) rabbi, I briefly applied myself to Judaism. But that ended with the end of the

Friends in High Places

relationship, which came breath-takingly soon. As a ten-year-old I'd joined the Rosicrucians (well, as I recall, it was only five dollars to do so), and for years inhaled their literature that promised, but did not deliver, "the secrets of the ages."

One time twenty years ago I found a local Methodist minister who was a secret Buddhist, and I joined a clandestine Sunday-night group in his basement. But it involved too much silent meditation for my tastes, and after the thrill of the secret meetings wore off, I dropped out of that group too, though the letting-go-of-the-world part of Buddhism is appealing. I attended a black church briefly, because there was so much feeling in the gospel singing, and I respond emotionally to music I love. But I was the only white person, and after four visits I realized that, kind as they all were to me, they were wary of what this crazy blonde writer was doing in their midst. I befriended one of their members, a woman about my age who also came to Weight Watchers with me, and we walked together for several months. But there were chasms between us: race, class, education, experience, and religion turned out to be barriers that confounded us. I persisted long after she realized we weren't destined to become close friends.

My quest in this book is to find out what, if anything, happens when our earthly lives end. Each chapter represents another step in what I guess you'd call one woman's spiritual development. I think I do offer proof that humans—at least some part of humans—can (and maybe always does) survive death. There has never been a time in my life that I wasn't fascinated by this mystery, but an accident when I was fifty-three set my feet on a path to finding out. Our culture is silent on how to die, and what happens after death. My work with Hospice has taught me how separated we are from dying, from death, in modern America.

This memoir is about how I came to believe that we survive death. I need to add that at no time have I had one of those transcendent at-one-with-God experiences that often turn infidels into believers. I read hungrily and enviously about those, knowing at the same time it would probably scare me to death to have one.

But I am a believer. I have become spiritual as a result of a lifetime of searching for light. If nothing else, the numbers might convince me. So the first thing I do is offer some new ghost stories that came to me following the publication of *My Neighbors' Ghosts*, which is about exactly what the title says: ghost stories *others* have related to me. I wanted so fiercely to tell the truth that I published only the stories that respondents would let me recount with their names attached.

I tell about our ghost-busting, more reasonably called "spirit retrieval," as we don't bust anything. We sent spirits into the light. What light? Just THE LIGHT. We probably all understand it a bit differently. Herein I use the words "Light" and "Darkness" loosely, to signify knowing or ignorance in spiritual matters, ecstasy or despair.

If the dead were really dead, no stories like the following ones would ever come to our ears. And in fact, they come every day, all the time, from every culture in the world. People tell them to me because my last book was a book of ghost stories related to me by friends and family.

This first one is very old, told to me by my friend and neighbor, Taylor Sanders, professor of classics at Washington and Lee University, who translated it from the original.

"I found him on the beach, murdered. Taking pity, I buried him and marked the spot.

"Sometime after, I was planning a trip by ship. The dead man came to me at night and told me not to go. I did not go, and the ship went down and the three of my friends who went were drowned.

"So I returned to the burial place and marked it with a new marker: 'Here lies the man who saved Simonides' life.'"

Simonides of Ceos, Fragments, 550-460 BC

Friends in High Places

The most recent ghost *story* I heard literally this evening, when I had a friend, a recent widower, to supper. He asked what I was writing (everyone does, of course, since that is how I am known locally), so I told him a book about *talking to the dead*. Immediately, Uncas, a law professor, said, "You know, that's interesting. Anne (his dead wife) comes to me in the guise of a crow. And sometimes she just gives me hell!" There was no doubt; he spoke matter-of-factly, and went on to tell me several stories of recent unusual "crow" contacts he'd had. He had no doubt they were his wife from beyond the grave still talking to him.

I know that a whole bunch of folks out there would probably put me in an insane asylum for taking seriously the idea that after death, the dead are still in some sense alive. I mean, that would be a requisite for communicating with them, right? (And I do!) As a skeptic for my first five decades plus, I deeply understand that doubting point of view; in fact, it is the firm, unrelenting view of two of my closest women friends with whom I interact several times a week.

So when I was fifty-three, I happened to lurch out looking for a writing assignment, and instead discovered the spiritual home I'd been looking for all my life. The information on the subject of life after death is, of course. all anecdotal, since we can't demand that Granny come back and talk so *others* can hear, and then record her comments. But in the last two decades I have come to know that often we can learn from the dead information that we did not have before speaking with them. So I visited and interviewed Bob Monroe, and this book contains a chapter about my introduction to The Monroe Institute.

My friends Fletcher and Margaret Collins (dead now for half a dozen years) lived in Staunton, Virginia, in a house built and lived in by Jedediah Hotchkiss, Stonewall Jackson's Civil War mapmaker. When Hotchkiss's maiden daughter Nellie died at age ninety-four in the 1940s, the Collins bought the house, so there were no other inhabitants between

Katie Letcher Lyle

the Hotchkisses and them.

Both Margaret and Fletcher have felt the spirits of Nellie and Jed in the house; Fletcher, especially, says he feels the spirit of Jed breathing on his neck when he attempts to repair something in the house. Fletcher has found some big rocks buried in the yard, and believes that Jed buried them there because Nellie said, "Get those ugly rocks out of the house!" Fletch claims to understand Nellie's personality through sixty years of association with her spirit, and avows that he and Jed are "intellectual companions." This from a sane and highly intelligent patron of the arts who has mentored sixty years of Mary Baldwin college students.

Once you begin looking for "evidence," of ghosts, it's all over the place. For example, my book *The Man Who Wanted Seven Wives* was about a West Virginia ghost story; it's, in fact, the only case in the annals of American law in which the testimony of a ghost has ever been allowed in a court as evidence, which I of course found fascinating, though at that time I was still a disbeliever in ghosts. In that case from 1897, there was only circumstantial evidence that the death of a young bride of three months was by her husband's hand—except for the surprising fact that the ghost of the young woman returned from the dead to tell on her husband!

Zona Heaster Shue's death appeared at first an accident. But her mother reported widely that in the weeks to follow, the dead girl had appeared to her four times, appearing in the flesh and in the gown she'd been buried in. Zona told her mother how she'd been strangled by her husband, and that the first knob of her spine was crushed, and other specific details, such as that her husband had killed her in a rage because she had no meat prepared for supper.

Her mother took the story to the prosecuting attorney, and apparently was persuasive enough that, a month after the funeral, the girl's body was dug up for autopsy. Her top vertebra was found crushed, and there was *no meat in her stomach*. Her husband was convicted of her death on

Friends in High Places

circumstantial evidence, since there were no witnesses. The ghost story as related by her mother was part of the trial transcript.

At the time, I disbelieved the mother's testimony about the ghost, and came up with what I thought was a convincing rational explanation of the ghost's supposed testimony.

But I got a letter from the famous Ian Stevenson, with whom I became friends after he'd read my book, telling me that in 1897 the head of the American branch of the Spiritualist Association of Great Britain (the SAGB), re-investigated this case. Richard Hodgson returned to the scene of the crime, re-interviewed everyone involved with the case, and came to believe that there was a strong case for the information about the young woman's death having been supernaturally received. He decided that the ghost's telling her mother how she had been murdered, and the subsequent disinterment and autopsy providing the exact information about how the woman had been killed, was inarguably true. Thus this became one of the most solid cases on record of the return of the dead. I actually found another explanation for the events, but you'd have to read the book. A doubter, a skeptic, as I was then, can always find another explanation.

Now I believe that Zona Heaster Shue indeed returned from the other side and talked to her mother, in the end, balancing the scales of justice. As an attempt to "right" my mistaken conclusions, in 1995 I published a second edition of that book with the SAGB information added.

So what actually happened to make me a believer? That's what this book is about. And it's not esoteric. Many, many people, it turns out, are visited by dead loved ones or friends. And we can visit our beloved dead. It's natural, and normal, and anyone can do it.

In January 2009 an old friend, Bob Moore, feeling low, called to talk. His wife Ellen had recently died. He asked what I was writing these days.

When I told him, he didn't miss a beat, just solemnly said, "Oh yeah. Ellen's been here every night. She told me to repaint the living room, and she told me what color. It's almost done." He was completely blasé about it.

Before I could stop him, Bob went on: "Y' know, when I was a kid, my grandma told me this story, many times. When one of her kids was sick one time, after several days, she was real tired taking care of him, and he wasn't any better. One night she went out on the porch and sat down in the rocking chair. Didn't mean to, but fell asleep. My grandfather, who'd been dead sixteen years, walked up the front steps. She woke up, said, `What are you doin' here?' And he said, `You need to take that kid to the doctor. He's real sick.' She woke up and he was gone, just like that. She almost didn't do what he said, since it was just like a dream, but then she did, and the kid had spinal meningitis, and would have died if he hadn't been taken to the hospital right then."

Ghosts often speak to people in dreams. If ghosts exist, this makes sense because our brains may be less protected, more vulnerable to subtle communications, when we are asleep. In the daytime we have to focus on the here and now, our day-lives. It's recorded, for instance, that the night before Julius Caesar's murder, his wife dreamed he fell dead across her lap.

Angela Gibson, a lovely, earnest woman who called me up after my last book, *My Neighbors' Ghosts,* came out, told me a rather astonishing story about a dead man speaking to her baby. When her son Johnny was only nine months old, in Abilene Texas sixteen years ago, he suddenly went from not talking to talking in whole sentences. As if that weren't enough, his mother would listen in on the baby monitor from the kitchen to him apparently gabbing with someone. When she went and asked, "Honey, who were you talking to?" he replied, "The man."

"What man?" his alarmed mother said.

Friends in High Places

"My guardian angel," the baby, still under a year old, replied. Then he said something odd, something that puts shivers up his mother's back even today: "His name is Stonewall Jackson. He told me he loves me, that I'm a smart little boy, and that he will watch over me always."

What an odd name her baby had come up with! His mother couldn't imagine where that came from. Stone Wall Jackson? She wrote down the name, fortunately kept a record of everything, including her son's claim that the guardian angel with the strange name had a smashed-down cap tilted over his face, and a beard.

As any Civil War buff knows, Virginia's hero, Stonewall Jackson, reportedly wore his cap like that. But Angela didn't know that, didn't know anything about the Civil War, and had in fact never heard of the famous warrior.

Moreover, the child of nine months of course knew nothing about the Civil War general and hero to millions, nor could he have known anything about guardian angels!

The clincher of the story is that the child's father twenty months later (when the baby was two and a half), got transferred from Texas to teach at a place Angela and her husband had never heard of—Virginia Military Institute in Lexington, Virginia—which is where Stonewall Jackson taught, lived, and was buried following his accidental death by his own men in 1863.

The child John is now grown and has long forgotten his conversations with his babyhood friend, which his mother fortunately wrote down. John attends VMI, where Jackson taught.

My artist friend Mark Cline, builder of wondrous gigantic dinosaurs and creator of a tourist attraction near Natural Bridge called Foamhenge, Virginia (it's a ¾ scale styrofoam model of Guess What), as well as a local columnist for our paper, wrote a while back of being at our local downtown celebration on Memorial Day of 2007. He noticed fondly the veterans and speakers leaning against the wall of the old bank building. He was glad to see among them his friend, World War II vet Carl Camden. A few weeks after that, Mark sauntered into McDonald's one day and nodded to a bunch of his friends there, including, once again, Carl.

As he stood in line to order, he noticed an article about Carl Camden tacked up on the bulletin board. He was shocked to see that the first sentence said Camden had died in late October of the previous year.

To quote Mark, "No way! I had just seen him sitting there at the table. I'd seen him before that on November 12. He'd have been deceased—by then—at least two weeks. How could it be? I saw him there! Or did I?"

Mark got out of line at McDonald's to go back and look, and Carl was not there among the others, though Mark swears he'd just seen him.

My friend and fellow seeker, the blogger and writer Frank de Marco, in his online book details his year-long communications with a dead man. In *Chasing Smallwood* he writes:

"Common sense says that we cannot talk to the dead, nor they to us. But this 'common sense' depends upon unstated assumptions: (1) that only the present moment exists, with the past gone and the future not yet created, and (2) that the dead either cease to exist or exist beyond the range of the living. Despite these assumptions, stories of people seeing the future and communicating with the dead are in all the world's scriptures, and are scattered throughout recorded human experience.

"The souls of the dead remain alive, outside of time and space, with all times and all spaces available to them. Thus, when we communicate with them, they interact with our minds from the inside, so to speak, knowing what we know. Thus we can communicate about the things in our life, getting the benefit of viewpoints formed in different space and time environments."

Friends in High Places

By far most of the messages from the dead are benign, and comforting to the living. This is the only really sinister story I have personally come across. When Angela Gibson (the lady whose child was protected by Stonewall Jackson) was about four, she had an ultimately frightening series of night-time events that involved conversations with an apparently dead child. A little boy with "a cold presence and a ghastly look" came one night to the edge of her bed. He had a vivid cut above one eye, and a ball under his arm. He asked her to come and play ball with him in the street.

Angela told the boy that her mother didn't allow her to play ball in the street out front because she was afraid she'd get hit by a car.

"Is that what happened to you?" Angie asked innocently.

"I guess so," the little boy said. Then he added, "Okay, can we just go in the living room and roll the ball back and forth?"

Angela agreed, and for a while they sat on the floor doing just that. Then Angela told him she was tired and wanted to go back to sleep, and asked him if he would come back in the daytime.

"I can't," he said. "Your mother's awake then. She can see me and told me not to come here."

So for a time in her young life, "Bobby" came at night and they played.

Angie continued: "Then one night, he asked me if I would go with him. At once, I looked up and saw a mean, white-haired Victorian-looking woman surrounded by a group of really sad-looking children. The scene terrified me."

She told the boy she didn't want to go because she didn't like the looks of the woman and the other children. And she was still worried about the road, and about disobeying her mother. Bobby (she thinks his name was) left after that and never came back.

Angie's impression to this day is that the woman was evil, some sort of spirit-magnet, and was looking to steal her soul as she had apparently stolen the souls of the other sad-faced children. Had Bobby been sent as bait to lure her to destruction one way or the other? How many children who have died in "accidents" have been seduced away from safety, been less cautious than Angela, and never returned?

❧

In a book lent me by a distant cousin, I found a great ghost story. The book is *Taproots*, by Paul R. White, Sr. This story, from sometime after the Civil War, comes from the memoir of Martha Ayres Cheairs, descended from my great-grandfather Governor of Virginia John Letcher's sister's family (she was Mary Bretonia Letcher Blackwell). Their family home was called Humanity Hall, Virginia.

"Aunt Matt lived nearest Humanity Hall, about two miles away, and one afternoon she decided to go there and look for a table she thought she'd left there. Her thoughts as she walked were on Humanity Hall and when she got there and was walking up the front walk she thought about when she lived there and those who had lived there or had loved it. Her memories were many, and of many things about it. She went in the front hall but the table wasn't there. It wasn't in the parlor on the left, or in Grandmother's room on the right, and not in the dining room back of the parlor and under the steps going upstairs. She went into the back hall and it wasn't there, and seeing it was growing late she decided to wait until another day to look for it upstairs.

"She came back through Grandmother's room instead of from the back hall. As she came into Grandmother's room through the door at the end of the front hall she saw Grandmother sitting in her usual place at the end of the hearth, where she sat in cool and cold weather.

"Aunt Matt said to her, `Mama, what are you doing here?' and Grandmother said, `My child, I'll always be here.' Then she was gone.

"This was told to Aunt Mary, Aunt Matt's and Mama's oldest sister, by Aunt Matt when Aunt Mary came on a visit from New Canton. Aunt

Friends in High Places

Mary told it to Mama on a visit to us when she came back from visiting her daughter Mamie in Plattsburg, Missouri, and on her way back to her Virginia home.

"Aunt Mary said she asked Aunt Matt, 'When you saw Mama, weren't you scared?' Grandmother died in 1897, and this was told to Mama twenty-five years later. Aunt Mary's answer was, 'No, I wasn't afraid for I felt just as I did when I'd come home when Mama was living.'"

❧

On a public radio (WMRA) call-in program about *My Neighbors' Ghosts,* a man named Brian called in and told this story about a message from the other side: his mother, a spiritualist minister, had died eight years before, leaving him with an unpublished manuscript that she wanted him to finish. He'd looked at it shortly after her death, found it confusing and overwhelming, and abandoned it. Then recently, her voice came to him from the beyond in an odd way, reminding him that he'd agreed to try to work it up for publication.

One day he put what he thought was an old empty tape or CD into the appropriate machine, and clicked it on. Immediately his mother's voice said, "This is to remind you to finish my book." There was not a single other thing on that tape, just that message.

❧

Tom Graham, the host of that "Virginia Insight" segment on WMRA radio, had been a lifelong skeptic until this happened to him. He told me before we went on the air, then retold the story during the hour-long program featuring *My Neighbors' Ghosts.*

He was visiting a friend named Gwen on the west coast. She was involved with some psychic group. He made fun of that, but eventually he laughingly assented to a psychic reading from Gwen during which she remarked, "There's a relative of yours here."

"Oh?" said Tom.

"He's died in the last year," she said.

"Nope, there's no one like that," Tom said. "I've had no relatives die in the last year."

But the psychic politely insisted that he had.

Tom couldn't think of a single dead relative. Gwen said, "I'm getting a really warm climate."

Tom shook his head. No connection he could think of.

Then Gwen said, "Florida."

"Oh my God," Tom responded, as the state name jogged his memory. His great uncle Edgar had indeed died within the last year, in Orlando. Gwen had not been reading his mind, he is sure, because he'd barely known his grandfather's brother, and had obviously totally forgotten about his death. He recalled, with Gwen's prompting, a conversation he'd had years and years before with Edgar, which had helped him decide on a career in broadcasting.

So Tom believed (no, he still believes) Edgar really did send him a signal from the other side of death—maybe only to let him know that the dead do talk to us, and are still in some sense with us.

A friend of mine, Elizabeth Wassell Sauder, artist and sign painter, had an experience with a spirit on Memorial Day a couple of years back. She had rented a VFW Hall's upstairs room in Lexington for her art studio. To get to it, one had to climb stairs and go through a door, so while she was painting and listening to modern music, she was a bit startled to "feel" a presence in the room with her. She'd heard no steps on the stairs. Slowly she turned around to face an African-American man in a brown uniform of some kind. In her confusion, why did he "seem" a bit threatening when she never really saw his facial features? She decided to "collect" herself, to turn and put down her brush and cloth before she

Friends in High Places

greeted or addressed him. Doing so deliberately, she then turned back around to face—nothing. No one.

The room was empty. It made her feel creepy; as she pondered, she intuited that he "disapproved" of the music she was playing on that Memorial Day, and perhaps preferred patriotic music, or at least that was her impression. She has no real idea why she concluded that. But she soon found another studio, never again feeling comfortable in the VFW Hall.

A confirming postscript to this story is that the building she was in has traditionally been the gathering place for African-American, not Caucasian, veterans. "Brown" is the color of the uniforms American troops wore in World War I; khaki, also brownish, was worn in World War II. She thinks the first, but isn't sure, being unfamiliar with Army uniforms of different wars, and entirely unfamiliar with the fact that the hall was a center for Negro soldiers. The soldier did not speak words, but he conveyed a message to her.

⁂

This is a story about a ghost that many people saw, over many years. In the 1970s, attorney George Warren and his wife Paula bought a gorgeous house in Montpelier in Hanover County, Virginia, that had been built by a local physician born in the 1850s. The house dated from 1896. Much loved in the area, Dr. Stanley cut a memorable figure with his distinctive black bag, old long coat, and high hat, which he wore on house visits out into the nearby countryside for over half a century.

After Dr. Stanley died, the house passed to his son, then to the church next door, which used it as a parish house awhile, and eventually rented it out.

When word got out that George and Paula were buying the house, a man working at the local service station said to him one day, "I have to tell you something. Don't buy that house. That house is haunted. We rented it when we first moved here. I saw the figure of a man in a long dark coat and high hat passing the door. We started hearing a baby's cries.

Katie Letcher Lyle

We got so scared we broke our lease and moved out."

Then another person, a Swedish woman George and Paula knew—logical, cool, and skeptical, the president of an insurance company—also told him the house was haunted. One day, while arranging flowers for the church in the house, she said, she watched the figure of a man in old-fashioned black garb walk down the steps and out the front door, where he vanished. She also had heard the crying of an infant, or a cat, or something. She felt she had to tell George these things about the house he was planning to buy.

Another local man a few years before had rented an insurance office in the house, where he worked with just a secretary. One day while he was gone, the secretary heard a noise and turned around to be confronted with a tall man in an old-fashioned coat with a black bag and a top hat, standing not five feet from her. She screamed, ran out of the house that day and refused to return.

But George and Paula, both skeptics, decided to buy the house anyway. They loved the house, and agreed that a ghost might even be fun. They didn't take the stories seriously, being rational people. George opened a satellite law office in the doctor's old office, downstairs in the house, away from the Richmond hubbub.

One day, Paula, working temporarily as his secretary, had two clients in the office. All three heard the front door open, footsteps in the hallway, a knock on the inner door. As the husband and wife sat on the couch, Paula went to open the door. No one was there.

She cheerfully explained about the ghost to the young couple, both of whom looked horrified. They left and never came back.

A while later, George's aging father moved in with them. He claimed to hear chains being dragged across the attic floor at night. George and Paula still weren't concerned, didn't really believe. The ghost had never hurt or even bothered anyone.

Friends in High Places

Then one night as George, Paula, and their two daughters were eating dinner, talking about their daughters' school matters, George just happened to look up to see the very figure he'd heard described so many times, crossing the hall just beyond the kitchen, between the bathroom and the back stairs. George saw the wraith clearly for several seconds, fifteen to twenty feet away, looking as solid as any living person. Warren knew immediately that it was Doctor Stanley: the long black coat, the doctor's bag, the top hat—all fit his description.

"I'm a skeptic," George repeated to me over a Sunday brunch. "I was just flabbergasted. I didn't know what to think. I did get the feeling he approved of us, what we were doing to preserve and restore his house." They continued to live in the house for several years, but no one of the family ever saw Dr. Stanley again.

While living in that house, Warren had a friend who was custodian at Scotchtown, Patrick Henry's home. Henry's second wife had schizophrenia, and was "detained" in the basement of the house, which was the only treatment known in those days. George says the custodian was upstairs one day, closing up the museum house, when he heard a woman's voice from the basement, asking plaintively, "Young man, could you come downstairs and help me?" Horrified that a guest had perhaps gotten injured, he rushed downstairs. Absolutely no one was in the basement. The custodian quit that day and never returned to the house.

George Warren's own theory is that the dead exist in another of the numerous dimensions physicists posit, but which we cannot access, and that sometimes people dead or alive pass from one dimension to another briefly. How? That he doesn't know.

Ben Lawless, a museum designer and an old friend, told me a story from one generation back in his family. His great-aunt Marie had a favorite nephew killed during World War II. Here's the story: Aunt Marie awoke one night to find her nephew, in full uniform, sitting in a chair in her room. In the way of dreams, it didn't occur to her that there was anything odd about this. "Are you all right?" she asked.

"I'm really tired," he replied. "Can I just sit in this chair for awhile?"

"Of course," she replied. Soon she fell back to sleep. When she woke in the morning, the chair was empty. Of course, she recalled the dream.

Two days later, word arrived of the nephew's death, at or near the time he appeared to her. Marie said he looked exactly as he had alive, and that she had no sense of his death. Many stories like this one came from World War II, when a time-lag in reporting meant that families didn't learn of deaths for several days. Frequently the ghost was seen of a person not yet known to be dead, the information coming to the recipient some time later.

American legal historian of the Marshall Plan, Jacqui McGlade, reported her grandmother told her of frequent visits and communications from her deceased husband. At night, he would come and lie on the bed beside her, *with his mouth sewn shut,* according to her grandmother, and talk to her about things.

One time when Jacqui was riding in the old car her grandmother still drove, night fell. When Jacqui suggested switching on the lights, it turned out the headlights were both burned out. "Grandma!" Jacqui admonished. "You have to have those fixed. You can't drive in the dark without headlights!"

"Nonsense!" her Grandmother replied, "Grandpa told me not to let anyone touch the car!"

Grandpa had at that time been dead twenty years.

(Jacqui had no idea if her grandfather's mouth had been sewn shut at the time of his death, before burial, though sometimes undertakers do that to keep the jaw in place.) Grandmother kept on driving the car, and nothing bad ever happened. She died insisting to the end that her (dead) husband talked to her all the time!

~~~

My friend Kay Lera, now of Lexington, Virginia, who was raised in Midland, Michigan, grew up as one of four siblings—along with a number of foster children taken in by her parents in the 1950s, who had been in abusive situations—and kept them for varying amounts of time. One of those children, Becky, was mentally retarded and never got adopted, and so Kay's parents eventually took her as their own. "When she came to live with us," Kay recalled, "whenever she was tired or scared, Becky would hide in a coat closet under the stairs to the second floor, and just go to sleep. We quickly learned that that's where we'd find her whenever she was missing."

In 1969, when Becky was eight, Kay got married and invited Becky to be in the wedding. Soon after, Kay had written a thank you note for a gift Becky gave her. Becky hardly ever got mail, and so she was excited about the thank you letter she knew was coming. She went to get the mail on the day it came, and was opening Kay's note on the way back across the street to the house, not paying attention, when she was fatally injured by a car.

"My father got to her," Kay recalled sadly, "but her extensive internal injuries killed her." Kay left Michigan for California with her new husband in October of 1969.

Kay had a childhood friend, Carol, adopted at birth, who had premonitions about tragedies. She would tell her friends, but they never paid much attention. Carol hated the "talent" she had, and it scared her that she would "know" ahead of time about tragedies both local and elsewhere. Carol, being Kay's friend, of course knew about Becky's death. Carol stayed in Midland, and Kay and Carol kept in touch for years.

Later in life, Carol found solace and meaning from being in "psychic groups." Eventually, they lost touch.

Then one day, out of the blue, Kay got a call from Carol. Someone in her psychic group, Carol explained, was living in Kay's old house, and kept hearing a child's voice. It seemed to be saying, "Remember me." She had tracked Kay down in California. "I know it's Becky," she told Kay, "but why does the voice always seem to come from that closet under the stairs?"

"It gave me chills," Kay recalled. "That's exactly where Becky always went, but Carol didn't know that. Further, after Becky died, Kay's father had given Kay a bracelet to remember Becky by. It was engraved with the words, "Remember me."

———

Linda Law Krantz, a dear friend, was for many years the head of the Rockbridge County Library. She is probably the most sane and skeptical person I know. Her grandfather was a railroad telegraph operator. When he and his wife (her grandmother) wanted to talk about something private, they had a habit of tapping each other in Morse code on the kitchen table.

Her grandfather died when Linda was a child, and her grandmother moved in with Linda's family, to live with them until her death ten years later, while Linda was in college.

After her grandmother's death, Linda's mother began to notice the sound of Morse code tapping on a television set which was not turned on—a color set which had been given to them by RCA when Linda's dad, Harold Bell Law, invented the color picture tube at the David Sarnoff Research Laboratory in Princeton, New Jersey.

Linda's mother, Ruth Workman Law, still alive at ninety-nine, reported this Morse code activity continued for years—and through two house-moves—but did not follow her into the Pennsylvania nursing home where she now lived. It was fast, and she (Mrs. Law) could not "read" Morse code, though she felt strongly it was her dead mother trying to contact her. Linda swore that both her parents were (and her mother still is) very scientific—and not prone to giving any attention to ghost stories or any other paranormal goings-on.

And Linda's mother, as a young woman, had an operation, and died—briefly. She saw tiny little miners with light beams on their heads going into a tunnel in a mountainside, like a mine. She was invited to go with them, and was attracted by their lights, but she decided not to go. To this day, she is sure that if she'd gone with them, she wouldn't have returned to life. Yet, despite these events, Linda's mother still did not believe that the soul survived death even though she was confident that her mother was trying all those years to contact her after death.

How well I know how the mind protects itself!

Linda used to be a blood donor, until the day she flat-lined (a term that means she died). What happened to her is that she rose above the chair and watched her body slump to the floor below, watched all the people running around trying to save her, while she thought about how needless all their panic was. She tried to say to them, *Don't worry if I die; you are suffering on my behalf so needlessly, and I'm not suffering at all. I'm just fine, and it is wonderful here where I am.* She was quickly aware that they couldn't hear her. She was never again allowed to give blood.

A friend, Natalie Chadwick, suddenly began to have her covers jerked off the bed during the night while she was living in Winter Haven, Florida in 2007. The action always woke her up, but she had no sense of who or what was doing it. It happened every night for a week or so; then on the seventh or eighth night she awoke and saw a woman sweeping the floor in a gingham dress, who paid her no mind. Natalie never had the covers removed again after seeing the woman. It seemed to Natalie that

"seeing" the woman achieved whatever notice had been needed in the first place and resulted in the nightly cover removal.

Paige Campbell of Buena Vista, Virginia, did—and still does—see spirits. Before 1952, when a new hospital was built in Lexington, Stonewall Jackson's home (now a museum to his memory) had been the hospital for the town.

Paige, a child then, was in the hospital with appendicitis. She awakened in the night to see standing next to her bed a nurse in a "Florence Nightingale" sort of uniform; even at her young age, Paige knew it was old-fashioned. She couldn't tell facial features but asked the nurse to please get her some water as she was thirsty. When she spoke, the nurse vanished.

She continued to call for a nurse, who came a few minutes later. She told the second nurse about the other, old-fashioned, nurse. The nurse said thoughtfully, "That was Sarah. Many people have seen her. It's not a good sign, for usually it prefigures a death or serious illness. Usually within a week or two." Paige wasn't worried, for she was mending well from her appendix operation and was due to go home the next day.

Exactly two weeks after leaving the hospital, Paige was re-admitted with peritonitis, a potentially deadly infection that was the eventual result of her appendix removal. She was given a fifty percent chance of survival at the time.

Paige collects Sarah stories, and says that Sarah apparently still visits patients at the "new" Stonewall Jackson Hospital—three blocks away—on occasion. I also heard that from another nurse who works there now. Usually her visits do seem to precede (and therefore predict) deaths.

Friends Dick and Judy Halseth and Kay and Bob Lera took a trip together to Natchez, Mississippi. In one old tavern, Dick experienced a

Friends in High Places

ghostly communication. Dick is a believer in spirit survival, as is Kay Lera, but both their spouses are not. Here is the story.

The barmaid where they'd stopped for a glass of wine on the way into the city for dinner one night mentioned to them that the house was haunted. It was commonly known, she said, that the ghost was a woman named Madeline who had long ago been the mistress of a man who owned the tavern.

When the tavern keeper's wife discovered her husband's treachery, she allegedly killed Madeline and concealed her body somewhere on the premises.

Cut to the last decade of the twentieth century, and four visitors sharing a late afternoon cocktail in the otherwise empty bar. "Would you like to go up to the third floor where Madeline lives?" the lady bartender asked.

They all gamely said sure, they'd love to meet Madeline. So up they traipsed, to "experience" the ghost, provided she was "in residence." The bar girl explained that the way her whereabouts were felt was if there was a warm spot on the bed.

The first to feel were the women, Judy and Kay, and both agreed that there was a warmer spot on one side of the bed. Bob Lera became nervous and would not even try to feel the bed. But Dick, the believer, not only felt the warm spot, but wanted to stay a bit and "feel" the atmosphere.

The others went on back downstairs, as Bob was feeling anxious, and the ladies were not especially affected by the warm spot. (Dick says he suspected a trick and looked around for electric wires or something that might have concealed a heating pad.) But the room was sparely furnished, and there was nothing.

When the others left, Dick began to take photos. There is an unexplained bright spot on one of his exposures, right where the warm spot was. Today Dick says that, as he stood there alone, he felt behind him an unmistakable presence. He knew there was someone else in the room with him. He felt peaceful, unafraid, though his back and neck grew icy cold, and goosebumps broke out all over him. He says he has never felt anything else like it in his life, and believes he encountered Madeline. He yearns to go back and see if he can recapture the feeling. Dick has recently been back to try to contact Madeline again, but this time had no sense of her at all. His wife Judy has died in the interim, and he has remarried.

Kelly Harris, my massage therapist, and her new husband moved into a house that turned out to have a ghost. Her husband's parents owned an estate built in 1747 in the country near Richmond, Virginia. As both his parents died within a year of their son's marrying, he and Kelly inherited the house. His family had a long-standing joke about a ghost named Mrs. Spalding, that being the name of the wife of Dr. Spalding, the builder and original owner of the house. So already there was the suggestion that the estate house was haunted, though Kelly doubted its validity.

Casey, Kelly's husband, had grown up there with his parents. From time to time, anomalous and unexplainable things occurred. The family fancied Mrs. Spalding was still trying to rule the manor; maids had heard chains rattling; repairmen left the premises abruptly and would not return. One of the hired help swore he saw the devil, and left for good.

"Whenever Casey and I fought, things would happen," Kelly recalled, a quarter century later. One night they looked outside to see a bush burning. When they went outside, nothing was amiss. At one point, Kelly found footprints in the snow that neither started nor stopped, a row just laid down in the middle of the big yard.

In their years there, Kelly said, Tupperware jumped off a kitchen shelf into the middle of the floor. A cradle in the attic that had been stored broken got mysteriously mended without human intervention. One night when Casey and Kelly had a fight, all the furniture on the third floor moved around crazily, even stuff too heavy to be moved by one person. Once when they were having a big party, with a record on a turntable, the needle zoomed across a record, and the machine shut off. Kelly "felt" that Mrs. Spalding didn't like strangers, or crowds—or the music they'd chosen.

Kelly and Casey eventually divorced; when Kelly returned to the house twenty years later, she felt in it a new peacefulness. New people had bought it. Perhaps, Kelly thinks, Mrs. Spalding liked them better than she had the young, discordant couple that Kelly and Casey had been.

So many stories surface about the dead returning to communicate with the living! Clear messages in real words, intuitions on the part of the perceiver, sometimes just feelings. It's increasingly clear to me that the great majority of paranormal experiences go untold because people fear being laughed at or thought crazy. Most of the stories people have shared with me have been told furtively, secretively, often with the desire expressed that I keep the story private.

My last book details many more such visits. There is a ton of evidence that the dead indeed—and frequently—visit the living. And, I ask, what other interpretation can we make of an entire history and community of "imaginary" common, similar, ghostly experiences?

If it is true, if the dead talk to us, perhaps we can learn how to answer them, converse with them. Every society we know of on earth has believed that life goes on beyond death, in some form or another. Why is that? Modern psychology will argue that is because we cannot stand the idea of a universe so absurd that we are born, live, die, and are forgotten. Man, these psychologists argue, is deceived by his own mind into believing what is untrue: that we survive death.

Another argument that makes just as much sense to me is that all societies believe in life after death because there is something to it. There have probably always been people who "died" and then

"recovered" with near-death experiences on their lips, including the child in the Hospice chapter.

We can't begin to know how many people have been visited or spoken to by ghosts, or so-called "dead" people. Many people who have secretly told me they have been visited by a dead relative are embarrassed to reveal it, as though it might betray gullibility, stupidity, even lunacy, on the part of the perceiver. Yet in September 1993 the London Daily News reported that over fifty-three percent of a sampling of over 1000 British widows believed they'd been contacted by their dead husbands.

If you by chance wanted to try what I've learned over the last twenty years, here's a way to start. Use your breath to lead you to a state of relaxation. Breathe deeply, focusing only on your breath. Say to yourself, I am open to intuition. Ideas and insights and communications flow into me easily. I'd like to talk with _____. Then wait. Whatever you get, you could write it down on a pad or in a notebook. Don't edit what you see, hear, feel, smell, taste, or even just sense. Listen trustingly and record. It's good to note details. You might just surprise yourself. You might hear from a ghost.

Friends in High Places

2. The Light of Reason

Said, Pull her up a bit will you, Mac, I want to unload there.
Said, Pull her up my rear end, first come first serve.
Said, Give her the gun, Bud, he needs a taste of his own bumper.
Then the usher came out and got into the act.

Said, Pull her up, pull her up a bit, we need this space, sir.
Said, For God's sake, is this still a free country or what?
You go back and take care of Gary Cooper's horse
And leave me handle my own car.

Saw them unloading the lame old lady.
Ducked out under the wheel and gave her an elbow.
Said, All you needed to do was just explain,
Reason, reason is my middle name.

~Josephine Miles

Katie Letcher Lyle

Like the truck driver in this poem, I want to be reasonable, and to show you reasonably so you can see, along with me, how the dead are still alive, and how therefore, we can indeed speak with them.

In order to do that, the mind, or some part of consciousness, would have to be able to survive the body. That would mean the mind can function separately from the body, yes?

Are you with me? We can observe this happening here and now: take a look at a school of fish, or a flock of birds. They are separate individuals, each able to function singly away from their flock. Yet their individual minds communicate with their fellows; otherwise they'd fly or swim into each other, and all would be chaos. Clearly they function not only individually, but also *like a group mind,* all together.

And the things they can do! Much as I love watching swooping flights of birds in big groups, I was absolutely blown away in 2002 on a Caribbean trip with my friend Lu Ann to see below us in the water off the edge of the ferry we were on, a gigantic fish: ten or twelve feet long. I pointed it out to my fellow travelers with a shout, and the guide told us it was not a fish, but a tight formation of tiny fish that protected themselves by forming themselves into that fish shape. To my eyes, it was a big fish with a rhythmically-moving tail, exactly the right shape for a twelve-foot black-as-night fish.

When another came by soon, the guide invited (or was it *challenged?*) us to dive into "the big fish." She assured us we would feel nothing. Though fearful, my friend Lu Ann and I both dove in. Neither of us ever felt a single fish touch us; they opened out as we dove, and closed again around us. At one panicky instant I was in total darkness, though it was broad daylight, surrounded by those fish in such tight formation that no light came through. I was in the middle of the "fake fish." But when I swam upwards, they opened to let me through without one ever touching me. How did they do it? And how did they as a group "know" how to shape themselves into what looked from the boat exactly like a huge fish? Group mind, *or mind that exceeds the limits of the body,* is the only possible answer.

So, if animals can communicate with other animals, it must mean that part of their minds are non-local, and therefore able to communicate with other minds of their kind. Likewise, as the animals we are, perhaps our own minds can also leave our bodies enough to communicate with someone away from us. It's a part of nature, of all the DNA on earth, and it follows logically that if other animals can do it, so might we be able to.

Our pets often communicate rather specifically with us, letting us know if they want water, food, love, or to go out. All pet owners speak "pet." How do we know what they are saying? I think because we are in some sort of hypercommunication with our beloved pets; we have learned to "resonate" with them. Obviously, many people also "know what he will say before he says it," about their mates or children.

My friend Hope told me of a time when her oldest daughter Penny was eighteen months old. Hope was trying to think of a way to leave her daughter without the child having a meltdown. As she mentally decided that the best way was to sneak off without telling Penny goodbye, the tiny girl astonished her mother as she looked up at her, and said, clearly and threateningly, "I'll cry...."

In one famous experiment described by Lewis Thomas in his essay "Warts," a number of people with warts on their bodies were hypnotized and told that the warts on the left side of their bodies would be gone in a week. In every case except one, the warts vanished as predicted. In one case, the warts vanished on the right (which was the wrong) side of the body. When the patient was asked to raise his left hand, up went the right. No one of the experimenters knew how their bodies had achieved the cure.

All of these people cured their own warts. Not a one of them knew how to do that. *Our selves are more than what we think.* So are our minds.

Though these invisible connections are unquantifiable, the entire medical community now accepts that they are real. We think we don't know how to cure warts, but we do. Part of us (what part?) is clearly non-local.

I also think it's reasonable to say that we are wrong to think that we are in every way more knowledgeable than were folks in the past. A good example: planting by the phases of the moon has been proven without a doubt to result in better crops than planting without heeding Mother Nature. My Appalachian forbears knew this, but then the world forgot it for a century or more.

We still have no idea how ancient stoneworks all over the earth were made, but we no longer have the laser-fine cut edges to stones that the ancients obviously did, to build megaton walls at Tiahuanaco in Mexico (aka Tiwanaku) or the Pyramids at Giza, or Sachsuahuaman near Cuzco in Peru. We have forgotten how to cut stone like that. It's there, so at some point we had that knowledge. (Unless, of course, as some people believe, more advanced beings than we came here from space and did it for us.) Come on: the proof's there. A reasonable person cannot really ignore the evidence. It's there; it's monumental; it's lasted all this time. And we can't duplicate it today.

When *The Power of Positive Thinking* came out in 1952, it was hailed as totally new thinking. Now it's become a touchstone for a good life; everyone knows about its ideas of creating reality for ourselves; kindergarteners learn that thinking happily and positively actually leads to positivity. Laying on of hands was among medical cures mentioned in the Bible. In modern times, laying on of hands had been discarded as not scientific. But we have circled back to understanding its power to heal. In his books, Larry Dossey proves over and over how prayer, even at a distance, even for people who don't know they're being prayed for, achieves a better outcome than not praying.

I don't need to tell you that our culture obviously discourages such

Friends in High Places

things as talking to the dead, and that our society silently but surely teaches us from childhood that it isn't possible. Politicians who consult the dead are not taken seriously. Yet all over this planet, other people and peoples believe in spirit survival, and spirit communication with the living.

It's difficult, sometimes well-nigh impossible, to outgrow childhood beliefs, even when we come to know they weren't right in the first place. For example, my parents taught me I'd catch cold going outside with wet hair. It took me a long time to be sure it wasn't true. But of course it isn't. Colds are caused by viruses.

༺༻

Lots of evidence exists for the functioning of consciousness outside the confines of the body. The near-death experience has been a popular topic of hundreds of books. Many people, including children brought back from the brink of death, recall hovering over their clinically dead bodies, watching all the hullaballoo. Recently on NPR an emergency room physician told the story about a young boy who officially was dead, and they were trying to revive him with paddles. The paddles wouldn't work for a long time. The child later told the doctor, "They weren't plugged in. I was on the ceiling and could see. After you plugged them in, they worked." The "dead" child flat on a gurney could not possibly have seen from his body the fact that behind his head a nurse had inadvertently knocked the plug of the machine out of the outlet. But that is exactly what happened. Even if adults (for whatever reason) might lie, children don't. Because they can't.

༺༻

As the speaker in the poem at the beginning of this chapter says, "All you needed to do was just explain...." So here are a few more statistics to help loosen you up—or just make you think.

According to at least one Gallup Poll, two out of three people believe in some sort of "paranormal" activity. Polls (which of course vary hugely, as they poll randomly) tell us that a majority of people believe in the truth of psychic phenomena, in angels, in the spiritual survival of the dead. Yet in general, as I wrote a few pages back, our society proceeds (governmentally, medically, commercially, politically) as if there is no spiritual dimension to our lives. If we really believe, why doesn't that belief influence our political and social lives more?

In 1946 J.B.S. Haldane, eminent British geneticist, wrote, "I have no doubt that in reality the future will be vastly more surprising than anything I can imagine. Now my own suspicion is that the Universe is not only queerer than we suppose, but queerer than we can suppose." He also wrote of humans having four stages of acceptance of anything new: (1) "That's nonsense!" (2) "That's an interesting, but perverse, viewpoint." (3) "So what if it's true?" (4) (as the scale slowly tips) "I've always said it's true!" I suspect many beginning to read this book will still be at the first stage, as I was for fifty-three years.

We are as a society ambivalent about spiritual things; we may believe them when they happen, but discard them when it's convenient to do so. Believe me, I know, and understand.

Thomas Kuhn popularized the terms "paradigm" and "paradigm shift." Paradigms are those seemingly *irrefutable truths that "everyone knows."* Paradigms change, as the last person investing in carriage whips learned. As the Swiss watchmakers learned when the quartz watchworks were beginning to be manufactured in the sixties.

Only a generation ago, "everyone knew" that tan was healthier, as well as more beautiful, than pale. My mother's favorite health instructions were, "Don't sit around reading. Go outside and play in the sun! Eat your meat. Drink your milk!"

Here are some more paradigms we ought, in my opinion, to examine, and perhaps even toss out.

Friends in High Places

1. *The only worthy science is replicable science.* But science deals only with physical matter, and not with the broader spectrum of reality—which is increasingly hard to ignore. Truth is many-faceted, multiple, slippery, and contradictory. Consciousness has many levels. Reality obviously includes things beyond the three-dimensional domain of physics, including energy systems and dimensions that science does not yet recognize. And, by the way, remote viewing is documentable, as you will see.

2. *Things happen regardless of thought.* I will try to show in this book that thoughts influence things, so much so that one might correctly claim that "thoughts are things." Thoughts actually make all the difference in the world. We do all create our own realities.

3. *All that we can know is the visible physical world.* Yet everyone knows that we can't see some of the most powerful things: electricity, which powers the world; radio waves and microwaves, all invisible yet powerful. Hatred is invisible, as well as love, yet who would argue that either has no power? Imagination, also invisible, may be one of the most powerful forces in the universe. And the truth is, that which is visible often fools us: the earth seems flat, the Caribbean sea looks blue-green. The sun appears to travel around the earth.

4. *Ghosts cannot exist because when you're dead you're dead.* How long can we continue to ignore the overwhelming evidence, from time immemorial, that the dead live on in some form, and interact with the living all the time?

5. *You can't talk to the dead.* But you can. Looking back, I see that it has taken the shattering events of the last few years to bring me to where I find myself today: a believer, no—a knower—that we live with divine protection, that we are more than our physical selves, and finally, that a part of us can leave the body and return with information that can be verified, not only by speaking with the dead but most particularly by remote viewing. I hope to prove to you that we will transcend death, go

somewhere else but not be gone, and that we too will be able *from the other side* to contact our loved ones who haven't gotten there yet.

But it's still the overwhelming number of personal experiences that wears down the scientific paradigm (which is that you *can only believe what you can* (1) *control, or measure, and* (2) *replicate)*. To value theory above zillions of experiences seems arrogant to me, yet this value is what feeds "scientific reality." Even though science is quick to declare impartiality in judging, it is anything but impartial.

"Talking to the dead?" (Eye rolling.)
"Even if you could, why would anyone want to?"
"Isn't it dangerous? I think it says so in the Bible."
"They're dead; how can anyone still talk to them?"
"You must be totally insane."
"How in the _____ (fill in the blank) can anyone do that?"

And those are only a few of the more polite questions and comments I've gotten. I can imagine a whole lot more out of earshot!

Yet here's a typical story told to me recently by a friend: Angie Gibson's mother called her one day about twenty years ago from a distant city, and out of the blue congratulated her daughter on being pregnant. Angie had told no one, not even her husband, of her suspicions that she might be.

Her mother explained that she had been visited by her mother, Angie's deceased grandmother, in a dream the night before, telling her the information, and saying "Angie needs you now."

The thing was, nobody—not even Angie—knew she was pregnant, and when her mother called she was at that moment just opening a pregnancy test kit to see whether she might be. And of course her (long dead) grandmother was right.

Friends in High Places

"Talking to the dead?" Thomas Moore, famous for his *Care of the Soul*, wrote in his column for *Spirituality and Health* in 2007 about a grieving parishioner who asked him the question, "Is it all right if I pray and talk to my dead daughter?"

Moore's reply, though sidestepping just a bit, is interesting: "...we modern people live surrounded by an invisible circle of belief in reason, proof, analysis, machinery... [which] has made life convenient and comfortable. But it is also a fence that keeps an entire world of the spiritual and soulful out of sight and unavailable."

He goes on to advise, "You can step outside that circle and from there pray and talk to the dead with certitude and intelligence.... As one who speaks for life outside the circle, I encouraged the man to enjoy his new relationship. I don't need to know exactly how the living and the dead interact. The fact that religions around the world honor them and ask for their help is enough."

I personally have had two widowed hospice patients and a younger friend tell me unblinkingly that their dead spouses still told them how to proceed in daily matters. All were completely matter-of-fact about it.

"Even if you could [talk to the dead], why would anyone want to?" Well, it's useful to realize that people the world over have been talking to the dead forever, asking their advice. Chinese worship their ancestors *because* the ghosts of those ancestors give them such good advice (often in the form of dreams). In the Latin classic, *The Aeneid*, its hero Aeneas visits the underworld and receives guidance and prophecy from his long-dead grandfather, and so do the twin founders of Mayan mythology, in the classic Mayan epic, the "Popul Vuh." Out of the world's religions, none that I know of asserts that the dead are really dead (though all of our earthly senses assure us that they really are). Tribal people worldwide consult their "dead" ancestors on issues of importance to their current lives. Christianity promises that we will continue to exist in Heaven. Perhaps this is because the dead exist not in time or space, but in eternity, which has no past and no future.

Although doubters say that man invents religion because he needs to believe in something beyond this life, maybe we should place the unseen world in the context of the spiritual universe of which it is a part. *All* the world's religions address the afterlife, describing it as numerous levels of spirit activity. Buddhists for two thousand years have had a sophisticated understanding of types of energy bodies and states of being that are experienced by the departed, as did the ancient Egyptians. The Tibetan Book of *Living and Dying (the Bardo Thodol)* and the Egyptian *Book of the Dead* are remarkable for their similarities, their instructions to the living about how to go through the process of death, to school oneself in how to die. Hinduism, from which many of the world's great eastern religions arose, including Buddhism, has a literature of unrivaled understanding of the realms, high and low, that may be experienced after death. Spiritualism today may offer the best description of a western view of an afterlife of many levels of development, from hell-like (though temporary) suffering to realms of light from which masters like Jesus guide our planet, and guide souls who have passed on. It's interesting, in view of the scads of information about the afterlife in other religions, that Christians are so silent on what happens after death beyond the baffling contradiction of Heaven: almost cartoonish golden gates and winged angels in nightshirts; and the other view of every Christian napping until judgment day, and every sinner consigned to Hell.

The dead were, after all, our teachers when alive—our friends, our older relatives, those who gave us their DNA. Sometimes they are children we lost too early. Usually, the people we loved the most and miss the most

Friends in High Places

are the very ones who taught us how to live. So of course we might want to talk to them again. *The good news is that we can.*

Some might argue that when we talk to the dead, what we're really doing is a kind of remembering: a tapping into our memories of them and retrieving (through memory) the wisdom they imparted to us while they were alive and we were young and foolish. But I have firmer proofs, I think, that there is direct contact, if we choose for there to be and allow it to happen. All it takes is the desire to do it, the imagination, and listening.

Wouldn't you love to tap in to your favorite deceased relative or friend? or have a conversation with some historical character you admire or find interesting?

I promise you, it's not some supernatural thing; it's a human gift every one of us is capable of.

There is a ten-minute exercise I have my Elderhostel (or other) writing classes do: choose someone in history you'd like to have known. If that historical figure interests you, you probably already know some things about him or her. On a spiritual level, you might say you've already established a "dance" or a common vibration with that individual. So the assignment is: Engage that person in an imaginary conversation, and write it down as it occurs. Just do it. Don't overthink it; just "go" contact that person, say howdy, and see what direction the conversation takes. The more detail you can get, the better. Note the surroundings you find yourself in, and record that. Note clothing, the age of the person, any detail such as what the person holds in his (her) hand. Any of those may be significant.

The results are often nothing short of amazing. Try it yourself, giving yourself at least half an hour. You will come away from the exercise astonished.

You wish you could recall your mother's recipe for blueberry pie? Actually, you can. She will tell it to you. Call it a trick of memory if you're more comfortable that way, but many people already know you can do such things—that the so-called "dead" still "vibrate" or "resonate" in us as they did when alive—and we can still and always connect with that resonance.

༄

Once after my father's death I had an important question to ask him about the stock market (about which he'd been something of a genius). I set the question as an intention when I went to sleep one night: Do I stay in or get out of the falling stock market?

Next morning I was aware of having dreamed about him. We'd been on a forest path, he stood over at the side looking at me; I was sitting on the path trapped beneath a bunch of fallen tree limbs, stuck but unhurt. But he never answered my question. A few days later, I told this to my stockbroker.

"But he did answer your question!" John told me. "Don't you see? It was to stay where you are." Amazed, I did see it then, and I did stay where I was, with results that proved wise.

We all have (and can learn to access) all the information in the universe—past, present and future. Thus you too can learn to access anyone, anything, any time. Often that universal information is called the Akashic record, from the word Akasha in Sanskrit, meaning "empty space" or "sky." Access to it might be how Remote Viewing works. Another theory is that we carry, through our DNA, specific ancestral memories that can surface spontaneously or at will. Going back only a hundred generations, everyone in our county could be kin. Perhaps the world is the same way, and that our memories can go all the way to the beginning of human consciousness. After all, we all share DNA.

༄

"Isn't it dangerous? I think it says so in the Bible."
The Bible wisely warns us to beware false prophets, Satan, devils, and

so on—in short, evil spirits of any sort—on the other side of death, certainly, good advice to follow. But my guess is we should avoid them here, too, on this side. The problem is, how is anyone to know the false ones from the real ones? "And many false prophets will arise and mislead many." "Even Satan disguises himself as an angel of light." "The miracles of Satan look like miracles of God." Deuteronomy (18:11) warns against ..."one who casts a spell, or a medium, or a spiritist, or one who calls up the dead..." It is clear to me that they're speaking, all of those New and Old Testament voices, of people who employ dark arts for evil purposes, and who try to persuade others that they are on the side of the angels.

But come on: we learn pretty quickly to avoid unsavory characters (though humans often are led astray by glitter and glamour). So how can we know the difference, we mere mortals? Is it okay to try to get in contact with someone you love who has died? My answer would be, if our intentions are pure and loving, no harm can come from contacting the dead. Intention is everything, and we intend with our imaginations.

"You must be totally insane." Well, maybe so. Isn't that what the so-called rationalists always say about people who perceive or look beyond the rational world (call us the *meta-rationalists*)? Just the way creationists simply ignore the proofs of archaeology, debunkers and skeptics (someone I know called them "psiphobes") think they are being logical and scientific, but they are ignoring an *enormous* amount of evidence.

At the current moment, we in our advanced Western civilization are of two kinds of minds. The first kind clings to the rational (Newtonian) view of the world, believing in what can be seen, measured, proven and replicated—and no more. Their creed is that time is linear, we exist in three-dimensional space, and when we die, we are gone, vanished, earth to earth. Thus one could say the ground for the rational view is *seeing is believing*. Therefore, if a person of that persuasion were to experience something outside that paradigm, he would do what I did for over fifty years: pass it off as "just my imagination," or "just a coincidence," or "something I made up," or "a mistake in my perception." People of the rational mindset brush off as false all claims they would call "paranormal," or "beside" normal. That is to say, according to them, *not* normal. They believe nothing can happen outside the parameters of space and time as we now understand them.

The second mindset (mine now) is hard-won if you're raised and taught to believe the above, as I was. The people of this second mindset, meta-rationalists, experience the world differently, believing in such things as intuition as opposed to mere accident, clairvoyance as opposed to dumb luck, synchronicity as opposed to coincidence, psychic aid from beyond—in short, in the possibility of all sorts of so-called "paranormal" abilities. In fact, we believe those abilities to be a part of the range of perfectly normal human abilities. *Believing is seeing. Because we believe, we see.* I believe all of us have paranormal abilities, but we certainly interpret them differently. Time and space are ways we on earth measure our world, and if we are honest, they aren't steady and linear. Vacation days may speed by so fast we "can't believe it," or the opposite: a week of snowed-in days can seem like a month. Five minutes of a root canal is not the same as five minutes drinking coffee with a close friend.

I've learned through ghost-busting that those concepts of time and space apparently don't exist after we are dead. It's the exact opposite from the first kind of thinking: in the meta-rationalists' minds, it is belief that allows us to begin to see: thus, *believing is seeing.*

Elizabeth Lloyd Mayer, in her recent book *Extraordinary Knowing*, writes, "The perceptions that characterize potentially anomalous experience appear to emerge from a state of mind that is, in the moment of perception, radically incompatible with the state of mind in which perceptions characterizing rational thought are possible." So, in a way, the rationalists and the meta-rationalists seem doomed to totally contradictory positions.

It is my hope that this book can change that.

If in your mind it's an impossibility to talk to the dead, then should you happen to receive a message from someone who is dead, your mind will of course find other explanations, including probably the logical, left-brain explanation that "I must be crazy." Or you will say to yourself, "That's just my imagination."

On the other hand, if in your mind it's possible to communicate with anyone present, past, or even future, then your mind can accept what you get if someone from the other side visits you. Hank Wesselman, America's most famous shaman, has recorded experiences across time with his own descendant, perhaps five thousand years in the future. His books are also a great read!

Naturally, the meta-rationalists would like to "prove" the truths of what might be called our "soft science" to the rest of the world. Before you decide this is nuts, please read the chapter on Remote Viewing, which is the practice that finally and surely convinced me that the intelligent part of us can have adventures on its own as we lie quietly and safely elsewhere.

The rationalists, believing that you can't influence your life's events, would call the ability to manifest the kind of life that you want coincidence or good luck. Meta-rationalists know that we all create the lives we live. It's not insane; moreover, it's the natural law. The way you see the world (and this is true of every living soul) does not merely affect what you think and feel about all that is going on. The way you see the world determines how your world will actually be.

"How in the world can anyone talk to the dead?"

The sections of this book can be read, actually, in any order, because every chapter, in one way or another, addresses that question. The stories, interspersed and not always in order, are illustrations. So, assuming our intentions are pure, and loving, how do we talk to the dead? You can do it. Anyone can. This book tells you how, many times.

When my mother had been dead about three months (1979), an interesting thing happened. I awoke one night, and "knew" somehow that my mother was downstairs in the kitchen and wanted to talk to me. In my been-asleep confusion, I thought she was alive, and felt mortified that it had been so long since I talked to her. We had during her lifetime usually talked every day. I grabbed my bathrobe, donned it hastily, and started downstairs.

My husband, coming upstairs to bed late, said, "What are you doing?"
"Going to talk to Mama," I replied.
"But she's dead," he said, and that was the moment when I "returned to my rational mind" and realized, Oh. Of course she is. I went back up the stairs feeling foolish, never got to the kitchen, went back to sleep. My failure to believe caused me to reject the possibility of her being there.

Here is an example of my attempt to solve a family mystery. (This was in 2005, and by then I'd been going to The Monroe Institute for fifteen years, and was participating in one of their programs when I experienced this.

My great-aunt Lillian Paul Flynn was one of the family mysteries. "She went insane," my father said, any time her name came up. He loved her, knew her as a child, and from letters I know that she was my grandmother's favorite sister, and I could see a spicy, loving personality and vivacity in her letters. The third sister, Virginia, was slow and lumpen, never married, never even left home.

"What do you mean?" I always asked when Aunt Lillian's insanity came up. Insane is scary. It's big. It's final. It's family! Would I end up crazy?

But that is all Daddy knew. He was not a particularly curious man. It was over and done. She went crazy. She died. Puzzled, I asked about

Friends in High Places

Lillian a lot for a time, then forgot about her when nobody seemed willing or able to talk about her. But it bothered me intensely that a member of my family had gone insane. My family spent a lot of time talking about who was like whom, who resembled whom, who inherited what from whom. My brother John was tall and gangly like our great Uncle John. I was sociable and chatty just like Aunt Jennie. My father was opposed to my becoming an English teacher because his Uncle Letcher Harrison was an English teacher who also became a spendthrift drug addict and owed thousands of dollars when he died on the streets of New York in 1950, homeless. So I was steeped in believing that family traits persist through the generations.

In college, enrolled in an introductory psychology course, I learned more about family traits and inherited tendencies, back in the fairly unenlightened mid-fifties. And I asked Daddy about Lillian some more. He admitted she was his favorite aunt, but said he couldn't remember much about her more than that she was a kind and loving mother-substitute when his own mother was so often hospitalized. Once in the early fifties (perhaps after Lillian's death) we got a brown package of photos and clippings, with a note, from her husband Jack Flynn, who seemed to be living in South America. No one talked about him either. My father "didn't think much of him." Daddy was dismissive of anyone you mentioned that he didn't like, "He wasn't much..." he'd say. Even if I'd known to ask about Jack, I wouldn't have gotten much information.

Lillian died in 1953 at seventy-one, and her death passed me by without notice. I was in high school. My grandmother, her sister, had been dead already for four years.

Later, while researching the family for other books (*When the Fighting is All Over* 1998, and *My Dearest Angel*, 2002) I learned that Lillian was confined in St. Francis Hospital in Pittsburgh from 1936 until her death in 1953. It was a mental asylum. Everyone who could have shed some light on Lillian Paul Flynn was dead by the time I focused on her. The mystery stuck in my head.

I told myself that surely, since she was institutionalized in 1936 at the age of fifty-four, her trouble *must* have been related to menopause. Many women have a particularly difficult time at menopause, and they were often regarded as insane when those hormones began to close down—and nothing medically could be done to alleviate symptoms or replace the hormones until the nineteen-sixties. Hysteria, with its dismissive and negative connotations, was still a diagnosis during Lillian's (Idge's) life.

I tried to research Idge, but St. Francis in Pittsburgh (which still exists, and is still a mental hospital) had no records that predated 1973. No microfilm, no old storage, nada. They had destroyed all the older records.

Jack apparently did not remarry; he went to South America to live with a widowed sister around the time Lillian died.

Jack and Idge had met in 1909 while Lillian was a nurse in Panama, and Jack was working there as an engineer on the Canal. Their love story was a rocky one; after a whirlwind courtship, they were engaged to be married—but then the wedding never materialized. Jack was not mentioned in letters from Lillian to her sisters (my grandmother and their sister Virginia) for over eight years.

And then, on the brink of World War I, in June of 1917, Lillian and Jack suddenly married in a Catholic church in Staunton, Virginia, neither his home nor hers, the wedding plans hastily tossed together at the last minute by my grandfather, including a supper afterwards, "with cake." (He wrote about this to my grandmother, who did not attend, though she lived not forty miles from where her favorite sister got married, an easy hour's train ride.)

None of that helped explain anything. I already knew my grandmother suffered from something like agoraphobia, and never went anywhere, not to parties, not to church, not to meetings, not even to her only son's (my

Friends in High Places

father's) wedding in Washington, D.C. in 1936.

In 2002, I visited my cousins, who still live in the house where my grandmother, Lillian, and their four siblings grew up. My cousin and his wife generously gave me access to all the papers, including some letters between Idge and Jack. To my surprise, they were much warmer and—dare I say? sexier—than any of the ones I had discovered between my grandfather and grandmother while researching *My Dearest Angel*. I remember such phrasing as "our bed is cold without you in it." The Pauls, and subsequently the Letchers, kept all their letters, which is how I fell heir to both sides of my grandparents' lifelong correspondence after my father's death in 1994. Jack's letters would have landed at Ottobine (the family farm) anyway, and I suppose that Jack must have returned Lillian's to her brother John Paul, a judge, at some point after her incarceration.

I never got from the letters that I found at Ottobine any inkling of anything wrong about the marriage. Jack and Idge wrote lovingly to each other. The letters abruptly stopped after about six years. Of course, maybe letters were somehow lost or destroyed. I satisfied myself with the menopause explanation, as I had come to a blank wall.

Then, at the Monroe Institute, at a program run by Mark Macy, "The Afterlife Communication Workshop," I invited Lillian from the other side to come and tell me her story. What I got I had never considered or imagined. Here is her story.

I invite "Idge" to walk the beach with me, from my imagined beach house (at the Monroe we prepare afterlife dwelling places for ourselves). We start out over the dunes; she has on a white embroidered, slightly wrinkled cotton dress. She's thin, blonde, small, and has a sweet "rubbery" face. She seems around thirty-five. Here is the gist of our conversation.

"Idge, why were you in an insane asylum?"

And her answer: "I went back and forth with Jack. He drank too much, but would be sober for months at a time. When sober, he was oh-so-charming.

"I knew that when he drank, he chased women. I always knew that about him—he could not be faithful."

(Idge is wispy, slow, smaller than I'd thought, delicately built, kind of hesitant, as if she hadn't thought about all this in a long while.)

"I got paranoid—that was the word—about his behavior, and he had me committed to an asylum while we lived in Pittsburgh. Divorce was not an option for me. But I could not stop my mind from thinking about his infidelity.

"For awhile he took care of me, but Jack had no staying power. The time came when he asked John (Idge's, Virginia's, and my grandmother Katie's brother, a judge in Harrisonburg, Va.) to take over my care; John of course agreed, appreciating what I'd done for his wife Frances before her death while he was overseas in World War I. (Idge nursed Frances Paul throughout a long illness to her death). I did have psychotic breaks, times when I'd fly to pieces and scream and cry, and they would shock me or sedate me, and I would wake up with my head bursting. I was depressed, as any prisoner would have been. It was such a blot on the family escutcheon to be insane. I finally died in 1953 of blessed pneumonia. They had no drugs. Katie (my grandmother, her sister) was not much better, but Green (my grandfather, Idge's brother-in-law) took care of her with such constancy. He was steadfast.

"Jack was restless, and moved about the world in his engineering work. Panama, India, Brazil—he died of alcoholism, never remarried. Ironically, at the end of his life there were no women; he was impotent."

"So it wasn't menopause?" I asked.

"Well," she said, "that naturally exacerbated my depression. Again, there was no medication, and nothing to live for. I adored Gee, by the way (my father's older brother, who died at fifteen, in 1916)—his death was a terrible shock, too. He was a people-pleaser, an honorable youth with such great charm and determination and promise."

Friends in High Places

Suddenly we hurtled though space (and time?) out among the stars. It felt like I was riding a pneumatic tube. The point of that strange ride seemed to be to show me how insignificant are all our "lives" here on earth. The tape (with its sounds that had enabled my altered state, of which you will read soon) ended.

That story fascinated me, but it was too one-sided; and so a day later at the same workshop I decided to invite Jack from the other side to tell me his story.

And here is Jack Flynn's "version" of their lives.

"I am Irish Catholic. Drinking is cultural. I adored Idge from the moment we met. I called her Anne, from the second half of LilliAN. She was reluctant to marry, having the example of her older sister Katie's unhappiness, and a strong desire to serve her family. She went and nursed anyone in her family who got sick. Her family was more to her than me.

"Despite my failures, I kept after her, and knew she wanted me too—despite her doubts, (which, by the way, nobody clearly understood in those days). Finally she agreed to marry me on the spur of the moment—it was wartime, I might have to go; a lot of people married rashly in those times—and for six years we were happy. I went on benders occasionally and I guess women were part of that, but they meant nothing to me. I once got the clap, but got it treated at once. I recall none of those women; it was just blind animal instinct doing what drunk humans do.

"She got wind of it via a Panamanian friend, confronted me, and I confessed. After that she just couldn't stop fulminating on it. It ruined us. She cried all the time, accused me, and one day she was just not herself, staring into the distance, did not seem to recognize me. She had some kind of a split with the world. I had to work, so I took her to St. Francis—just for a while, just to get her well—never intending her to stay there.

"But it was as if her heart turned to stone, and she would not budge. She could not see things differently. There was no talking therapy or medicine that could change her. As a nurse, she knew about things like this. She could not change, or would not, whichever is true.

"In later life I moved to Brazil and lived with my much older sister, whom I didn't know well. She was widowed. After a while, I didn't have the money to care for Lillian—Ann. I'd sold the house, the silver, the furnishings, everything we owned, to keep her at St. Francis."

This is an exact transcript of what they told me. The word "fulminate" was not in my vocabulary until I looked it up.

There is no way I can prove anything. But it all makes sense: the Irish name Flynn, the religion (Lillian's family were Episcopalian, and from many family letters I know that her family (my family) were fairly strongly anti-Catholic), the hesitation on Idge's part to marry despite a strong attraction to Jack, her breakdown—all of it.

Did I just suddenly make up this story? It wasn't a thing like the version of their story I'd settled on for myself so many years ago. All my life, I'd had in my mind a *different* story.

I looked for letters from Jack Flynn to Uncle John Paul, Lillian's brother, but found none. In other cases in this book, I have absolute proofs of the veracity of messages I have received from the dead. Unfortunately in this particular case there seems no way at all to prove the truth or untruth of the stories Jack and Lillian told me.

One time at the Monroe, in the interest of fairness, I decided to contact the only one of my four grandparents that I didn't much like, my mother's mother. She was called Laolo. Boppy, my grandfather, her husband, was a USMC general. I got an interesting response, one which also helps explain why I didn't like her much! And I was sure she didn't like me. I have no nice memories of her. Once in high school when she was sick, I made her some custard, and she asked me nastily if it was poisoned. I was shocked. Here's what I took down from my contact with her.

"Why didn't you like me?" I asked.

"It wasn't just you. I wasn't child-oriented. Neither are you."

"What happened to you? Polly [her daughter, my mother's sister, and my beloved godmother] said you once were humorous and charming."

"I was ill. Out of balance. Boppy retreated. I was lonely. He was passive-aggressive, furious, and did the very minimum. I'd been a Marine Corps General's wife, and I didn't think many other people were up to me. Look out; you have the same tendencies. I thought it was funny to make fun of people, that others would be amused. I was wrong; it was unkind. Be careful of your tendencies in the same direction. I couldn't imagine why anyone should like me, for I knew I was mean. Therefore I became paranoid in my elder days, thinking people might want to be rid of an old quarrelsome woman. I was taken in, as you are, by people humoring me. Be careful to change that in yourself."

So, reason, reason. If you don't open yourself just a little bit, you may find yourself stuck in non-belief. As I was until I attended the Monroe Institute. If I hadn't allowed the information in, I'd probably be where I was at fifty, where my spouse was until his death, loudly denigrating everything that didn't fit with rationalist beliefs.

Try this yourself, and you may be surprised. Sit with a tablet and pencil. Center yourself with a few deep breaths, and a centering intent. Imagine that it is easy to talk to someone who is on the other side of death's veil. Ask to speak to someone who is dead that you'd like to speak with, have a conversation with. Imagine that conversation. Record each side of it. For this to work, don't question it; just do it. Don't overthink it!

Your rational brain is used to being in control when you are awake, and it can quickly persuade you that all this is hokum. So ignore it, and try!

Katie Letcher Lyle

3. Midlife School: The Monroe Institute

> *We are separated from the dead not by time and space,*
> *but by vibration.*
>
> *All frequencies are jumbled together;*
> *just as you can tune in to TV or radio frequencies with ease,*
> *you can do the same with the spirit world.*
>
> *All our lives, during waking and during sleep, we're flickering along the living continuum. Even when we're unconscious, we are conscious.*
>
> ~Robert Allan Monroe

I went over the mountain when I was fifty-three to interview a man I'd never met, in the summer of 1991. I wrote the following article, which explains.

Friends in High Places
Robert Allen Monroe

For the twenty years since I read his *Journeys Out of the Body*, I had been curious about Robert Monroe, who lives just over the mountain from me, near Charlottesville. Finally, today I have come to meet him, ending the fear that I might come across his obituary in the paper before I got around to visiting. Monroe, whose accounts of out-of-body travel stretch the rational mind, certainly doesn't appear crazy or deluded. Elderly, shabbily elegant, he looks a little weary, but that's only what you'd expect from a man who claims that he has not slept in the ordinary sense for more than ten years.

Monroe tells me he has discovered, among other things, that there are, on other planes of existence, millions of human spirits belonging to people once alive and now lost in a hellish sort of limbo—desperate, tormented, ex-people who do not know they are dead, and do not know how to "move on." He has of late been leading a program devoted to helping these pathetic souls to find peace in the Afterlife. Monroe is the founder and owner of The Monroe Institute, a pleasant mountain-resort sort of place near Afton, Virginia.

Who comes to The Monroe Institute? Well, Monroe's answer is vague; but "a lot of people" come, for "a lot of reasons."

"Most self-help groups," Monroe comments, "are heavily attended by women. But for some reason we have more men than women coming for the Gateway programs."[1]

The Gateway Voyage to which he refers is a monthly week-long experience for a group of paying clients "dedicated to the development of human consciousness through exploring profound states of expanded awareness." Participants, he explains, are from every walk of life: physicians, therapists, housewives, house builders, stockbrokers, diplomats, retired military, young yuppies and old hippies. Some of them experience

---
[1] That statistic still holds, though it seems to me there's about the same number of men and women at most of the programs I have attended. The one exception was a program that Bob himself taught called High Adventure around 1993 in which there were twenty-five participants—twenty-four males and me. And Bob. It wasn't the Paradise I expected; I felt left out and among the men largely discounted, without a single other female to talk to!

Katie Letcher Lyle

leaving their bodies as he did, Monroe says, though he emphasizes that this is not the focus of the program. So far about five thousand people have made the Gateway Voyage, and a sizable percentage have returned for more advanced week-long experiences, one of which, "Lifelines," teaches Monroe's methods for "helping those many dead-but-unresting people to places in the Afterlife that might be compared to Heaven."

A soft-spoken man, Bob Monroe is as matter-of-fact about all this as if he were discussing the pizza and iced tea he has chosen for lunch in the Tower Club, built for the convenience of the staff—the unassuming restaurant which is part of the grounds of the isolated Monroe Institute. In another part of this building, program participants live, sleep, listen to tapes, meet for discussion, and have meals.

Monroe insists that his interest is and always has been—since his first, accidental Out-Of-Body-Experience (OOBE) at age forty-two—first, finding evidence to prove the unbelievable things which he says happen while he is in his bed, apparently asleep and second, applying what he learns to human spiritual growth.

He accepts his experiences as the reality he perceives them to be, which I suppose is what all of us do. He first left his body in 1958 while living in a house in Croton-on-Hudson, New York. He soon found himself traveling astrally to places far removed from both the physical and spiritual realities of his life.

Monroe explained that he was the owner and director of two radio stations in North Carolina and a private corporation in New York at the time of his first astral projection. He traveled (in body) between the two locations frequently, and noticed how much nicer life was in North Carolina than in New York. As he was trying to decide whether to move, he searched for a climate similar to that he'd lived in as a child. He accomplished this by running a line from Lexington, Kentucky, his birthplace, to Richmond, Virginia, and looking for land somewhere

Friends in High Places

between. Simultaneously, he purchased a third radio station in Richmond.

He established The Monroe Institute of Applied Sciences in 1975, on land near its present site. Its purpose was to gather data that would help him understand his own paranormal night-time activities.

Eventually, he found the beautiful 500-acre tract for his sodality now called The Monroe Institute. To its rolling fields, hardwood forests, hills and valleys of red clay, quartz, wildflowers and narrow winding roads, all against the backdrop of the Blue Ridge Mountains, the Institute attracted a surrounding community of sympathetic souls. A sign within a mile or two of his land announces The Institute of Synchronicity. Down the road from the Monroe Institute, an outfit called New Visions is the dream-come-true of a Monroe disciple, Suzanne Evans Morris, an internationally famous speech-language pathologist specializing in feeding disorders for children with neuromuscular impairment. Suzie combines mainstream speech and occupational therapy with tapes Monroe has developed, called Hemi-Sync© because they cause the hemispheres of the brain to function in sync with each other, or synchronistically. "The technique employs a system of audio pulses which create a frequency-following response in the human brain," the literature explains.

Monroe calls Hemi-Sync a process of facilitation. Listening to the tapes, claims Monroe, facilitates the brain to work more efficiently; like-minded folks like Suzanne Evans Morris reason that Hemi-Sync may allow damaged brains to mend more readily, or enable functioning brain parts to take over (in the case of handicapped folks) the work of the non-functioning parts. The tapes also can "hold" the brain at certain wave-lengths, thus imitating reverie, deep sleep, trance-state, mystical states, healing mode, concentration, and other normal as well as unusual brain wave patterns. Monroe is interested in recruiting other experimenters to duplicate his experiences, to validate the astonishing events he now takes for granted. His programs have now been going on successfully for more than a decade.

A dozen or so people show up for lunch while we are in the Tower Club. A notice listing today's specials, pizza and quiche, reminds us to record everything on our bills, as the food is priced at cost. In this cozy sunny room with an honor system, everyone is friendly, everyone speaks, and there is a lot of hugging. The place seems reassuringly normal, with meat on the pizza, plenty of excellent coffee, a fresh and varied salad bar, and even a few people smoking.

But I want to get down to business. This is a man who says he is dedicated to obtaining scientifically acceptable proof for the unusual events that occur to him. If he travels out of body, I ask, can he then bring back information that proves he was wherever it is he thought he was?

He nods Yes. When asked for an example, he thinks a moment, then tells about the time that not he but one of his researchers agreed to (astrally) enter a heavily-guarded, high security government agency and report later what he found there. In his OOBE the researcher "went" to the designated office, found no one there, and so moved to another office nearby where a man stood, reading a letter. The researcher looked over his shoulder, read and memorized the letter.

Monroe tells that when he (Monroe) revealed what the researcher had seen there, it "scared the Hell out of the agency." He tells me of a personal episode when he pinched an old friend while on one of his own out of body trips, causing a non-astral bruise on her body.

Monroe says he has been on other planets, to the back side of the moon—and that he "told the government long before they photographed it" what it would look like.

He has discovered, he goes on, in communion with other entities while he is out of body, that he has lived many lives. For example, while traveling in London and Paris several years ago, when he got near certain twelfth-century buildings, he felt a dreadful heaviness and became so ill

Friends in High Places

he had to leave. This was before it was "revealed" to him that in the twelfth century he lived as an architect in London who became so upset at the unsafe conditions of the construction workers, who were killed with shocking frequency, that he badgered the king for safer working conditions, and for his efforts was banished from England. He then moved to Paris where the same thing happened, only this time he was guillotined for championing the laborers. This, to his way of thinking, explains his present-life deep discomfort while in these cities.

But he was determined to check the historical records, to attempt to verify the possibility that he had lived as his spirit communicators said he did. He could not, however, persuade his spirit guides to tell him what his name had been back then. "You have the name," they said. He insisted that he did not. "But you have the name," they repeated. He gave up, and came home to America.

But the story is not over yet. Robert Monroe tells me he has long had an interest in architecture. Several years ago he designed and built the Institute Center with its Tower Club on this mountaintop as the meeting place for his programs.

"You want hard evidence?" he asks, for I admit that I am not convinced by his stories, fascinating though they are. They do seem self-serving (a past life as a champion of the little people!) and unsatisfyingly vague. I am suspicious that no past-life I have ever heard of is that of a murderer, Nazi general, cruel plantation owner, or serial killer. Sometimes they are merely ordinary, but most often they seem, as his does, self-aggrandizing.

He leads me outside the Tower Club to a vantage point from which he bids me look back. "Note the octagonal tower built into the building," he tells me. He points out the iron railing on the roof surrounding what appears to be a small rooftop viewing deck. I comment on the gorgeous view from the Alpine-like building, then add that his designing a pleasant modern building hardly constitutes evidence of his having been an architect in a past life.

But Monroe knows how to keep an audience on the edge of her seat. "Just wait," he tells me calmly. "Come over to my car. I want to show you something." As we cross the gravel parking area slowly, he tells me that two years ago, his brother visited Scotland, and discovered there a Munro family castle built in 1234. He says offhandedly that neither of them had previously known of its existence.

"Who built it?" he asks rhetorically, then answers his own question. "Donald Munro was the architect, along with his son, Robert Munro."

Oh, now I see the point: "You have the name."

By his car, he reaches into the open window and pulls out of a heavily-taped brown paper wrapping a framed enlarged color photograph. "This just came in the mail yesterday," he says casually, and hands it to me. It takes only an instant to notice that the ancient stone castle in the photograph has an octagonal tower built into the building, with roughly the same proportions as the Tower Club's octagon. And there on the roof is an iron railing like the one on the modern building. If the story is true, that he built his club four years ago, and didn't until two years ago know of Munro Castle, it's a pretty impressive coincidence. He remarks at my skepticism, "Now that I know the name, I've got researchers trying to find records in London and Paris of an architect named Robert Munro who was guillotined there," he says.

He adds that it's no good telling people who aren't believers: you have to arrive at your own knowing, which is different from believing or not believing. I certainly want to keep an open mind; but I associate the guillotine with the French Revolution, which is five centuries past the time he is talking about.

And all of his stories, when I repeatedly ask for proof, are still, it appears, "being researched."

He, for his part, has concerns a lot more pressing than convincing me.

Friends in High Places

We part cordially.

On the way home I listen to "the Patrick tape," which he claims is an actual "rescue" he made of one of those lost spirits he'd told me about, through a medium, that he happened to catch on tape.

The entity Patrick believes himself to have been clinging to a log in cold water for several hours. On the tape, Monroe asks the confused and unhappy Patrick what happened. It seems the man was a cook, named Patrick O'Shaughnessy, from the ship Laura Bell, sailing from Oban, a "small town in Scotland," in the year 1879, when his ship exploded. His parents were already dead of smallpox.

By gentle leading, Monroe convinces Patrick that he is dead and sets his spirit free to go join his parents and friends, who have presumably "found" their appropriate afterlife slots.

Dramatic stuff, yet why should I believe it's anything more than just a good old radio show? After all, that's what Monroe did for a living before he started his institute.

I decide to go on a mission. Oban, it turns out, was indeed a northwestern Scottish seaport of about 6000, according to The Encyclopedia Britannica, Ninth Edition, 1889, a purchase I'd made once at a yard sale and lugged home in the trunk of my car, all twenty-nine volumes.

At tape's end, "researchers in England" are still looking; the fact of the sailor's life (or death) still has not been confirmed.

Monroe says that roughly a quarter of the 5000 or so people who have gone through the Gateway Program experience an OOBE, but he thinks that all participants deepen their understanding that the physical body and our current life in Time-Space are only small parts of all that we really are.[2]

In addition to the week-long programs offered each month, Monroe has put together an almost endless array of Hemi-Sync self-help tapes,

---

[2] By 2008, as of this writing, TMI estimates that over fifteen thousand have taken Gateway. And of course many, many have returned for other programs.

for everything from relaxation to stroke recovery, which the public can buy and use with or without going through the programs. The Monroe Institute will provide extensive materials to anyone wishing to learn about their experiments, programs, and materials: the address: 62 Roberts Mountain Road, Faber, Va. 22938.

Following acceptance of the previous article by the magazine for which I wrote it, and the receipt of a small check, curiosity tugging at my consciousness, I found myself wanting to attend a Gateway program to see for myself what all the nonsense was about. I wasn't convinced at all, it sounded frankly silly to me, and I certainly didn't want to waste my money, but...

Filling out the application form, I was stopped cold at a place where I had to sign a statement that I would not write about this experience without letting the Institute okay whatever I wrote.

Of course, I clambered up on my high horse, and called up the secretary at once saying, of course, I could not agree to that, as I was a writer and intended to write without censorship about whatever I experienced, especially during that program.

To my great surprise (I frankly thought they'd cave in when challenged) I received a polite note saying that I couldn't be admitted to the program unless I agreed to the condition.

Still unable to square that with myself, I proposed instead that I send them the article I'd written about Bob Monroe, to prove to them that I was a careful and fair-minded writer.

So okay, they said.

To my even greater surprise, the article, which I thought was balanced, polite, and fair, elicited a seven-page tirade from Monroe himself, through his secretary Helen Warring, to the effect that my whole piece was unfair and biased, that I was a "yellow journalist," without scruple,

Friends in High Places

and that I had "returned his courtesy with discourtesy."

His response, in part (his references are to the preceding article):

"might have come upon his obituary..." (I'm glad I met her before I saw hers in the paper. She could have been killed in an auto crash on the way home. Not in good taste as I see it, but I wouldn't edit it out.)

"whose claims that he has not slept..." (as used carries the implication they are not real or true. If she is a professional writer, she absolutely knows this, that's why she expresses it this way. She is trying to build a disbelief in the reader's mind. If she denies this, let her take a lie-detector test.)

"shabbily elegant" (Well at least she said elegant. Shabbily? I was in my work clothes, and she arrived while I was at work. I don't think the description is accurate. Did she expect a three-piece suit with coat and tie? I gave that up years ago. I don't remember how she looked, so I can't comment.)

"pathetic souls..." and the rest of the paragraph. (patently untrue! First I never use the label "souls" because it has too much connotation attached to it. Yes, I have not slept in the ordinary sense for many years, but definitely not because of any such discovery. I don't know that there is such a tragedy to the extent of millions. I could speculate, but that is what it would be. I have only partial knowledge in this respect. I would have edited this out as a reason for my sleep changes.)

Monroe complained of *something* from nearly every line of the article. He quibbled about "sympathetic souls" as if he had never heard that phrase, and groused, "but why list the Synchronicity sign some three miles from our entrance? It is a religious organization with whom we have little contact, and no relationship whatsoever. I would edit this as irrelevant with an untrue innuendo, i.e., that we have a subrosa religious connection."

Of the Munro Castle part, he wrote, "...both my brother and I would take any number of lie detector or other tests to verify: 1. That neither he nor I knew of the Foulis Castle and its tower on the Munro Fields prior to his trip there in 1990. 2. That he was not aware of the new tower in Virginia until November, 1990, when he received a promotional photo of it from the Institute. 3. It is a matter of Munro Clan history that Donald Monroe and his son Robert began the tower in about 1152 AD. Neither I nor my brother knew this fact until 1991."

"As to the guillotine, she may have a point. I don't know that's what it was. I had a hood over my head, neck down on a block, and a blade severed my head. It could have been a sword. That seems a petty issue compared to the rest. Even though she does say it is impressive, it is a feeble attempt to question the veracity of the incident."

He ended by writing, "...if the above doesn't convince Katie of the need for such approval I suggest that you tell her the Gateway program will not be helpful to her.... If she is the skeptic she appears to be, it would be a waste of her time and money and our efforts, and I don't know (sic) it would be meaningful for her

I wrote the following letter of apology:

October 31, 1991

Dear Bob,

I am very sorry (and surprised) that you found my article so offensive. I feel, given that I let you know I was interested but skeptical, that I treated you fairly, kindly, and respectfully.

Terminology is difficult; I thought you used the word "souls," but perhaps you didn't. You certainly implied that they were the non-physical remains of people, or what I know as souls.

I'm sorry I apparently misunderstood your explanation of the genesis and purpose of The Monroe Institute; I thought I'd heard what you said. I thought that you said it was another researcher, not you, who entered the government sanctuary; for that factual error, I apologize. I completely understand your point about one factual error undercutting other claims you might make. I noticed the Synchronicity Institute sign because it was on the road as I approached, but I have no idea what it is, and I intended no religious innuendo. In fact, it sounds scientific to me.

As to "shabbily elegant," I meant that as a compliment. I'd say the same thing of my husband. I also don't see how saying that I wanted to meet you before you were gone could be construed as tasteless. That, too, was meant as a compliment, as was referring to Suzanne Morris as a disciple, for she is an avid follower of your technology and ideas.

The phrase "sympathetic souls" is so commonly used to mean people of like minds and interests that I am astonished that you would delete it because it includes a word you personally find offensive.

The piece is nothing more than an interview with you. You knew I intended to write an article about you. I still feel that my piece is a fair summary of what you are about, and I think a good number of readers of the regional magazine that commissioned it would find you and your work of great interest.

Nor can I agree with you that there is anything misleading or deceitful in my piece. You did not seem to me the kind of man who would balk at an interviewer's honest skepticism. As the article implies, I found your responses to my questions regarding proof, while most intriguing, less than convincing, and I needed to say that in all honesty.

Katie Letcher Lyle

To close, however, let me repeat that I am genuinely sorry that I have offended you, for I mean you no unkindness and no harm. You were indeed gracious to me, and I thank you. Cordially,

◈

I never got an answer, and I certainly wanted no more contact with that unpleasant man. *But I kept thinking about the place.* Finally I decided no petty tyrant (which I had by then decided Monroe was) was going to stand in the way of my own investigation, and so I eventually signed the document agreeing that I would not write about the Institute without permission, and went to The Monroe Institute for the Gateway experience just before Christmas that year, 1991.

It took all the courage I could muster. I had no desire for further contact with the man I'd interviewed. But I just had to see what the Gateway Program was like. I was nervous, since we clearly didn't like each other, Monroe and I.

I forced myself the first night of the program to sit on the front row when it was time for us to be introduced to the great Bob Monroe. That evening, I saw him do for the first time a trick I was to see many more times; as he approached the front of the room from the back, he shed his jacket and tossed it behind him. Of course it fell on the floor. Showman that he was, he looked around, and said, with apparent surprise in his voice, *Sometimes it stays up.* "Oboy," I groaned to myself.

I even forced myself up afterwards to shake his hand, in an effort to dispel my own intense discomfort. Monroe appeared not to remember me, though later in the program he let me know clearly that he did, several times directing sly remarks to me.

The Gateway program changed everything for me, and I withdrew the article because, by the end of the week, I was convinced that Monroe was not a fraud, the coat in the air notwithstanding.

Friends in High Places

I am more than my physical body, is how the Monroe Institute Affirmation begins. A newcomer to TMI is asked to try to be open-minded enough to accept this as a possibility until he finds it out for himself. I didn't believe it for an instant, despite my (perceived) mother's message involving the butterflies. Soon after her death, as I was mushrooming alone in the woods, I was attended for an hour or so by a Diana butterfly that seemed to be saying Happy! Happy! Happy! To me. It *just seemed to be Mama.*

For years afterwards, occasionally a butterfly, usually a big colorful one, would appear, seem interested in me, and would "feel" like my mother. And it was always one of the ones she'd taught me about. She seemed to be coming down from somewhere, checking on me. Though it happens less frequently now, it still does happen occasionally.

My personal experience, though I have longed for something dramatic, has been gradual. I have returned over thirty times for week-long programs, long weekend programs, and personal booth sessions. I am sometimes assured earnestly by a fellow traveler that I am an abductee ("Your intense interest in UFO's is proof of it!") or that I have "healing hands." People have sometimes asked for my attention to their pains or diseases, and I have imagined pure white light flooding them for the energy to heal, then red light for healing energy and healthful circulation, then green light for new growth, then lavender light for peace, an end to anxiety, and tranquility. To my surprise, some of these people have claimed that *my intention to heal them has indeed healed them.* I use this perfectly human ability to calm my Hospice patients, all of whom are dying, and I experience that it works. Nothing magic about it, merely a focus of intention, an intent to soothe, to comfort, to help ease the difficulty, discomfort, and fear of dying. I firmly believe that all of us can do whatever I do. I am sure my fellow Hospice volunteers have experienced similar things.

Once, shortly after I returned from the Gateway program, as I sat with a dying friend, his visiting daughter asked me if it was all right if she went running for awhile. She was concerned about leaving because she'd brought her dog (now snoozing on the floor) and her baby (asleep in a little traveling crib). It seemed okay to me for her to go on, and I said so.

But the instant she left, the dog got agitated and began to bark. The baby woke and began to cry, and that woke her father, the patient. I picked up the baby, gave George a dose of the liquid morphine the nurse had shown me, sat down with the baby and the dog on the floor, and mentally sent calming and healing energy to the baby, to George, and to the dog. The effect was nearly instantaneous. Within two or three minutes, everyone in the room was once again calm, snoozing, and peaceful. I was impressed that the intent to calm worked on a tiny baby and on a dog. I'll give morphine the credit for George's peacefulness, but the whole episode was profound and dramatic. I was beginning to notice that there were really forces beyond rational fact that I might believe in, such as an intent to calm actually manifesting.

Many Monroe travelers have written extensively of their personal experiences while at the Institute (presumably with the Institute's approval). I see no benefit to detailing my own experiences while learning to use and using the Monroe technology, simply because all our experiences, all our symbols, are so personal. (At the end of the book is an ENDNOTE in which I do describe my own experiences, for those who might be interested.)

Let me make an analogy here: going to The Monroe Institute might be compared to going on a vacation to Mexico. You can go there, and do a lot of different things. You can have a good time or a bad time or a boring time. While in Mexico, you can focus on the heat, the mosquitoes, the

Friends in High Places

slow native waiters, the filthy conditions, how unpleasant your traveling companions are, and vow never to return; or you can focus on the warm clear waters and the great fresh food, the gentle and easy-going natives, the fragrance of the exotic flowers, the omnipresent music, the laughter. You could even decide it's just safer to stay in the airport until it's time to go home. You could go to a resort owned by Americans where all the food and all the language and even the decor are American. It's all Mexico, but we will every one of us experience it differently, and believe that our experiences are the "real" ones, the only valid ones. This is why my experiences are not valuable for you, nor will my experiences persuade you of anything; you must go and see for yourself!

These days, I go to The Monroe Institute for a week-long program once or twice a year as a vacation from the fairly "straight" life I otherwise live. At The Monroe Institute I can be open about my curiosity about everything "paranormal," hear marvelous stories, and make new friends. At home, I rarely speak of these adventures.

The technology of the tapes that are the heart of the programs is patented. It's called Hemi-Sync, which means hemispheric synchronization of the right and left sides of the brain. It is accomplished by "reverse engineering" which is this: the brain wave patterns of people in intense concentration, or under hypnosis, or deeply relaxed, or in meditation, or in the state between wakefulness and sleep, have been observed, mapped, and recorded. Healers have been brain-mapped as they focused on healing. Some tapes have been back-engineered from the mapped brain states of Yogis in their highly-focused trances.

In order to "persuade" a listener's brain to follow one or more of these mental states, two signals are recorded, the gap between them making the kind of brain waves associated with those states of mind. These signals are orchestrated to lead the listener from day-wakefulness into relaxation, a state of mind-awake, body so relaxed as to be asleep. Then to an expanded state of awareness, the place in awareness where time and space cease to exist; or into deep trances in which one can be in communication with loved ones who have passed on, or alien entities, or receive information not available to one in the alert awake state such as (incredibly useful!) an instant and permanent change in some long-held behavior. Examples include overeating and smoking.

Brain wave patterns are "persuaded" to change by listening, in exactly the same easy way that you absently—or intentionally—tap your foot to the rhythm of some music you are listening to. With Hemi-Sync, no subliminal suggestion is used, or hypnosis, or brainwashing. The listener is always in control. Unlike traditional ways used to induce trance states (drugs, starvation, pain, fever, intoxicating substances, sensory deprivation), one can stop the brain states at any time by merely taking off the headphones.

What you do physically at TMI during any week-long program is to go into comfortable cave-like beds called CHEC units (an acronym for Controlled Holistic Environmental Chambers), put on earphones, relax, and listen to tapes. After each tape, the group (a maximum of twenty-five) gathers for discussion, questions, sharing of experiences. One can choose to share or not. You learn how others experienced the tapes.

While in residence at the Monroe, you are served simple but good meals. Snacks, tea, and coffee are available at all times. Folks tend to stay up late to talk and eat popcorn or the leftover cake from dinner, and to share experiences.

Participants are encouraged to walk or exercise during breaks. There is a lake to swim or boat in when it's warm, if you are so inclined. There is optional yoga early each morning. You are nudged to healthy sleep cycles by gentle tapes that run all night in your CHEC unit (you can turn them off if you don't care to have your sleep influenced.)

TMI's stated purpose is to explore human consciousness, to encourage participants to expand, to learn, and to experience their own proof that they are more than their physical body. Skip Atwater, program chairman there, once wrote that the Institute's programs "encourage the evolution of human consciousness through personal experience." Bob Monroe was fond of saying, "The only way to know is to find out for yourself." In short, The Monroe is a nonprofit center where people come from all over the world for weeklong retreats facilitated by the sound technology patented as Hemi-Sync. The Gateway is the first, and there are many others.

For me, it was difficult to overcome my fear of the unknown, my stubborn doubt, the same doubt that many first-timers feel deeply—and the chatter of my intellect continually badgering me that this was all nuts. For me, the hardest thing was to give myself permission to go into something I formerly regarded as stupid, fringe-y, and impossible.

I was able to get over my fear of being in an altered state by recognizing rationally that all consciousness occurs along a continuum; on any day I might travel at the wheel of my car miles on automatic pilot without being able to remember having done so; I clearly have functioned in an altered state. Within our time/space framework we are forever slipping over the edge into the unknown; as we dream up ideas, dream in our sleep, go through that state of twilight sleep between waking and sleeping, concentrate so intently that we become unaware of time, fantasize, read, remember the past, envision the future, worry about possibilities, even when we are in the process of remembering, or sorting out dream from daylight reality—all those times we are in states of consciousness different from the here and now. In fact, it's fair to say that we are rarely entirely in the present time-space moment. The Monroe technique merely directs those altered states, so we can gain access to the truly spiritual aspects of the cosmos. As meditators know well, it is difficult to consciously stay in the present moment.

Katie Letcher Lyle

Dreams are an altered state everyone knows about. Artists and writers, creative people of all sorts, are aware of times when they feel they have transcended time and space, working so intently that they weren't really aware of where they were, couldn't believe so much time had passed as they wrote a scene, or played instruments, painted pictures, or inlaid a jewelry box. In any case, they were differently aware than usual. They were somewhere other than present.

Hemi-Sync is successfully used world-wide now to aid in learning, to facilitate creative thinking, to manage stress, sleep problems, anxiety, and pain, and to answer philosophical questions the person listening might want insights about. Hemi-Sync is powerful, yet all it costs is the price of the tapes (now CD's), and the only equipment needed to use it is a stereophonic tape or CD player, and headphones.

Visual imagery, guided by Monroe's voice (and other voices now, since Bob's death in the mid-nineties), is included on some of the tapes, but minimally, to allow you to imagine your own experience the way you wish to construct it, with your own knowledge, symbols, scenes, memories, intellectual training, beliefs, and imagination.

Various altered states of consciousness are given numbers arbitrarily assigned them by Bob Monroe. To some people, twenty-one is higher than, or better than, twelve or fifteen or three or ten. For me, personally, the numbers are only tags for remembering what I've imagined at each number. I can go where I need to go by simply imagining that I am there. The numbers to me are like numbers on a radio; 89.9 is not "higher" or "better" than 85.1. It's just different. Some "channels" may be clearer to us than others.

In spite of the fact that I am not a Christian, I find that in the Monroe Institute programs many of the familiar but mysterious sayings of Jesus are suddenly clearer and more "true" to me than they ever were before.

Friends in High Places

In my Father's house are many mansions, for instance; Knock and the door shall be opened; God is love; Ask and you will receive.

While listening to a tape during a program called "Lifelines," you might be instructed to "Go to Level twenty-three (to Bob, the area of lost souls), look around, and see what you can find." Your intention might be to "attract" a spirit or even a group of spirits to you, so that you can, in your imagination, take them to Level twenty-seven (the pleasant garden or park-like area you've created in your imagination where souls can rest and gather themselves together while they figure out the next right step for their spiritual development).

I can imagine you might be asking, How do you do that? It really isn't mysterious. You just *imagine* you are doing it. You just *intend* to do it. In the beginning, the tapes support your intention. But once you've learned the technique they aren't necessary.

The premise that underlies this particular activity of rescuing stuck souls is that many people, having never imagined an afterlife, have died without any concept of what comes next. Not knowing they are dead, they continue to haunt old locales, including their earthly homes, or even their earthly loved ones, unable to "move on." Or they are bound to earth by unresolved problems, guilt, or fear, or by another person's need of them. I once "encountered" a ghost who would not try to go towards the light because he was afraid of being rejected in Heaven because of a participation in a homosexual act; I once met a ghost who did not wish to go to Heaven, because he thought he'd have to rejoin his dead nagging wife there; I once communicated with a ghost who did not believe in Heaven and would therefore not even try to get there. If in life they believed they would never make it to heaven, then that belief indeed seems to keep some from doing so. The vibrational level of Monroe's "Focus 23" seems to be where at least some of these souls are.

After my divorce in 2002, I attended the Monroe more freely; my husband hated my going there, called it a cult, and often ranted that the Monroe was destroying our marriage, thus conveniently ignoring his increasingly abusive alcoholism.

This is a typical Monroe event. I take notes during the tapes, having decided from the beginning to learn to take notes in the dark throughout all the tapes. It is September of 2005, and I am at the Monroe doing a course called Afterlife Communications. It's after lunch, where we'd been discussing the plights of all the recent Katrina victims, and during the first tape I am swept into a scenario: a group of New Orleans folks, all black, all distressed and panicky. I know they are dead. It is my task to try to move these "stuck" souls on to the next level. I know I have been drawn to them through a sympathetic vibration.

First I say to them, with great authority, "You must be calm. I will take care of you." They stop talking, and turn to me, paying attention.

They are dirty, muddy, so I imagine for them a row of white stalls like Porta-potties, only they are porta-showers. I supply them all with towels and white cotton garments, and they go off to get cleaned up. Then I think they must be hungry, so I manifest a table nearby heaped up with what I think they'd like to eat: fried chicken, biscuits, cornbread, beans, peach pie, and iced sweet tea. Clean white plates. They head for the table.

I choose one lady to speak to, and ask her name. "Dixon," she replies. She tells me she is fifty-three, and that she doesn't have anywhere to go.

"Look around," I tell her. "You can see that this is a good safe place, and you can have any kind of house you want. What kind of house would you like here, Dixon?"

"South'rn mansion," she says quickly. But then she shakes her head

Friends in High Places

and corrects herself. "No, I wouldn't be comfortable there. A small house in the country, with a big porch and electric fans. I'd like my man George to join me. My momma too, but she's dead."

"Your momma can join you right now. Dixon, you are dead too."

Her face tells me she's already considered that possibility. All she says, slowly, is, "Ain't that something...."

I then turn back, and speak next to a small black man, who tells me he is Tin, or Tinge, or maybe Tiny. "Cut myse'f out of the roof to go get he'p," he says. "I was terrified, coz I can't swim. I lef' Nell and the kids in the attic. I fell in the water and can't get out. I don't know how I got here." I ask again, and Tidge seems to be his name. "You died in that water," I tell him.

"Then I can't see Nell no mo'?" he asks, and I get the impression that his family got rescued, but he did not.

"You'll have to wait a while," I tell him, "but it won't be long. You can go to any kind of place you like while you wait." And he then seemed okay, and seemed to wander off down towards a river.

Next a little girl approaches me, six or seven, with tight cornrow braids. "I want my momma," she says.

"What's her name?" I ask.

"Nell," she says.

And I realize. "Nell!" I exclaim. "Come with me; I can take you to your Daddy."

"He done went," she says. "He didn't come home." She tells me she is Tisha.

"But I know where he is," I say. "Come on." And we find him building a house already nearly finished. I leave Tisha with her daddy.

I then go to an old man sitting on a bench by the picnic table weeping. "I'm here to help," I say.

"I done lost evathing. In the hairicane." That's how he says it, *hairicane*.

"But you've come to a place where the lost are found," I tell him. I take his hand and we fly over the park to a place where everything he was dreaming of is. "You can rest here," I say.

"Thank you," he replies.

And finally I speak to a boy of fourteen or so who says his name is Cetus. "Bring them all with you now," I say, aware that my time here is short. "Hurry and get them together. There's room for everyone. Come on."

Together our group lands in the park, and I must go back, leaving them in the care of others who work in the park.

It's been twenty years since I began my association with TMI. Any changes that have occurred to me have come about slowly and subtly, not with a blinding transcendental light as happens to many people. I've not had a medical crisis that hurled me onto a different path, nor a Near-Death Experience leading to instant belief in an Afterlife. But I remember learning that most, if not all, tribal or "primitive" cultures worldwide regard Out-Of-Body experiences, yogic trance-states, and communion with the dead as perfectly normal, everyday events. And now, so do I.

Since December 1991, I have taken every program offered by the Institute, one of them (Lifelines) five times. I've taken several weekend and one-day seminars. I have also been back for many "booth sessions," or private monitored sessions in the isolation chamber on the grounds. The Monroe Institute shored me up as my marriage dwindled to nothing but a memory, my husband spending all his waking time twelve miles out in the country where I was forbidden to come without calling him first. Through the years of our marriage's gradual decay, my husband, wanting to divert attention from his escalating drinking, told me many times that the Monroe Institute had destroyed our marriage. At Al-Anon, I learned that all drunks say things like that.

The Monroe Institute gives participants more awareness of who and what we are. First, we become aware that we have many levels of attention, and that they are useful for different tasks. The training we do can be compared to a deer path through a woods: the more we use it, the firmer the path will be established, and the easier it becomes to access any focus level we choose. Beyond that, it's hard to talk about our experiences: as one participant remarked, it's like trying to tell someone who has never tasted vanilla about the taste of vanilla. Only when someone has tasted vanilla themselves can he understand what we are talking about.

My first week at TMI—at The Gateway Program—convinced me to withdraw my article from the magazine, as I already doubted my former conclusions. I returned the money I'd been paid. I have been going to the Monroe ever since, whenever I can afford to, and continued my efforts to live spiritually.

The most important thing I personally have learned at The Monroe Institute (generally in Lifelines) is that it is easy to "visit" the dead. You do it by imagining that you are doing it. Part of me still says, in keeping with my lifelong skepticism, that it is "all in my imagination." But part of me knows it's real, because I have learned—in those conversations with the dead—things I did not know before, things I have subsequently been able to prove.

For example, while I was at the Gateway program (the first Monroe program, which everyone who goes there must take as a prerequisite before taking any other), a man I knew slightly kept popping up in my mind, laughing. I found it puzzling. He never laughed in life, at least not that I saw. (Typical of my exchanges with him: one Christmas morning, I decided to take a short walk downtown, which was largely deserted on that snowy day. On the post office steps, I encountered him. "Hi!" I said. "Merry Christmas!" I wished him cheerily.

His deflating response: "Are you having a merry Christmas? It's hard for me to, with all the terrible news in the world.")

Perhaps a reasonable response, but surely not an endearing one.

He'd died the previous August of a swift cancer. While his wife is a dear, lifelong friend, I was unfond of this man: he was sarcastic, sour of disposition, unhelpful with their three children—and I sensed that he viewed me as sociable and extroverted, worldly and frivolous—clearly the kind of woman he didn't like. So his laughing when he appeared in my imagination in the tape sessions was odd.

The fourth time he appeared, I asked him why he'd died so young. The answer came in one of those complete balls of thought: I saw his childhood, which he indicated was miserable, with cold parents; he'd never liked the responsibilities of being married, having children, having a wife, even having sex; he'd always wanted to be a Buddhist monk; he could not wait to escape his earthly life. The message was clear and forceful, direct and specific. I did not think I could ask my dear friend, his widow, whether any of it was true. Though we are close, she is a private woman, and had not chosen to share any of this with me.

But when I had a chance to talk to a mutual friend, who had known the man's family growing up, as I had not, she confirmed the story pretty much as I got it. He'd been raised somewhere in England and sent to the states as a child at the outbreak of World War II; his mother was "something of a dragon" in my friend's words; and his father, while well-liked locally, (and a friend of my grandfather's) had been a remote parent. As a child, the boy was left with unsympathetic relatives, and he never adjusted well to family life. I could not have been more surprised that I should "receive" this communication, because he was not someone I resonated, or "vibrated" with, and I most certainly was not thinking about him at the times he appeared.

In the years that followed his death, as I resumed a friendship with one of my oldest friends, his widow, I learned that he'd been severely depressed more or less all of his life. Over a decade later, I did finally share my experience of him with her, and to my relief, she found it comforting that he seemed happy in his afterlife. Perhaps, in the scheme of things, that is why he chose me to communicate with, passing to me a message which I could eventually share with my friend. It may have been his way of "manipulating" an earthly event from the other side.

Another friend whom I'll call Faith—an only child, a Greek married to a Russian, with three children—nursed her loving but dominating mother through a final illness, hating her mother's difficult and demanding ways, and finally, months before death occurred, wishing her mother would just go on and die.

Afterwards, Faith felt guilty, for her mother had adored Faith's children and helped her raise them and in general had been extremely supportive of her and her family. She hadn't liked Faith's husband much, which had been a source of conflict. Faith, feeling guilt, asked me to contact her mother and give her the message that she was sorry for her unfilial wishes and her anger.

When I first tried to contact the mother/grandmother whom they called Vaga, I saw her in great darkness, agitated, too upset to even pay attention.

"You're who?" she kept asking; so finally I quit saying, "Faith's friend, Katie," and said instead, "Vaga, I'm Jennie's mother." Vaga had been fond of all children, and had been especially taken with our handicapped daughter. Then she apparently recognized who I was but remained upset, saying, "You're the first person who's spoken to me since I got here. This is a terrible place; no one's paying attention; it's dark, and there's nobody here." She seemed frantic and scattered.

I took her hand and led her to a bench in my imaginary park and told her to feed the ducks (since she'd had a strong need to nurture), and wait here until she felt better. Then I retreated.

I didn't report this experience to Faith, for I thought it would upset her.

Two weeks later, I contacted Vaga again. This time was different; I understood that she was much better, from her demeanor and from the light in which I found her.

So I delivered Faith's message. Vaga quickly said, "Oh, no, Faith did everything she could; she did more than enough; she was much better to me than anyone should have been." She further indicated that someone named "Chris" was now taking care of her. I at once thought Chris must be her husband, whom I never knew—though I did know their last name had been—I'll say Christopherou. As I thought it, she conveyed to me, "Oh, him? No, I only see him when I want to…" and I got the impression that she hadn't been awfully fond of her husband, and that the Chris she'd referred to was a handsome hunk of a teenage boy.

Aha, I thought, that would be just like Vaga, who in her eighties, until she took ill, still wore red stiletto heels and eye makeup and dyed her hair jet black and flirted like a teenager. As she seemed content, I left Vaga there with her "gigolo."

This time I was happy to report this incident, with all its details, to Faith, who has a great sense of humor.

Immediately Faith said, forcefully, "I know who Chris is. Sixteen years ago, we were still in graduate school and had no money and three kids, and I got pregnant again. We decided we just couldn't afford another child, and I had an abortion. That child, if it had been a boy, would have been named Chris, for my father."

Thus Faith is convinced that the message I got is a real one. Many

Friends in High Places

psychics say that children who die as infants grow up in spirit. Faith confirmed also that her mother had for years merely tolerated her father. This kind of evidence-based experience has persuaded me that I was really in touch with the spirit of Vaga.

※

In June of 1993 while at TMI, I "came upon" an atheistic friend named Esther who just popped up during a tape session. She wasn't dead, sick or dying, as far as I knew. "What is this place?" Esther asked. I knew she didn't believe in Heaven. In my imagination, I urged her to play along, inventing a place for herself to go to when she did die. At first she said, "On the Kennebec River." I knew she'd grown up there. But then she changed her mind, said she'd prefer someplace a little warmer, and said she wanted a simple, woodsy cabin. Her appearance in my mind puzzled me, because she definitely wasn't dead, as I was able to ascertain later.

Surprisingly, Esther died suddenly—while waiting for her appointment in a doctor's office, only three months later, of an undiagnosed brain tumor. Perhaps her soul (the God-part, that larger piece of us that is precognizant, all-knowing, all-seeing, and eternal) was in June already searching for a resting place.

※

When my close friend Jeanne's mother was dying, Jeanne came home to be with her. She had planned one evening to come from the hospital to our house for supper. Jeanne and I grew up together. Her mother was active in the Robert E. Lee church, sang in the choir, took care of the altar linen, polished the communion goblet and platens, and taught Sunday School. I knew her as well as any child could know the parent of a friend. From my observations all our years of growing up, I'd have said Jeanne's mother was an extremely devout Episcopalian.

Jeanne called from the hospital about four o'clock to say her mother had just died, so she didn't think she ought to come to dinner—though after a few minutes' conversation, she changed her mind since, as we both realized, she had to eat supper somewhere.

While cooking and waiting for Jeanne, I entered a reverie, and had the clearest sense of Jeanne's mother greeting me with great enthusiasm, from halfway up a long stone stairway. She said, "Katie, this is just marvelous! I hoped, but never really knew, that there'd be an Afterlife." I further perceived this woman I'd known as gray-haired all my life as having a shiny, wavy, marcelled blond hairdo, and being younger than I'd ever known her.

When Jeanne came, I told her about my "meeting" with her mother. She confirmed that her outwardly religious mother had always harbored serious doubts about Christianity. This I absolutely did not know.

I told her about the blonde hair, and Jeanne laughed and said, "Well, Mother always wanted to be a blonde!" In fact, she'd nagged Jeanne for years to lighten her light brown hair.

Jeanne stayed in Lexington for a while to clean out her mother's house in preparation for renting it. A day or so after the funeral, Jeanne, while cleaning out the bathroom linen closet, came across two hair bleaching products from decades ago, with names like Blonde-Glo and Moonbeam. They were stashed behind towels, in her mother's bathroom cabinet, both still unopened. To Jeanne, this was confirmation; her mother had wanted, even planned, to dye her hair blonde at one time while on earth—then apparently lost her nerve. In the afterlife, you apparently get to look just how you want. And to be whatever age you are comfortable being.

Once, after I'd researched the extant Pocahontas literature for many months, which work culminated in an article about her for *Virginia Cavalcade Magazine,* in 1999, I decided to invite Pocahontas herself to talk with me. (If Hillary Clinton could imagine talking to Eleanor

Friends in High Places

Roosevelt, why couldn't 1 imagine talking to Pocahontas?) So, one afternoon at home, I took the phone off the hook, put on a Monroe tape, entered a light trance, and had a fascinating visit with Pocahontas.

What I found was a feminine, gentle person who looked more English than the other Indians, who spoke English, who fit in easily with the English, who was sent by her father when she was only eleven to deal with the English all by herself. I found her charming, open, with a softness to her. She told me her mother was English. This squares with the fact that the Indians, when they took over other tribes, kept the wives for their own leaders' consorts, and took in the children of the conquered to boost their own population. Roanoke Island vanished without a trace a dozen years before the English settled Jamestown; certainly local Indians could have been the reason, or one of the reasons, for the disappearance of that early colony, and Powhatan could have taken an English woman as the wife, who bore his "favorite" among his documented twenty-seven children. Pocahontas' portrait is much more English-looking than other early American native portraiture. Her facial features are more English than American Indian.

Pocahontas never got over her "crush" on Captain John Smith, according to what she told me. She told me their English ships seemed as large as their towns, and she marveled at their technologies, and loved some candied almonds she was given by the English. When Captain Smith was badly wounded (his gunpowder pouch exploded as it hung from his waist), and returned to England to die, she was told he had died, but she could feel him still alive.

She was from the beginning entranced with Christianity and loved Mary the best of what she understood was a three-part god: a father, a mother, and a baby. It was easy for her to adopt that religion, which she did. It was simply a continuation of her own many-gods religion, in which water, thunder, and the sun were gods. She never denounced her own people's faiths, she told me—just added Christianity to the lot.

She married John Rolfe, she said, as a Christian duty to blend her people with his. He was kind and decent, but she did not love him. She adored their son Thomas, whom they took with them to visit England when he was eighteen months old. She was the Virginia high chief's daughter, and so was presented as a foreign princess to King James and Queen Anne, taken to Shakespeare's plays, and treated royally in London.

But London made her sick. The smog from the ubiquitous coalfires of London filled her lungs, she said, making breathing difficult.

She and John Rolfe decided to return early to Virginia, where he already was accumulating wealth from his vast (15,000 acres) tobacco plantation. Tobacco was the rage in London. It was time for planting.

Only days before they were to leave London, Lady Rebekkah, as Pocahontas was by then called (given that name when she "converted" to Christianity), weakened by the illness in her lungs, received a visitor whom she at first did not recognize, though by then she knew he still lived. When she laid eyes on her aged and diminished hero, Captain Smith, she had to withdraw—for three hours (he wrote), to recover her equanimity. But she had accomplished what she'd come to England for, seeing him still alive. She told me he was shorter now than she (she had been eleven at the time of their meeting, when he was taller than she by far). He'd been younger, and healthy. His wounding had aged him enormously in eight years, and he was now an old man. Their conversation was bitter and angry, and she told me she still regretted having created that memory, though he had hurt her deeply by never contacting her in all the years. He left, cutting short their meeting. Two days later, she, her husband John Rolfe, and their son Thomas left London on a ship, with her still very ill. Pocahontas died before they even reached the mouth of the Thames and the open sea. She was hastily buried at Gravesend, England, some fifty or so miles down the Thames

Friends in High Places

from London. She said she coughed up much blood in her final days, so probably she had tuberculosis. John Rolfe, changing plans precipitously, left baby Thomas with his people in Norfolk, England, fearing he could not raise the child by himself, who was still nursing at the time of his mother's demise.

I perceived Pocahontas as a gentle, amused and amusing person—in fact, a girly girl—soft, bright, and happy to be of use to her people and the English. Her marriage to Rolfe was political, not personal. Sadly for her, she could not have the man she loved.

Granted, I cannot use this fancifully-gathered material in any scholarly format, and I certainly could not prove any of it, but I could and did use it artistically, in a poem that has won a contest, and an award, and a performance monologue that's been staged twice. I also had an article in *Virginia Cavalcade Magazine* in 1998 outlining several reasons why I believe Pocahontas may have been half-English. Though I do not name the source of my idea anywhere in the article, the possibility makes a lot of sense, and my arguments were as follows: she was sent at age eleven to deal with the English: why? she must have spoken English; a persistent rumor around Manteo, North Carolina, today says she was the daughter of an English woman; she was "fairer to the English than the other Indian females;" her portraiture looks English; she was Powhatan's "favorite" of twenty-seven children; one of her Indian names translates to "white child;" Governor John White was the leader of the ill-fated 1587 Roanoke Island settlement, and his daughter, Eleanor White, could have been captured by Powhatan, and could have borne, around 1596, the baby Pocahontas; Powhatan may have kept her lineage a secret as a weapon against the English. (Her mother was probably dead by the time of English contact. Pocahontas's mother was never mentioned by any of the early chroniclers.)

Katie Letcher Lyle

My Greek friend Faith, two years or so after I'd contacted her mother, asked me to check in on Vaga again; when I did, Vaga told me plainly that she planned to be reborn on Corfu, and would be named Lydia. It was nothing that I could check on. At the end, Vaga remarked, "Oh. Tell Faith she has to do something about the purple dress." It sounded to me like a throwaway line.

But I telephoned Faith and duly reported all this (following our ghost-retrieval rule that, no matter how silly it seems, you have to say what you get, you have to not edit whatever you "hear."). When I got to the part about the purple dress—I was almost embarrassed to say it—both Faith and her daughter Tammy, who was listening on an extension, laughed uproariously. "That was Vaga, all right!" Faith said.

"What?" I asked.

The story they told me was that Faith had recently, since Vaga's death, needed a new outfit for her many public appearances, so she hired an old Greek seamstress, who had been a friend of her mother's, to make a jacket and dress for her. It was made of an expensive magenta silk, and to her horror, the woman charged her nine hundred dollars for making it. That was bad enough. But it gets worse. It was tight in the top, immense in the skirt, the jacket's tight armholes didn't fit, and, in short, the outfit was a disaster. But because her mother's friend had made it, Faith didn't feel she could make a protest about it, or ask the woman to remake it. (Also, Lord knew what she'd charge for adjustments!)

Since it cost nearly a thousand dollars, the whole family, all of whom referred to it humorously as "the purple dress," had discussed endlessly and fruitlessly what might be done. So Faith again believed I'd really been in contact with her mother.

When I first contacted my mother (she had died in 1979) while I was at my first program at the Monroe in December of 1991, I found her in a

Friends in High Places

beautiful garden, painting. The smell of summer roses was palpable. She was a painter in life, and loved roses. My father discouraged her from growing anything but vegetables (he had the crazy idea that anything with roots would undermine the concrete foundation of the little house he built us in 1950). A year or so later at the Monroe Institute when I "visited" Mama she seemed to be on a ladder pruning big, fragrant, pale pink roses growing on a massive stone or brick wall. She never grew roses, (though her own father, Boppy to me, was an avid rose gardener) so I mistrusted that "vision" and only later recalled that Mama had always wanted to have a flower garden, and loved roses, so surely would have had them in a wished-for place.

So, on later consideration, for Mama to be working on roses in a beautiful afterlife garden seemed not far-fetched at all.

Recently, 2007, at the Monroe Institute for the twenty second weeklong program I've attended since 1991, a fellow who had recently committed suicide in my home town, plagued by a string of debts then criminal activities, popped into my consciousness. I knew his parents; he and I had a speaking acquaintance only. I perceived him weeping so hard that the impression I had was of bloody tears streaming down his face, which was so distorted as to seem to be melting. Yet I recognized him. This is what he said to me when I said, "Talk to me."

"Suicides don't get to go to Heaven. It may take me years."

"Are you sorry you died?"

"No; I'm sorry I lived. It will be harder next go-round. In order to get out of here, you have to agree to go back under terribly difficult circumstances."

"Like what?"

"I have no idea. By an eternal contract, there must be evil in the world. Earth's obviously not Heaven. Hell is being forced to remember what you did and how you died."

"Why is there blood coming from your eyes?"

"I've wept so much. I did it all, all, wrong."

"But what about your work at the theater?" The little I had known of him was that he was a volunteer at our local theater. I was trying to point out what good I knew of him.

"That was escapism, and trying to win my father's approval. God weighs everything. No one is all bad. Criminals have themselves been criminalized. At first, crime is abhorrent, then it becomes habit, and finally it's the only way you know how to live anymore.

"There would be no gangs if parents loved those children. They're angry from being unloved. My crime is harder to expiate because I knew better. Pray for me."

Suicides especially seem to have abandoned the light for darkness.

True? Yes, absolutely. (I mean it is true that I experienced this.) Was it just my imagination? Maybe. But what does that mean? Who else's imagination could it be? Isn't imagination how we "see" everything that isn't right in front of us in the material world? In fact, what other vehicle besides imagination do we have for remembering, envisioning the future, "seeing" the people we loved but who have gone now, either back to their houses or to another life, and a zillion other such daily happenings? Imagination even plays into material life; we *imagine* the people we love are beautiful, whereas others may find them homely. We *imagine* a rainy day as a wonderful gift to the garden, or as a grave disappointment to a frustrated golfer.

My great-grandfather was governor of Virginia from 1860 to 1864, or for the majority of the un-Civil War between the states.

Once, at the Monroe Institute, I decided to try to contact him. I'd so love to have known him. I asked (at the Monroe, during a tape) for a meeting with my great-grandfather. There he stood, in a clearing in a woods, just as if we'd met on a walk in the forest. I told him I was his great-grand-daughter and introduced myself. I added that I feared that

Friends in High Places

he'd think me frivolous, but hoped he'd like me anyway.

"Why is that?" he asked.

"Well, I'm modern and liberal, and I love silliness," I explained.

"And a drink or two?" he asked slyly. The perfect question to put me at ease.

"Yes," I said.

"Me too," he admitted.

I said, thinking of his thirteen children, nine grown to adulthood, "I am Greenlee's grand-daughter."

"He was my favorite," he said. "I had to leave him too soon." (I quickly did the math: 1872 was G's birth, and his father died in 1884. So my grandfather was twelve.) "But he was the sweetest child I had. I followed his career on this side."

"Then you know he was called Guv," I said, "after you."

"Yes, I know."

I asked, "Was there a lot of laughter in your life?"

"Oh, yes. As much, I imagine, as there is in yours."

"Did you and Sue [my great-grandmother] love each other?"

He nodded solemnly. "We had a special love for each other."

"Did Sue like sex?" I asked.

"I believe so," he said, solemnly.

"Tell me about your other children."

"Lizzie was the most responsible, the oldest. Jenie [Jennie, Virginia Lee Letcher Stevens, Robert E. Lee's only god-daughter] was a great deal like you, now that I see you. Lizzie was more serious."[3] "Tell me about Andrew," I said. I knew he'd died of blood-poisoning from a flesh wound while still a child.

"He was a solemn child, like John. Yes, like John." [John was an engineer, a designer, and something of a wacky genius who became in

---

[3] All my life I've been told by Lexington old-timers how like my Aunt Jennie I am. No one ever thought I was like my grandmother, for whom I am named. I named my Jennie for her.

his later years a religious fanatic, to the distress of his relaxed Methodist-Episcopal family.]

"At nine, Andrew drove a splinter into his hand. We got it out finally, but it poisoned his blood. He died of tetanus, lockjaw. Dreadful, dreadful. He grew up in spirit here and guarded Greenlee in the war in Europe in 1918." [My grandfather entered the war at age fifty-five, five full years older than the Army allowed, and spent two years in France, emerging unscathed, to live until 1954.]

"Who was Frank?" [a name in a letter; I knew it wasn't one of the children.]

"A slave, then after the War a servant. He didn't wish to be free. We cared for him until his untimely death by drowning in 1873 in a flood."[4]

"In the Maury?"

Yes."

I waited a bit, but he remained silent. "What," I asked, "did you like most to eat?"

He hesitated for just a moment before answering. "A fine turkey dinner would be my choice, with all the family in attendance. I do love having my family all about me."

And so I asked him about the war.

"I saw war coming from, 1852 for sure, and worked for a reasonable resolution through talk and agreement, but there was no compromising about the slave issue, unless we had a separate country, with different rules and laws. And so we seceded from the Glorious union of the USA—I knowing it would not work, knowing it would lead to major bloodshed and chaos and grief among all American families."

My father's older brother died unexpectedly, while a student at prep

---

[4] In July of 1873 the Maury flooded after a sudden hard rain, the article describing it in the Lexington News and Gazette titled "As in the time of Noah."

Friends in High Places

school, at the age of fifteen, in 1916. He was Greenlee Letcher, Junior, known as Gee. He was a much-loved golden child, popular and promising, a handsome lad with the black eyes of the Paul family and black curly hair, unlike my wary, not-so-sociable, sandy-haired, blue-eyed father. He died of some flu-like disease, probably strep throat, high fever, some swift-acting infection, two or three days after being sent home on the train from Augusta Military Academy, where he was deemed apparently too sick to stay at school (so they sent him home by himself on the train). My grandmother nursed him until his death, and later wrote that *"at the instant of death, he gazed wonderingly at something no one else could see, a mysterious and haunting—awed and joyous—look on his face."* I always wished I'd known my uncle Gee. I sought for him, and he seemed delighted to talk to me.

"Ah, Miss Katie, I would love to have known you on earth. I chose to leave early, could have gone back to my body. I didn't like military school. A boy there raped me, and it destroyed my spirit. I could speak of it to nobody. Buzz [who became my father] was younger; I couldn't speak of it to Mama, not to Pops. It broke my spirit, and I did not want to live in such a world. After that, I couldn't face Kat Marshall [a girl he fancied at the time he died], and take her a body so defiled. I was sixteen and had nobody to turn to."

"Who was the boy?" I asked, looking as always for validation.

"An older boy," he said, and gave me the name. "He was kin to the headmaster. He threatened to kill me if I told. My family honor, as I saw it, was at stake. I saw no choice but death. I had no will to live. On this side, I had to be healed lovingly for a long time, of my humiliation and pain. I felt I had done wrong, was not angry at the aggressor, but at myself for being so weak and vile as to have 'allowed' it."

Later, I confirmed the name he gave me—but, curiously, not the first name—at the Augusta Historical Society, located next to the old Augusta Stone Church in Augusta County. A boy with the last name Gee gave me was indeed in the class ahead of his.

My devoutly Presbyterian mother-in-law was in something like a light coma for the last couple of years of her life. She suffered from dementia. Once, during a program at TMI, I decided to "visit" her and ask her (on the soul level) why she lingered when she could set herself free and move on. Her answer was immediate and forceful: "People choose the way of their death. Some people choose to cut off life suddenly; others choose to fade slowly."

"But," I said, "isn't it boring to just lie there day after day when you could go on and die?"

"Time isn't relevant where I am," she replied. "Get up and go to the window of your room and look: that is my choice."

Surprised, but doing what I was told, I took off my earphones, got up, left the CHEC unit, and did as she'd bid me. Out the window were, as far into the distance as I could see, layers of the Blue Ridge Mountains, fading at last into the distance. My dear mother-in-law had shown me a perfect picture of fading, which is exactly what she did, slipping away peacefully a year or so later. It is interesting that she indicated that we choose our own deaths on the spiritual level.

My father and I had a difficult, stormy relationship, which I have written about in *When the Fighting is All over*. I decided to try to contact him and ask about his [also-difficult] relationship with my mother. My visit with him was enlightening. (Kaish was his nickname for me, Russian for Katie, or something like that.)

"Kaish. I never knew that about Gee. Or Lillian. Now Bunny Hammond. She could have been your mother. But she tossed me over for someone else, a sailor. I met Betty [my mother] on the rebound. I realized I never loved her as much as I had Bunny, so I tried to break it off. When

Friends in High Places

I realized how devastated she was, I bit the bullet and went on. She couldn't say I wasn't honest with her. I told her the truth, and she said she'd die if I broke it off. So we got married. I don't know what she expected; she said she didn't care about nice things and comfort, but she did. She said she loved animals, but she didn't like dogs, and I did. So we never had a dog.

"I did the best I could, but at times my anger at that betrayal rose to the surface. I enjoyed my children—you most of all—but was short-tempered with them. I had the idea children should be obedient and excellent, and you were always boy-crazy. I worried to death about you. Johnny seemed unmanly—wouldn't do the things I wanted to teach him—so I sent him to military academy to straighten him out. Pete too. Betsy did everything she was supposed to do but then got pregnant with an actor. Children are supposed to turn out better than their parents. You should have joined the Marines."

"But I was a writer and a teacher!"

"You could have done that on the side. There were teaching opportunities in the Marines. Of course I see more clearly now, but you asked me what my story was. I'm all right now; I have a cabin in the woods, friends, a swimming hole in the river, a dog. Nice fellow named Tuffy (or Toughy)."

"May I tell this to Betsy?" (Betsy is my sister.)

"Yeah, I suppose it's nice how close you are. I understand my children now, but it's hard to condone things. Remember, you asked me. I have the big picture now; that's what happens after death. It's why we go back again and again. Trying to be better. At birth, we forget our goals and memories. Look at babies in the first months before they get attached to your world. They remember, they know everything. But as they have to deal with speech, walking, and so on, they forget what they knew on the other side, so by eighteen months they've forgotten. Almost always, they've forgotten by then."

"You know, Annie [daughter of Betsy—his daughter and my sister] is pregnant now."

"Maybe I could be born to her to try again."

I said, "You get to decide about those things?"

"Yes and no. You have guidance. You tend to go back to the same families—sometimes quickly, sometimes a generation or two apart. It's all guided. I have a lot of choice in the matter, and it's time for me to go back."

"When do you enter a fetus?"

"Days before birth. Sometimes only hours. It varies."

"Would you ever change sexes?"

And Daddy said, "Not now, not me. I'd be male."

"And you'd go into life with all that you know, all the memories we've just been over?"

"Yes, but I'd forget soon. Everyone does."

"Is there anything Annie and Sean could do to help you remember, if you go to them?"

"They could keep reminding me, keep asking me what I remember. Talk to me as if I am cognizant, which all babies are. It would be a great experiment, and maybe I could keep from forgetting my extended self, my rainbow self, my real self."

Then the tape ended.

Oh, by the way, Annie and Sean had a boy. He is at two at this writing, willful and energetic, as was our father (as reported by my grandmother, his mother). Aidan doesn't look to me anything like our father, but I didn't know Daddy as a baby. Time will tell. Once when he was eighteen months old, I asked him, "Aidan, remember when you were big?" He stared at me with a puzzled look, and did not answer. The mystery stands.

Friends in High Places

On the one hand, when you spend a week at a beautiful mountain retreat (The Monroe Institute) consorting with like-minded people, eating good food, sleeping and resting more than usual, eschewing alcohol (and other mind-altering substances) for a few days, lifted gently out of your normal life, who wouldn't feel better? Add to that meditation, a technology which you believe can lend you insights different from your usual ones, and support of your perceptions, whatever they are, and such an experience is highly likely to be transformative.

On the other hand, if the hemi-sync technology can persuade you to value your imagination, provide you with a safe diving board off dead-center and into a universe with meaning (as opposed to a "God-is-dead-and-so-will-you-be-soon" world-view), if anything can persuade you that your imagination is in fact not "just your imagination," but rather an entree to all other places and times—vibrations, states of consciousness—then what is so wrong?

It isn't at all difficult to have a chat with an ancestor. Center yourself by sitting down, closing your eyes, and taking some deep breaths. Think about your ancestor. Pretend to ask him (her) what life was like when he was alive. Ask her (him) for help with a current problem you have. Record what you "see" and "hear." If you are lucky enough to own something your ancestor owned, hold it or wear it with the intent of learning about its owner through its vibrations. Pictures have power; I think perhaps if you can find and look carefully at a picture of the ancestor you have in mind, it may help to create the necessary vibration that puts you in touch.

By the way, this chapter was vetted and okayed by Darlene Miller, Program Director at the Monroe Institute.

Katie Letcher Lyle

4. Reincarnation: Joseph's Case

So… do we truly return for another go at earth life? Dr. Ian Stevenson once told me he heard probably once a week from families with a child of two or three who claimed past-life memories, so they are apparently not uncommon. This is the story of a child I found, and whom Ian interviewed twice at my house.

The anecdotes were typical. Joseph's aunt was my friend Patsy, and she told me about him. Joseph at age two asked his mother, Jenny, "Remember when Daddy and I painted the roof red that time, and I got all that red paint on my leg?" In fact, the roof is now green, and has been for over twenty years, but a brother in the family, who was killed in about 1970 at age fifteen, had once helped his father paint the roof, and somehow got red paint all over one leg. How could young Joe know about that?

Joseph also had a "friend" he began to talk about at the same time, and used to report all sorts of odd items to the family about "Michael." After a while, he began to report that Michael was sick, and one day this two-year-old announced that Michael had died of AIDS.

And passing a store, Joseph would indicate that that was the place where he got into a fight with a man with studs in his boots, or remark that this field they were passing in the car was where he and another man plowed and planted corn a long time ago.

Once when looking in a magazine, Joseph pointed to a picture of one of those plastic pen holders that fits in a man's pocket, and said of his grandfather, whom he had never met, "Daddy used to wear that in his pocket all the time." It was true, but how did Joseph know?

It was that story that made the entire family stop and think. Why had Joseph always called his mother Jenny? The "Daddy" referred to was Joseph's grandfather, dead for many years. They decided unanimously that Joseph had to be David, returned to them fifteen years later as Joseph.

I contacted Ian Stevenson about Joseph. Dr. Stevenson lived in Charlottesville, just over the mountain from me. He came to visit within days, and Patsy and her young nephew Joseph and Ian and I drank lemonade out on my terrace while the great reincarnation scholar tried to ask Joseph about things. We ended up having two visits, and Stevenson felt that this was a genuine case of a child recalling a past life as his own uncle who'd died in a tractor accident fifteen years before the boy's birth. A brief version of this story is recounted in Tom Shroder's biography of Stevenson, *Old Souls: The Scientific Evidence for Past Lives (1990)*.

It is possible that one reason these facts came to light is that Joseph's family was entirely accepting of the possibility of reincarnation, and encouraged Joseph's recalling of events. The entire family agreed that there was no way Joseph had ever even heard of AIDS, or many of the other things he spontaneously came out with. They knew no one named Michael. The family knew of no man with studs in his boots, or any fight that anyone had engaged in, but they all remembered the painting red of the roof, and the fact that David helped, and got his leg all covered in red paint. And David had indeed helped neighbors to plant corn and other crops.

When I next saw Joseph, he was an adolescent, and claimed to have

forgotten what he was told by his family that he'd remembered at two and three.

※

When I was in Pompeii with two friends long ago in the summer of 1961, I had a strange experience: I wandered off from the group we were a part of, feeling drawn nearly as if I had no choice in the matter, down a narrow street in that tragically destroyed town with all the roofs open to the Mediterranean sun, into a house that had four rooms on the first floor. I walked directly to the right back room where the walls were green, with a fresco of a young girl: she had blondish hair, and fruit on her head in one picture, while in another she knelt and tended to some flowers. I felt I belonged in that room, and have never forgotten how strong that feeling was. But at that time, I had no belief in past lives, and suddenly became aware that I needed to run back and find my group. I found it somewhat odd that my experience there led me to a blonde girl; there are few blondes at Pompeii. In fact, I'm not sure I ever saw another.

I went back to Pompeii in 1986 with my then-teenage son, but could not recapture the feeling of belonging there, nor could I remember where the house was. I didn't look hard, for I was embarrassed to confide to my son what I'd felt in 1961 (and I had not yet been to the Monroe Institute!). Today I wonder if, in 1961, I momentarily accessed a past life. I've revisited that life under hypnosis, and it seems I died in extremely hot weather, shortly before Pompeii's destruction, of a fever that lasted a week, and that my body lay in that room after death for awhile. I am unclear how long. I think I was nine years old, though I remember the girl in the fresco as looking older than that. Yet I thought I had been the girl in the fresco. Since then I've had past life regressions, and indulged myself in stories of past lives in Tibet, Crete, Rome, Central America, Central Europe, Egypt, several in England (one about 300 AD, another about 500 AD, another in the 1550s, and one in the nineteenth century.) It is interesting that I've always been an avid Latin student (eight years of it, through all high school and all college), and forever interested in Tibet, the Greeks and Romans, the Mayans, the Incas, the Celts of southern England, the Minoan civilization of the third millennium before Christ, the vampire legends of central Europe. In one life I accessed, I was being bled to death in a big stone bathtub. I was not in pain, but I grew increasingly cold and numb as I died. Someone famous was going to bathe in my blood. The king (or an important leader) of the area was named Vlad.

I have a good friend who is Caucasian but has always, all her life, been a passionate champion of the black people in this country. Our town and county weren't even integrated until we were out of high school, but she always sympathized with people of color. Was she a slave in a past life? Has she *known* what it is to be black in a country at a time when many people undervalued the contributions of Negroes, perhaps even owned them? Certain features she possesses do suggest the possibility of black ancestry, and there's a new theory that people retain physical characteristics from incarnation to incarnation.[5]

It's difficult to discount the work of Ian Stevenson and other reincarnation researchers, because children can't make up these things, and so many of his accounts have been factually verified.

At the very least, I believe that the purpose of past life regressions in this life may be to tell stories that are helpful to us to begin to understand ourselves. At the end of any regression, it is useful to ask oneself:

"What did I learn in that life?"

"What have I brought from that life into this one?"

"How did I die?"

Such exercises have powerfully changed people's understanding of themselves in this lifetime, which is the only one, after all, that we can be

---

[5] *Return Of The Revolutionaries,* Walter Semkiw. Hampton Roads, 2003.

sure of right now. Brian Weiss is one writer to read to follow up on past-life experiences. His books are riveting, and all the stories come from the patients in his psychiatric practice.

A way to start waking up to the awareness of past lives, perhaps, is to look at what places and peoples interest you in this life. And you can *intend* to "go back" to one of those lives. Just close your eyes, have a pencil and paper at the ready, *intend* to revisit a past life, and see where your imagination leads you. Are you male or female? Describe your surroundings. Your clothing. Do you have a sense of when and where in history it is? How did you die in this life? These are some of the questions you might ask. If you have an unusual pain somewhere, it might be useful to ask what the origin of that pain is, intending to probe for past-life causes.

Friends in High Places

5. Spirit Retrieval, AKA Ghost Busting

> *In the end, the only events in my life worth telling are those when the imperishable world irrupted into this transitory one.*
>
> *That is why I speak chiefly of inner experiences, amongst which I include my dreams and visions.*
>
> ~Carl Gustav Jung

In 1992, I met David McKnight, because I signed up for a course in ghost-busting that he taught. He was teaching at a junior college when I met him, had once been a Presbyterian minister, and would remain a close friend and a true soul-mate of mine until his death a dozen years later. It was a loose group; new people showed up at every class; some fell away. Little did I suspect that the class would lead to a ten-year important hobby for me.[6]

I was impressed by David McKnight's credentials. A Harvard and a

---

[6] When David and Mary moved to Canada ten years later, without David in the group I didn't feel as protected and safe as I had with him there, and thus retired from the group. It has now disbanded entirely.

Katie Letcher Lyle

Union Theological Seminary graduate, he had held Presbyterian parish ministries for a few years, until teaching and a failing of his Christian faith tugged at him so strongly that he broke away from the church. That, and the fact that he held some unorthodox beliefs, which I was to become familiar with in the coming years. We three—his wife Mary, David, and I—all became close friends through the years. Mary remains my friend since David's untimely death. Unfortunately, my husband feared and despised them and wanted nothing to do with them.

About half of us that met in the ghost-busting class are frankly and devoutly Christian; the other half of us are not, but our mutual interest in sending stuck souls on to the Beyond erased our religious differences. We were a motley group: a fit ex-Marine, now a Domino's Pizza regional manager, a Lynk Systems Account Executive, a lovable and sensitive blue collar worker who's been employed locally at several stores; a (fallen-away) Presbyterian minister (David), his wife Mary, who's a Congregationalist minister on her own, and me: writer, professor, seeker. Occasionally, other curious or interested people would join us for a session. We always welcomed newcomers, as often one or more of us would be unable to attend a session.

When I agreed to do this I accepted the presumption that such earthbound souls exist. When these spirits, or ghosts, make nuisances of themselves in houses, by making noises, moving or misplacing objects, sometimes by appearing, or making a room threatening or just cold, people sometimes asked us to intervene. Out of ten years of these sessions, I took notes on only a few, never thinking I'd write about this, and always being in something of an altered state while engaged in this fascinating process.

In my ten years of spirit-retrieving, we found many "stuck" souls, and sent them "into the light."

The tragedy of these ghosts seemed to be that many of them died so quickly or so violently that they didn't know they were dead. Sudden violent death seems to produce ghosts, if I may generalize. Just as in live people, trauma (at death) seems often to bring denial. At the top of the list of traumas that occur to humans must be sudden death. At the first haunted place we met, dating from 1789, we encountered a man who died from a fall down stairs, a boy who "fell" from a second story window at age twelve, the man who killed him when he learned that he (the killer) was not the father of his "son." A black coachman was the final spirit we contacted that night; he was hanged by a mob who blamed him for the boy's death, when in reality he had only been passing the house.

Unable to accept their deaths, or even to grasp the concept of not being alive, these spirits stay earthbound. They may have died while drunk, or just without any preparation, or without a belief in an afterlife. These souls therefore have no idea where to go or how to get to somewhere else, so after death they hang around in a kind of timeless, spaceless limbo, attached to people or things or places they knew while alive on earth, without the skills or beliefs to move on, or sometimes afraid to go on. Most of them, when asked how long they had been "there," told us "I don't know," or "A long time," or "It seems like a long time," or, "I don't know…" One said, when I tried to pin him down, "…many hours, at least…."

The first time I participated in spirit retrieval, I had no idea what to expect, sitting on the floor of Jack Roberson's house, listening to him tell about the ghosts other people had encountered in his house through the years, one of the oldest (and surely the dirtiest) houses in Lexington, built around 1775.

I listened, but really did not believe, as people in the group "encountered" several spirits in Jack's house, but none of the ones he told us others had experienced did we experience. I took in the fact that stories got spun, about slaves being tossed out high windows in the attic, about jealous lovers and betrayed women, related by people in trances as they seemingly relived dramatically horrible deaths, including a lynching. Bill Walls, the man whom a lynched slave "came through," was glistening with perspiration and trembling as he apparently relived the terrible death.

The "spirits" spoke or "came through" the people assembled. I noticed that some of them seemed deeply entranced, and upon waking told us they did not recall what they had said. Others remained alert, reporting on feelings, personalities, even whole life stories, apparently able to stay in their bodies, to be themselves, and yet able to allow spirits to express ideas and speech through them. One of the participants, David's wife Mary, went into a trance so deep that her eyes rolled back, showing only the whites. She passed out and crumpled off a sofa onto the floor, moaning while "being inhabited" by a spirit. I was hugely interested and vowed at the end of the evening to return. But I wasn't anywhere near ready to "allow" any spirits to inhabit me. That took several sessions, several months. I never, in over ten years, actually *saw* a ghost with my eyes. Others said they did, but I never did.

At one house where children had experienced pinches, and every night brought bangings and other loud noises and flashes of light awakening the entire family, we contacted a spirit who came through one of our members, whose name was Keven: "I'm here," he mumbled, "I'm the one you seek."

"Tell us your name," David said.

"I'm too ashamed... I killed them all. All the family."

"Why?" asked David. There was no answer. "Where are you now?" he pursued.

"Nowhere," was the answer. Eventually he gave a name: Jonathan William Burk.

"For my own pleasure, I killed them," he said. "Then I killed myself."

Friends in High Places

Keven (Jonathan) began to weep.

"Take my hand," David said, taking Keven's. "God forgives. You need to leave this house, and these people, alone. There needs to be peace, for them and for you. Go to the light. All these acts of violence, turn away from them."

"I can't," he said. "I'm afraid."

"How did you kill them?"

"With a machete. I killed them any way I wanted to. And myself."

"How old are you?"

"Twenty-nine. Anyway, I wanted to. I couldn't let them catch me and put me away."

"What year do you think it is?"

"1888, of course. It's 1888."

"You have been trapped in time. It's 1994."

"No! It's not."

"Yes. Look down. Are those your hands?"

"N-n-no.... whose hands are they?"

"Keven's. Jonathan, it's 1994. You are dead."

"I'm not... dead."

"But you told us you killed yourself. You are dead, and you need to move on. We want to move you forward out of the Hell you have created."

"It's so dark here...."

"Turn away from the darkness. Seek the light. Do you see the light?"

"There's no light for me. That light isn't for me."

"Oh, yes it is. Go into it. There is forgiveness there, but you must take it," said David.

Eventually we talked that soul into moving into the light. There were no more disturbances in that house. When we called several months later to ask, the family living there told us things had been quiet ever since our visit.

Ghosts we encountered could somehow manifest sounds: thumps and bangs, and, on occasion, footsteps. They seemed in general to be dressed normally for their times of living, had no material substance, and vanished or faded with no trace. Some of our group reported seeing some spirits that were transparent, some solid-appearing. I never saw a thing. Some ghosts were never seen, but were strongly felt. Some interacted, and some never did—were seen only in passing, as shadows, lights, or even, once, as a flimsy cloth-like form. They were of different ages. My conclusions are the results of at least four or five, and sometimes as many as ten, of us doing the soul-retrievals—all of us with different sensitivities, different sensibilities.

Another thing we intuited was that if a *living* person is drunk or drugged or weak in some way, that weakened state seems to create "holes in the aura" which can sometimes enable earthbound spirits to enter them. It happened once at my house, when I perceived that my husband was not my husband; he took on, briefly, the face of a demon, red-eyed and deformed-looking. He was extremely drunk at the time, glancing up at or through or past me, evil-faced and transformed. I was so frightened I left the house for two hours, slipped back in, and went up to bed without speaking to him again that night. And I locked my bedroom door.

"What do you do?" people often asked me, when I mentioned that ghost busting—or my preferred name for it, spirit retrieval—was a hobby. "How do people hear about you?"

Word about our group traveled by grapevine; we neither advertised nor accepted compensation. When we were invited, we agreed on a time to go to the houses and listen to the stories of people who were being bothered by—we guessed—disembodied spirits. Our mission was always

Friends in High Places

to contact, then direct, these lost, troubling, and troubled spirits to the light. By this "light" we meant the next level a spirit is supposed to go to. We did this by going into a relaxed semi-trance state to try to open ourselves to contact by the spirit or spirits. We closed our eyes, took some deep breaths, thought of centering ourselves on our subject, and tried to be open to any spirit that would communicate with us. We asked for universal protection from evil, expressed our beneficial intentions, and stated that we wished to be contacted by anyone there.

At our sessions, the rule was that *we must give whatever we get*—that is, describe verbally what we're seeing in our mind's eye, any *emotions* that we feel arising in us, any *words* we hear, any *impressions* of any sort that we have.

Certainly, some souls have, in some of these sessions, seemed to come through me. In the altered state of consciousness that we experience, I (and others) have a different experience of time and space than usual. (I have to add that I often questioned of myself whether I was just making all this up, trying to be an agreeable member of the group.) I remember one woman who came through me, at a house where the current renters could not sleep at night because of all the aural kitchen disturbances; the sounds of crashing pots, breaking china, slamming doors, and visual disturbances: lights going off and on. When she was "in me," I felt how suspicious of us she was, how she argued that she certainly wasn't dead, that of course it wasn't 1998, and told us in no uncertain words that she wasn't leaving her house. I was aware of her in me, a rather stubborn and ignorant farm woman of the 1890s, with little joy in her life, and, at the same time, I was aware of being me, blue-jeaned, a hundred years beyond her time, trying to persuade her to look for her husband and go into the light. Eventually she left, though it was with her children, emphatically *not* her husband. Her world seemed—or felt—dark and joyless to me.

Although some ghosts apparently just choose to stay on in "their" houses, for instance, rather than going on to a higher level after death, many are fixated on unresolved situations left over from their lives on earth. Some souls fear to meet their Maker, or, as in one of our cases, a nagging wife on the other side, and so are reluctant to "move on." Twice I've encountered souls who hesitate to go on because they believe they are undeserving of Heaven, and feel reluctant to even try to advance. One was a vicious murderer, the other a guilt-ridden participant in a childhood homosexual act with a teacher in the 1840s.

Since time apparently has no meaning on that other plane, ghosts may think they have been wandering around in the dark for "a while," or "a long time," when it may be scores or even hundreds of years in earth time. We tried to ask spirits what year they thought it was, and then we told them what year it really was. We showed them our hands, to persuade them that we were not them. In fact, they seem somewhat disoriented about pretty much everything. Sometimes they were embarrassed to realize they didn't even know their own names: Never did they know just how long they had been dead, and many denied they were dead at all. Presumably, love is the connection that allows them to go on to whatever awaits them. Apparently one of the "jobs" of the dead is to greet their loved ones when they die. Their love may even be the light. There is literature that confirms this, and our own Hospice nurses confirm many visits from dead relatives just before the death of patients.

At a local Domino's Pizza Parlor where there has been continual ghostly activity for years leading to rapid turnover of employees, in a dozen sessions we discovered spirit after spirit. Perhaps, as some of our group think, the building is a gathering place for spirits, or, in the word of one psychic, a "portal," where spirits can more easily than usual enter this realm. In general, from our sessions we learned that our information jibed with what we can know locally of the history of the nineteenth-century building. It has been a railroad rooming house, a brothel, an apartment house, a washer and dryer store, a television store—and there are apparently many earthbound spirits either passing through it or living in it (and what is the difference between passing through or living if there is no concept of time after death?).

In digital photos of the rundown and dirty empty rooms now used only for storage, we find many orbs that our eyes cannot perceive. The stories that we dis-cover or un-cover at our sessions at Domino's have been dramatic, horrifying, mundane, complicated, or simple. Most of the ghosts we have encountered seem to have died suddenly or violently. If the passing had been sudden, it seems that often the spirit is not aware of having passed on at all, and thus attempts to continue to exist on earth. This may be a key; presumably if you die with time to contemplate your death, you may not be so disoriented. Clearly some discarnate entities (ghosts) are confused because others seem to be living in their houses, and they can't seem to communicate with these new people or understand what they're doing here.

At Domino's we have spent twelve three-hour sessions, and sent into the light among others the following spirits: several children; a young woman who died in childbirth; an abortionist-preacher; a British airman from World War I who died over the English Channel; two railroad loafers, both alcoholic, who had died earlier in the twentieth century, named themselves as Lester and Red Hawk; a girl named Becky who, around 1930, fell off a cliff in the adjacent mountains while gathering berries and broke her neck; a black tramp; a man who fell out of a boat and drowned; a man named Eugene Topping who was endlessly looking for his wife; a frightened runaway slave; a morphine-addicted woman named Lilly, who after death still craved morphine. All of these and more we have coaxed or coached to follow the light, to go into the light, to look for someone they love in the light, and to go on to whatever is next for them. I declare that we did not make up these entities. Furthermore, Bill and Tim, two of our group, talked to people in town and found several old-timers in Buena Vista who remembered or heard of Lester and Red Hawk hanging around the railroad hotel in the twenties and thirties.

Meanwhile, the employees at the pizza parlor to this day still hear ghost babies crying, watch objects from the kitchen levitate off the counter and float in the air, see flashes of light at the edges of vision, feel ghostly hands on their backs, or, in the case of some of the women, ghostly pinches on their bottoms. Apparently, we haven't yet cleared out all the stuck earthbound souls that seem clustered there.

At Domino's early one Sunday morning before the place opened at eleven, we met upstairs in the usual spot, a dirty messy storeroom, when an angry, enraged man came through Bill, probably the gentlest of our ghostbusters. He was staying there, he insisted belligerently; there was no one who could make him move. He wouldn't tell us his name. Hostile, furious, he yelled at us, through gentle Bill, to go away and leave him alone.

Then, suddenly, the spirit of his daughter came through a girl named Christa, who was visiting that morning in the group. The spirit told her sad story, which the rage-filled father constantly tried to interrupt and deny. He had impregnated her, she said, his own daughter, then killed her when he discovered she was pregnant. He had thrown her body into the river across the field that lay beyond the railroad track in front of the store. She was cold, and did not know how long she'd lain in the water. The man, inhabiting Bill's body, would have nothing to do with our coaching him to go into the light, convinced that only Hell was waiting for him. He admitted he was dead, but he refused to go on.

As Christa tearfully relived the daughter's horrible death, and her chilled condition, her father, coming through Bill's large and powerful form, unable to stop her telling her story, suddenly leapt to his feet,

Friends in High Places

picked up a board lying near where we sat on boxes, boards, cinder blocks, coils of wire, and stacked up tiles, and headed for David McKnight, clearly intending to whack our leader with the board. The women scattered, the guys all intercepted him and forced him to the ground, and called Bill to return to us.

It was the only physically scary moment I ever encountered in all that ten years.

Finally, together we persuaded that man, who continued to refuse to give us his name, that God forgives even the worst sinner, and at long last we did convince him to go when he made out the form of his mother in the light. In an instant, the charged atmosphere of that store-room vanished. We all were exhausted when it was safely over. Bill had a hard time getting over the fact that he nearly attacked our leader while possessed by that strong evil spirit. Perhaps Bill, the gentlest of men, but also probably the most psychic one of us, was easier to "enter" than the rest of us. I myself often "held back" from allowing anyone to come through me. I think Bill never did.

Space and time seem at the least *irrelevant* when we are communicating with the dead. They are always "right here" when you communicate. They're not off, far away, somewhere. They are in you, around you, often occupying the same apparent space as you are. Physicists will tell you that's impossible, but that is what we experienced.

Some earthbound spirits are bored. They are the ones that are apt to show up when the kids play with ouija boards, and spell out that they are Napoleon, or Jesus, and give silly messages. According to what I've read on the subject, ouija boards are the easiest way for spirits to communicate, so easy in fact that it is difficult for users of these board games (?) to screen out bored, or impish, or evil spirits.

On the same fairly low vibrational level, David McKnight believed, are some innocent spirits who may be stuck, unable to move on simply because they haven't ever heard or thought about dying and what follows death. If you haven't got a roadmap, how would you have any idea of how to get to wherever it is you're supposed to go? Before I went to the Monroe, before I took any of this seriously, at our old country house one weekend I had charge of three of my nieces, and two of their friends. I had to leave them for an hour or so for some reason. But before I went, to entertain them I hastily drew a Ouija board on a poster paper, gave them a juice glass, and told them how to ask spirits for information. By the time I got home, they had "conjured" a man who had died in our farmhouse in the last century, whose wife had killed him with a poker, then dragged his body into the fireplace, where damage by fire covered up her crime, and it looked as if he'd fallen into the fire. One of my nieces, Emily, looked up at me with big eyes, and said, "Katie, we made this up, right? None of it is true, right?" And, because I believed it at the time, I said, "Honey, you all just made it all up. It's not real."

Those without any idea of what occurs after death—or any idea that they are dead—seem to experience boredom, panic, confusion, frustration, anger, denial; sometimes they experience these emotions with enough energy to cause a haunting. It's like being lost somewhere, with no idea of what to do next, or where to go. Help is always available, but you have to know to ask for it. (It occurs to me that perhaps the same thing is true on the earth plane. The light is always there, but you have to "go to" the light.)

We've found that people we contact on the other side, even if they acknowledge that they are dead, don't all experience death the same way. For those with a sectarian view of death, such as fundamental Christians, the Afterlife may appear at first to be composed only of people like them, a world of Baptists or Presbyterians. If you are Muslim, then perhaps your heaven will be a Muslim heaven. If you are a Native American, your Afterlife may be a version of the Happy Hunting Ground. After all,

Friends in High Places

among the living, your imagination is the vehicle on which you are taken to wherever you go. It may be the same with the dead.

Jesus said, "In my father's house are many mansions." That to me means that the afterlife will be as different as the souls inhabiting it. Imagination seems to be the critical factor.

Spirits who need to rest awhile before going on seem to be drawn to a beautiful park, or an area that has come to be known in the literature as Summerland. For folks who can imagine it, this is Valhalla, the conventional idea of Heaven, a place where desires formerly unfulfilled can be fulfilled, where old friends and family that we thought lost to death are restored to us. Thus, if you died cold and hungry, there you can experience warmth and satisfaction. If you died of cancer, over there you will be healthy and whole, and any age you want to be.

Another universal that we have experienced is that those on the other side come for their dying family members. We have tale after tale of Hospice patients being greeted, and I can't think of a single example in my years of spirit retrieval of nobody being there to usher the newcomer into the light. Once, a horse appeared, the beloved pet of a ghost who came through me, to lead his mistress into the light. Here is what happened.

One night in a store in downtown Staunton near the railroad, I became the medium, the channel, the physical person through whom a spirit speaks. We six ghost-busters of the evening had been invited, and were holding our meeting in the store. The owners had experienced some unsettling phenomena, the nature of which I now can't recall. They asked us to come communicate with the spirit or spirits.

As I quieted my perception and entered an altered state, the impression that came to me is that this simple woman was a circus Fat Lady, that she was born of midwestern parents in a small town that bore their last name. At least one of her parents shared her glandular disorder and both were also obese, though not as fat as she was. She was their only child, and her name was Sarie (sounded like "sorry"). As a child, she'd had a pet horse that she loved. She informed us that she had died near the spot where we were, probably in the nineteen-twenties, as part of a circus that was being moved by railroad.

I "saw" her in a ridiculous dirty, fluffy, ruffled yellow—and childish—dress, obviously designed to increase her bulky appearance even more as "The Fattest Lady on Earth." She seemed lonely and sad and depressed, but not really ill. In fact, I sensed an immense dignity in her. My impression was that she had died of a massive stroke following a train wreck, of fear rather than injury, and because she had no concept in her mind of Heaven or an Afterlife, she became "stuck" in some gray timeless landscape, like someone in a never-ending dream. Perhaps it was what people speak of as purgatory. She could not tell us what year it was.

But when she could not believe it was 1999, and that she was dead to the physical world, we convinced her by asking her to look down at her hands (actually my hands), and then she "saw" that she was in someone else's body (mine) and not her own.

We asked her who had died before her that she loved. She named her chestnut horse. We asked her to look for her horse, and to look for the light. We sent Sarie into the light, riding bareback on her chestnut horse. When she did, I then "saw" her as a normal-sized person. In recollecting the event of that evening, I felt her in my own body and saw her history in my own mind.

Ridiculous, you say? We have, believe it or not, rid several houses of bothersome and frightening ghosts. We add to each other's impressions as we "sense" information, and on occasion, as with Sarie, I feel another person's whole life, and can sense many things about that person. But still I am embarrassed, for I feel fake about it, feel I am making it up.

Unfortunately, I have never been able to find proof, such as a newspaper account of the circus train wreck and names of the dead, of the life and

Friends in High Places

death of any person I've sensed, or who has communicated with me, though two of our group have confirmed the names we got in one session as the names of those two railroad bums who hung around Buena Vista in the nineteen thirties.

※

In one house we were invited to de-haunt, we discovered that a woman named Louise, the sister of the husband, had died of alcoholism eight weeks before. The house was now being disturbed by thumps and noises; the shape of a young woman showed up clearly in a photo taken of the husband and wife leaning against a car. One morning all the goldfish in their aquarium were floating dead on top of the water. But what worried the parents was that their two young children kept reporting seeing Aunt Louise, hovering footless above their beds, dressed in a white leather-fringed garment. The wife was worried about Louise's influence on the children, though she admitted that she felt Louise was staying around to "protect" the kids. There had been bad blood between the wife and Louise, the dead alcoholic sister-in-law.

When we went into our usual seance mode—relaxing, focusing, opening, praying for protection—I felt strongly that there was a blonde pony-tailed girl in a blue sweater sitting at the top of the stairs just behind us, hiding and listening. I reported this.

"Louise was buried in her blue denim jacket," the husband told us. He added that in life she often wore her blonde hair back in a pony tail, though it was "styled" for burial. When we pooled our impressions, it turned out she didn't trust or like her brother's wife, and was trying to protect the children from their own mother. It was a complicated case, but eventually we sent Louise into the light, and the hauntings stopped. People sometimes die with unsolved problems on their minds, which keep them hanging around instead of moving on.

Katie Letcher Lyle

One autumn afternoon in the mid-nineties, David McKnight and I walked up on Sitlington Hill near McDowell in western Virginia, where the Battle of McDowell had taken place during the Civil War, on May 8, 1862. The area where we walked is believed to be haunted by some of the spirits of the 720 casualties of that battle. David, tape recorder in hand, asked me to go into trance and see if anyone might "find" me. I closed my eyes and breathed deeply, covered us both with white light, and waited.

Within mere moments, I was in psychic conversation with a young Union soldier from Delaware who had died there. He was confused, felt that the battle probably was still going on, though it seemed to him hours since he'd seen any of his fellow soldiers. As usual, I asked him what year he thought it was, and eventually told him the Union had won the war. He professed amazement, for he felt the Rebs were winning the battle he was in. (I later learned that the Battle of McDowell was, in fact, a triumph for the Confederacy.) I tried to urge him to "look for the light" and go towards the light.

He said hesitantly that he couldn't do that. I asked why, and he said he thought the light led to Heaven. I said I thought so too, and he repeated he couldn't go to the light. The story he reluctantly told was that he was certain he would not be accepted into Heaven, because he had once been a participant in a homosexual encounter with a school teacher of his in the late 1840s. He was not homosexual, but he cooperated because he feared and respected his schoolmaster. He felt that his part in the event had tainted his soul and precluded him from going to Heaven, despite the fact that he had not wanted or initiated the event. I tried to explain about forgiveness, urged him to look to the light, asked him to look and see if there wasn't someone he knew in the light. Though it took a bit of persuasion, when he saw his mother, he forgot about his prohibition and went with her into the light.

Friends in High Places

A postscript to this story is that I eventually found a list of those who died at that battle. There was a soldier with the last name he gave me, but a different first name. There were two others on the list with his first name, but not the last. Maybe the exchange of information between us and the dead is necessarily iffy. After all, we exist in two different worlds. I continue to search for validation.

※

Several years later, after David had died, and two weeks before *My Neighbors' Ghosts* was published, Mary McKnight, David's widow, whom I had not seen since his death, came to visit me. I told her I was working on a second book about the work David and I had done together, and asked her if she still had any of the tapes of the sessions we had done that I might borrow, even though I had notes of my own.

She brightened and said David had transcribed many of them, and had intended to do his own book on our spirit-retrieval before his unexpected death. Would I like to see his unfinished manuscript and perhaps make use of it?

Yes, I said. I told Mary I worried about taking credit for someone else's work, and would not even look at it unless she assured me it was all right to use David's name, and attribute anything of his to him. She was delighted, and said she felt that David had been telling her to give me the manuscript and see what I could do with it.

David did lots more retrieving of unhappy spirits than I did, and in other parts of Virginia, with other spirit-seekers. What he transcribed, in the papers given to me by his widow Mary, included, unfortunately, only one of the sessions we did together, the one above. My own notes are sketchy—I never thought at the time of needing to tape the entire evening, which naturally often ran to several hours of tape.

Throughout the ten years when I went with David to some haunted site, the tape recorder would often malfunction, only to function fine when we got home. We learned this was not unique with us. The theory is that ghosts use earthly energy, and "take" energy from wherever they can find it. Including tape recorders! Or sometimes nothing was on the tape, though we'd been in a group, talking, with the tape running the entire time.

The following are from David's later translation of our encounter, in the same part of Sitlington Mountain where David had been before with others, and encountered spirits often. The following is from David's manuscript.

Katie picked up William, who said, "You're going to have an experience, my dear." (William is my spirit guide I met one afternoon in the Washington and Lee Library. He seems eager to help me do this work.)

K: William, will you help me?

Wm: Oh, this is the most excited I've been in a long time.

At the same location where our previous group picked up a young soldier calling for his mother, Katie suddenly felt a soldier:

K: He's on the shoulder of another soldier. He's saying, "My brother, where's my brother? He's back up there, and he's hurt."

David: William, bring this young man along, and we'll talk to him up on the hill.

K: I think his name is Bill, and his brother is David. He's worried about his brother. His name seems to be Bill Bell. Oh, here's another one coming down the hill. (pause) His name is Perry. Lieutenant Perry, I think. He wasn't badly hurt. He was calling for someone to pay attention to him. More scared than hurt. I can "see" soldiers moving around this hill, almost like boys playing games. Not a lot, maybe twenty. God, they look young.... Now someone is saying, "We're safe because they're shooting higher than we are." I'm picking up a shock to the shoulder, which had to have been a shot. The soldier with the bad shoulder is thinking, *This is what it's all about. This is what it's like to die.*

Friends in High Places

The bullet spun him around. It's not so much pain as shock.[7]

Katie stops at exactly the spot where Bev (another spirit-retriever who met with us occasionally) stopped last time.

K: It's another one. He says his name is Andrew, or Andrews, not sure. Nothing wrong with him, that I can see. He's greeting me. He strode down here and said, "Andrew, Ma'am," and saluted me. He has a dark blue uniform. I guess he's a Union—a Yankee.

David: Ask him how the battle is going. What's happening on the hill?

K: He says, Old Stonewall has come up here. We don't know how many others there are. They're up there. They seem to be retreating down this way.

D: Ask him where he's from.

K: He's a private. It's something like Harbin. It's out west of here. He has on a uniform from some school. He's a Virginian.

D: Ask if he's retreating.

K: He says, "Oh, no, we're gonna lick em."

David: What's his first name?

K: "Joseph," he says.

Katie keeps walking, and there's another soldier in front of her.

K: "Meecham, Ma'am," to my question about his name. David, there are three people hiding behind that rock outcropping up to our left.

Twenty yards or so before our destination (Nancy Walker's cold spot) Katie felt cold, and a breeze. [Nancy was another of David's friends who did some ghost-busting.]

K: I get a name, Harry Camden, right here. He's lying down. He's from Trentfield, New Jersey, saying, "I'm just a-going to rest here for a bit." He doesn't think he's dead.

D: Ask him how's the battle going.

K: He says he doesn't know. He sees lots of soldiers in the ravine, lots of running back and forth. But he says a battle doesn't ever make sense to him. It's

---

[7] I have no recollection of "seeing" all those soldiers, but I must have at the time.

not orderly. He says, "It's orderly the way we're told to do it, but it's not orderly in action."

D: How old is Harry?

K: Eighteen.

David: Is this the first fighting he's engaged in?

K: "Yes, Ma'am," he says.

D: How does he feel about being in this war?

K: Says he's confused, just going to lie here and rest. He wishes he could go home.

David: Has he been hit?

K: Says he can't feel anything in his legs.

D: Could I ask him some direct questions?

K: Yes, he seems to be telling me.

D: I want to point out to you, Harry, that if you can't feel in your legs, that's not a good sign. A doctor would not like this, and would think you'd been hit in the spine.

K: He says he thinks he'll just lie here and rest.

D: Harry, can you move a toe?

K: He says he can't.

D: Harry, we want you to rest. But you need to think, also. If you're going to get out of here, you're going to have to figure out how. How are you going to do that?

K: Says he isn't going to think about it.

D: That's fine, Harry. But you appear to me to be mortally wounded. You're resting in another world.

K: "No, I've just been here a while. I just wanna rest!"

D: Harry, can you see us?

Katie turns to me, says, What's that pungent odor on my hands? Can you smell it?

D: Possibly it's Harry. Harry, I'm here with a machine that wasn't invented

Friends in High Places

in your day. In fact, 135 years have passed since you fought on this hill. It may sound silly, but how do you explain that I'm here talking to you?

K: He says that's even more confusing.

D: Harry, it's not 1862. It's 1997.

K: He says no.

D: Do you see any fighting going on right now around you?

K: He says no.

D: Well, everyone didn't just disappear suddenly. But you're hearing us. You don't see anyone else. There's just a bunch of trees and rocks. This battle's over, Harry. Why haven't your comrades carried you off the hill? Doesn't that seem strange?

K: He says, "If I can just go to sleep and not think, it will be better. What you're saying is more confusing than the battle." [Obviously, I am repeating to David what Harry's telling me here, though I have no memory of this. From here on, I appear to be speaking directly as Harry. Again, I plead ignorance.]

D: I know. I understand. But this is no place for you. Nothing but a lot of weeds and trees and rocks here. Don't you have a girl back home, or a family you'd like to be with?

K: Yeah, I'd really like to go home.

D: Harry, you can do that. The northern troops retreated just a few hours after this battle, when nightfall came.

K: Well, that's why there's no one nigh.

D: Harry, would you like me to take you to your family? Who are you really close to?

K: My mother.

D: What's her name?

K: Gerta.

D: Harry, can you picture her real clearly? Just rest, and imagine that your mother is coming toward you, and that she's surrounded by a wonderful light. She sees you and calls to you. Can you see her?

K: Yes, and she's got the dog with her.

D: *Good! What's the dog's name?*

K: *Trig.*

D: *What's going on now?*

K: *They're comin. I'm... I'm runnin' towards them. She's saying, "Welcome home, Boy. Why son, you're in Heaven. You died in that battle."*

K: *I knew there was something wrong. I can walk again! I'm walking with Mom and Trig on this path that's really beautiful. The sun's going down, and the trees are green green green! It's a path in the woods. Don't know where it goes. How'd you do that? Who are you?*

I then asked Katie if she could see Harry. She told me, "Yes, he had a darker skin than you or me. He was chunky, short, probably 5'6" with brown hair, and bulky through the chest though spindly in his arms, and bow-legged, like he'd ridden horses a lot, or had rickets maybe. The dog was largish, nondescript, shaggy. His mother was taller than he by about two inches."

That same day, we picked up a soldier that I felt had been hit in the head and couldn't even hear us. I saw a streaming yellow and red liquid on his face, and he couldn't respond. David directed questions at William (through me), who said he was aware of many troops still there. But my friend William added he doesn't understand the insignia of this war, having been a Quaker and alive a century before the Civil War. He notices a gaunt soldier with pale skin and black hair and a thin beard, about twenty, who was so still because he was afraid if he moved he'd hurt himself more. He kept his eyes wide open as he tried to hold the world in his vision and stave off death. His name was James Evans, and told us his father called him Junior. He had a sweetheart named Janie Carr, and was from Washington.

David asked him if he believed in the Lord, told him he was dying, and that Jesus would come and take him home.

And I said, "David, that's interesting! He died. He knew he wasn't

Friends in High Places

going to make it. He just disappeared. And I could tell that he was seeing Jesus coming towards him in a light. Just amazing!"

⁂

There's a story in David McKnight's collection that's really typical, and instructive, and complete. I wasn't there, but I'd like to present that story here. David calls it "A Civil War Battlefield Rescue." The following story is entirely in David's words, from his manuscript:

A Civil War Battle Rescue

On May 6, 1862, Major General Thomas "Stonewall" Jackson began moving a confederate force of over 9,000 troops from Staunton, Virginia, toward the tiny farming village of McDowell, some thirty-five miles to the west. In concert with Brig. General Edward "Allegheny" Johnson, his objective was to dislodge a Union force of almost equal number that from the opposite direction had been gathering in the McDowell area. The Union forces were at first unaware of the Confederate approach, Jackson having feinted a movement of his men toward Richmond to the east before reversing his direction in a rapid movement toward McDowell. General Jackson and a small group of the 52nd Virginia reached a point of the Staunton-Parkersburg Pike approximately one mile east of McDowell. At this point he and his men left the road and climbed up a rocky wooded ravine to the top of a hill owned by a local farmer Robert Sitlington. From the top of Sitlington, Jackson was able to observe the Union forces camped on the Bullpasture River a quarter mile below them, clustered around the McDowell Presbyterian Church located at the juncture of present-day Route 678.

When the Yankees noticed the Rebels, General Milroy ordered skirmishers to advance up the hill, and the Battle of McDowell, said to have been Jackson's first victory in his Valley Campaign, commenced. The fighting took place from late afternoon, by which time Jackson had a dozen regiments in place in the mountains around Sitlington's Hill, past nightfall. In the battle, which included hand-to-hand combat, approximately 400 casualties resulted, with 116 Confederates and thirty-four Federal soldiers killed or mortally wounded. Of the battle, Jackson wired "Today God blessed our troops with victory."

We were eight in number, led by Marilyn W. of Highland County. She had tramped the battlefield several times looking for minie balls and relics. She had told me several months before that she had noticed a "cold spot" when she was walking the hill several years before, causing her skin to break out in goose-bumps. On a subsequent relic search with her metal detector, she chanced upon the same spot and again experienced goose-bumps. She told me she was not really a believer in ghosts, but that if there were such a thing, this was the only experience in her life that might suggest such an explanation.

I asked if she would be willing to lead me and a group of rescue workers to this spot some day; and on July 12, 1997, a group of ghost hunters met at my house, and we made the trip. When we had proceeded only 100 yards above the remnant of Robert Sitlington's farm lane through the rocky, wooded slope, Nancy H, who had driven down from Baltimore, said she "saw" in her mind's eye, a young Confederate soldier lying beside the land calling for his mother. Tears welled up in her eyes, so strong was the impression. About fifty yards further up the farm lane, there was a steep slope to our left, and Bev McT. could perceive psychically a group of retreating Confederate soldiers, some wounded, stumbling, and falling down the boulder-strewn slope in their flight, with several actually dying where they fell. Marilyn had found numerous Union minie balls on this hillside through the years.

"Soon Marilyn made a right turn, and soon we were standing in a circle of small trees at the cold spot, and again she broke out into noticeable goose-bumps clearly visible to us all. So we sat down in the long grass and prepared to tune in to what might have occurred there. Bev was the first to speak: 'I sense four bodies here. Three are Confederate soldiers." I suggested that she try to tune in to the mind of any of them, and eventually she said, "I'm actually getting a northern soldier. His body is here with southern soldiers. He had some

superficial wound in his left leg, where his pant leg is torn.

Bette G. then added, "I'm picking up the name Bartholomew."

Bev went on: "This soldier chanced upon the Confederate dead here after the fighting ceased at this spot. He was actually looking for the body of a relative of his who was fighting with the Confederates. It's strange, but I think he took his own life at this spot after finding the three Rebels dead. I'm seeing he was young, maybe not even twenty, and a sensitive person who could not process in his mind the carnage of the battle. As he found the Rebs while searching for his kinsman, he was filled with revulsion, and simply sat down and cut his wrist. He did not want to die at the hand of the enemy, as these boys all had. But he's thinking he failed in his attempt and is in an agitated state of mind, fearing that his commanding officer will find out that he did the dishonorable act in the heat of battle. He does not want to deal with us in any way for fear we will learn his secret and report to the commander."

I then asked Bev if she could try to bring through one of the Confederate soldiers whose bodies she had perceived there. As we sat silent, meditating, she spoke, in a deep southern drawl. "It's me, Donald." (I'll call him D throughout.)

David: Where are you from?

D: South of Atlanta.

David: When'd you leave home, Donald?

D: Long time ago.

David: What did you do back home, farm?

D: Yeah, me and my dad got a little place.

David: What you think about this war, Donald?

D: We're gonna win it. That's why I'm here. But I never saw such rocky land in my life. You couldn't grow nothin' on his land. Rattlesnakes and bears, I reckon.

David: How old are you, Donald?

D: The truth?

Bette: Yes.

D: I'm fourteen. Big for my age, though. I said sixteen when I signed up. I'll be fifteen soon.

David: Been fighting, Donald?

D: Not too much. Got this big ole blister on the bottom of my foot. I did a lot of kitchen detail. I've not done a lot of fighting. I been with the army for some time.

David: Donald, you know what day this is?

D: I don't read, so I can't tell what those papers say that tell you what day it is.

David: Where'd you get those shoes, Donald?

D: Smokey give em to me.

David: How do they fit?

D: Not real good. I lost some of the leather comin' over them rocks. They just eat shoes right up. They'll eat your feet up too, if they get a chance.

David: Which direction did you come from to get up here?

D: I just followed a bunch of other folks. I didn't know where I was going. They said, "Go this way," so I went.

David: Then what happened?

D: Don't ask me. Don't want to tell you. It was bad. No place to go. Lot a guns. I got a ball in my stomach, but I don't think it went all the way through. What you folks doing settin' around here?

David: Beverly, why don't you introduce Donald to us, and tell him what we're doing here.

Bev: Yes. My name's Beverly, and...

D: Howdeedo, Ma'am. Why, you ain't got no uniform on. I didn't know they had women in the army.

Bev: I'm not with the Army.

D: You better git out of here, then. This is a war. This is where men kill. No disrespect, Ma'am, but ain't you a little balmy to be up here?

Bette: Donald, we're here to study history. Do you know what history is?

Friends in High Places

D: Yes, something that done happened.

David: That's right. And what this lady's getting at, Donald, is that you actually have done happened.

D: It don't make no sense.

David: What I mean to say is that you getting hit in the stomach with that minie ball, that's history, that's the past, Donald.

D: Yeah, I know. That happened day before yesterday.

David: Donald...

D: Yeah?

David: It happened 135 years ago. What do you think of that?

D: I think you're crazy.

David: I know. But I have evidence. For instance, there are women sitting around you here on this battlefield, not in uniform. They're here to study history 135 years after you think it is.

D: Well, you know, when that lady was talking about comin' here, I got this real funny feelin' about maybe I was it.

David: Donald, there's nothing wrong with being history. You've been hanging around here a lot longer than you realize.

D: Am I going to get in trouble for this?

David: No, certainly not, because your officers have been gone a long time. Some have been in their graves for a hundred years. What do you think of that?

D: Some of 'em, that's a good place for 'em.

Bev: You've been fighting this war long enough.

David: You know what she means, Donald?

D: Well, I just plumb quit two days ago. But I might understand what you're saying like when you think it's gonna rain a couple days from now, you jest feel it in your bones, and you better get your crop in. It's that kinda feeling, that maybe there's some truth in what you folks sayin.

D: Yes, Donald. Any one of these ladies can explain that a lot of time has passed since you got hit with that minie ball, but you feel like it was yesterday. You know, if a man gets hit with a minie ball in the stomach, surgeons don't even try to operate. They just set them aside and give them something for pain. And that's what's happened to you.

Hazel: Would you like to leave this mountain, Donald, and go somewhere you can be comfortable and happy?

D: I'd like to go where my buddies are. You know, they went off, and didn't take me.

David: Why do you think they didn't take you?

D: I asked that question too. Why didn't they? I think it's cause I wasn't dead. They took the dead, and I wasn't.

David: Or it could be the opposite. They may have taken the others because they were alive, and you weren't.

D: Ooooh.

David: It's something to think about. If they took people off this mountain, and left you, practically everyone would know why. Doesn't take an education to figure this one out.

D: I guess I'm stupid. I didn't figure it out.

David: Donald, it's not a matter of being stupid. You didn't want to die.

D: I thought I didn't. I told 'em when I joined, I'll go, to save my paw's place. Save southern womanhood. Come right down to it, mister, I don't want to die.

David: That's why you haven't realized that you did die on this hill. You lost a lot of blood with that bullet in your stomach; your body lost consciousness, and you passed on, like so many of your buddies you saw die. But you were still conscious, Donald, like you are now, because our spirit never dies when the body quits. Many continue on without realizing what happened. We think we're still living that old earth life, unaware that we've really entered another world. You haven't been able to take your attention off the old world and begin to look around for something new.

Friends in High Places

Hazel: Donald, we can show you where to go, and how to go.

D: Man, how do you know that? You know where my buddies are? Oh, I guess I don't need to ask you how, as long as you know.

Hazel: Yes! Would you like to go with them now?

D: It's real quiet here. Is the battle over?

Hazel: Yes. Who is one of your good buddies here?

D: I come in the army with a guy from outside Atlanta, name of Simon. Now I lost track of Simon when I got the blister, don't you know. But then we found each other when we climbed this hill. And I don't know where he is now. We used to have these tobacca-spittin contests. We're real good.

Hazel: You'd like to see Simon again?

D: Yessir. Reckon I'm as close to him as anybody. My ma died when I was born. I got my paw. But he's still…

David: Donald, I'd like to mention something, if it's all right. You're talking to us like you didn't lose your body in that battle. The litter-bearers didn't take you down the hill. I've said you died in that battle. Now, what do you think happens to people when they die?

D: Oh, they go to Heaven or Hell.

David: And you likely feel they'd know which they were in.

D: Yessir!

David: And you don't feel like you're in Heaven?

D: No sir.

David: Do you feel like you're in Hell?

D: Not from what I've heard.

David: And this is the reason you think you can't have died.

D: I reckon.

David: Now Donald, what if all this you were taught about isn't entirely true?

D: Well, it won't be the first, will it?

David: Maybe some preachers don't know what happens when we die.

Maybe it's like sitting on a log denying that this body on the ground is their dead body. But we need to test what I'm saying. If you can find Simon, and he tells you that both he and you have died and are in another world, would you believe him?

D: *Yes.*

David: *We can leave it up to Simon, then. I'm guessing Simon is somewhere like Heaven.*

D: *Maybe you don't know him like I do.*

David: *Well, maybe the preachers are wrong about some things, Donald.*

D: *I believe it!*

David: *Okay, how are we going to find Simon, since he's died and gone beyond?*

D: *Maybe whistle?*

David: *Let's try it. (All whistle.)*

D: *I done seen him! He's coming up over that hill.*

David: *All right! What's he look like?*

D: *He looks fine. He's smilin' and wavin'!*

Hazel: *Why don't you call to him?*

D: *Hey Simon, whacha doin?*

David: *What's he say?*

D: *He said he came to get me.*

Hazel: *Good! Now go on, just start walking towards Simon. He'll tell you where he's been, and what all happened. Tell us what Simon tells you.*

D: *He done come up and put his arm around my shoulder and clapped me on the back and said, I done found a place. Over here! Now we're walking, walking, and the hill's disappeared.*

David: *What are you seeing now, Donald?*

D: *Just a bunch of light. He's still talkin to me; he knows the place. He says I'm gonna like it. I can see the sun shinin' over some funny-lookin' hills over there—they're kind a white!*

Friends in High Places

Hazel: Well, just keep going toward those hills.
D: Yes, thank you, Ma'am."
And there the session ended.

❧

One night we were invited to a house up in the mountains near Harrisonburg where a woman, her daughter, and her granddaughter had all been experiencing frightening episodes in the small hours of the morning of "a heavy black shadow with red-coal eyes" lying on top of them and seemingly trying to suffocate them.

Let me explain here that the house, and the area, were full of hostile and unpleasant vibes. The woman, the mother, had come home to this property owned by her father after leaving her abusive husband; *her* father, who lived in another cabin on the property, was angry about his daughter's coming home. Her daughter, the man's granddaughter, was pregnant for the second time without benefit of wedlock. Her first little girl was about two. The teenaged mother and the little girl both were drinking soft drinks, and eating Little Debbie confections the whole time we were there. The daughter smoked non-stop. The child whined, cried, created distractions.

The grandfather had said absolutely that he did not want any ghost-busters there, but the woman had ignored him, begged us to come, asking us to cut off our headlights before coming by his house, and to de-haunt her house. So already we felt unwelcome, and debated going there at all.

But the woman, who called David on a payphone after reading an article about him, and us, in the Staunton newspaper, begged us so entreatingly that we agreed to go. I felt alternately cold or burning up the entire evening, as though I was coming down with some illness. I also could not stop worrying about the child in the girl's womb, feeling tremendously sad for its future life. It, another girl, I felt, seemed to be begging me for help, and I had no help to give it. I did finally gently say to the mother that smoking and eating that way did not serve her baby well. She just sneered, gave me a withering look, and didn't look my way again the entire evening. I guess I understand that nobody likes to be criticized, and of course she already knew she should quit smoking and eating junk food, but did not care.

I was uneasy the entire time we were there, wondering if the father, the landowner, might just decide to come down and shoot us. I did not invite any spirits to contact me. The entire place felt dark and depressing, as well as menacing. One of our members felt the presence of an ancient and very proud Indian chief on whose burial ground this farm had encroached. He seemed to have been alive around 500 years ago, and did not at all like these unpleasant people who were living atop him and his kin and ancestors, and did not understand why they wouldn't leave. They had only negative emotions, and he wished to be rid of them.

I wanted to be rid of them too. That evening, I felt anger, anxiety, and even a little fear. The "thing" the family had encountered never would respond to requests that it communicate with us. It may have been the angry Indian, or some other entity entirely. It did not feel human to me.

Later, on the way home, we all agreed that the atmosphere had felt frightening and "haunted." David was the one who always followed up, contacting folks later to see if we had successfully sent spirits into the light. But these people had no phone, and I think we never had a follow-up report. It's the creepiest I have ever felt in my life, and I have no idea if we helped those poor people at all. We all agreed later that we'd felt unwelcome, fearful—of the dark, of the drive up the mountain—of the place itself. Our usual protections seemed flimsy against the almost palpable evil in that place. I felt an unusual hopelessness and sorrow about the small child and the unborn one, and a deep distrust and dislike of the pregnant girl.

Friends in High Places

One Friday afternoon in the late summer of 2002, I answered my phone to a timid woman's voice: Mary McKnight had told her when she called their number that David was coming to spend the night at my house, in Lexington. She lived in Washington, and her mother lived in Buena Vista, just six miles from my house. Her mother was being haunted by something, and couldn't we—David and I—come to their house on Sunday morning and try to de-haunt it? David wasn't even due at my house for several hours. I told her we'd call her back as soon as he arrived. As I talked on the phone, I became aware of somebody standing right behind me, too close for comfort, and that somebody wanted a drink badly. Since my husband was an alcoholic, I thought I was imagining him behind me, or just making this up. The girl on the phone had told me nothing. I could not shake that presence, and told David about it when he arrived. We called the woman back and said we'd come Sunday morning. But this man's continued presence haunted me all weekend. He was big, he was right with me, and he craved booze.

When we met the woman being haunted, I asked right away if her dead husband (I was certain it was he who had dogged my footsteps the last two days) was a drinker.

"Big time!" was her frank response.

She, his widow, confirmed my impression that her husband had been a big man, and an alcoholic, and quickly told us that his death in 1966 was the result of a drunken car accident. Then she described the paranormal activities which had been bothering her for a year or more.

I did not become a channel for him, but he spoke only to me, which never happened before that day… or after. We had barely begun when he told me he was haunting the house where he had lived because in his view it was time for his wife to come with him.

I pointed out that he was scaring her to death with balls of light, boot-stomping around her house, lights and television going on and off, apparently by themselves, and that she would come when it was the right time for her.

He seemed a bit confused and said he had not realized that he'd frightened her. He agreed to leave, and did so. We sent him into the light.

We have learned from our sessions of talking to the dead that death doesn't seem to change anything but the physical body. Personality, values, beliefs, memories, addictions, and obsessions—all appear to survive the grave. Perhaps, in that particular case, the man's mind was unclear because of his drinking problem. He had been drunk at the time of his death in the traffic accident. The dead seem to be, somehow, literally and figuratively, in the dark.

When I "saw" this big man, he seemed to be flanked by two small black men. When I told his wife of my impression, she replied that he had always been a champion of not only minority people but also of "the little guys" as she put it, the underdogs. Perhaps I got a metaphoric vision of that, though I did not understand its meaning until she explained.

When we called the widow back a month later, she told us her house was free of any disturbances.

A year later, I dropped in on her one afternoon. She said that for a long time after our visit, everything was quiet. But on Hank's (her husband, the ghost) birthday, a book she'd never seen appeared in the morning on her coffee table: a children's book called Happy Birthday Mother and Daddy. She said to me, "You'll think I'm crazy, but I know it was from Hank. No one else was in here."

Sometime later she had several strokes, and she has heard, three times, loud explosive noises. Though she says the gas company has been all over her house "with a fine-tooth comb," no one has been able to find anything wrong, or any source for the noise which she says sounds "like a refrigerator dropped three stories onto concrete."

Friends in High Places

Shortly after David McKnight died, I wanted to contact him to ask him about the experience of death. I knew that he died quickly, of an abdominal aneurysm, knew his death was imminent, was made comfortable with morphine, and died two hours later without regaining consciousness.

We had the kind of friendship in which we could discuss anything, and we had actually planned this conversation.

Relevant facts: David loved sweets, but lived for years avoiding sugar, as he believed sugar "fed" cancer, which he'd fought for several years and finally conquered. He loved baseball, and coffee, and swimming in mountain rivers. He'd had a lifelong disappointing relationship with his father, who had openly disapproved of him. We had agreed years before that whoever died first would attempt to contact the other. I expect David had this arrangement with others besides me.

And so I put on a Hemi-sync tape, and asked for David to come.

He appeared instantly, smiling with pleasure, alive and well and glowing. "Was death as you expected?" I ask.

"Oh, more. Much more. More beautiful than our home in Highland County. I'm in the most beautiful place I've ever been."

"Is there food there?"

"Anything you want. Lots of sugar!"

"What's a day there like?"

"Well, so far I'm not bored. I'm told I will be, but not yet."

"So, can you go to a baseball game?"

"Yes, anything I want."

"You could see Babe Ruth hit the ball?"

"I presume I could."

I repeat my question about what a day's like on the other side.

"I wake up. I send Mary love, and you, and all my other friends. The coffee's fantastic, and someone else serves it! The time goes by but I'm not aware of it. There's so much to do, to learn." He continues to be vague.

"Did you reconcile with your father?"

"He has his Afterlife, and I have mine. It's absolute harmony."

"Do you get to swim?"

"I've swum in unbelievably beautiful places. When you come, we'll go together."

"Do you worry about things and people on Earth?"

"Not yet. But that's the service I'll join eventually."

"Could you tell me the names of some of the friends you visit with?"

(Here he names both living and dead friends) Clyde, Elisabeth (Kubler-Ross), a boyhood friend named Gerry, Harry, or Jerry—something like that—his mother, even Jesus. "I visited with Jesus!" (I asked his sister Kay, who remembered no one in David's boyhood by any of those names, but she admits she was older, and wouldn't necessarily know.)

"Thanks, David. I have to end for now."

And his last comment to me, gleeful: "See how easy it is to communicate?"

Someone recently asked me, If the dead are still alive, then where are they? My answer would be: obviously they are not in physical space, yet they always seem nearby when I am in contact. Right here.

You can pose this parallel: Where are dreams? They are where you are. They (ghosts) don't come from anywhere, and it doesn't take a while for them to get to *where* we are. They are already there. I'd say that they exist in some where that is analogous to dream-space. We all know that dream space is as fully "furnished" as any physical space, as rich as the world we live in daily, yet vanishes entirely when we wake up. It doesn't abide by physical rules, yet when we are in it, it seems just as real, just as physical, as the world. Two people that I know of have written about this, both in the middle of the last century. There are undoubtedly others I haven't run across. Professor Henry Habberly Price, a British philosopher and

Friends in High Places

professor at Oxford University, who wrote the classic *Thinking and Experience,* and Professor William Ernest Hocking of Harvard, who wrote *The Meaning of Immortality,* concluded the same thing (at least as I understood it), only with many more complications. I read them years ago, and this theory made sense to me.

We tend to think of ourselves generally as living *here*. Where do I live? *Here*. In this body. On this street. In this town. On this day of this particular year. All that seems true. There is physical space, and there is time.

But it may surprise you to hear that we really live *there* much more. Here's what I mean: we daydream, night-dream, imagine, worry, fear, anticipate (those are all living elsewhere, in the future); or we *remember*, or mourn for things and people lost to us, like our mothers or our own youths (those are all living elsewhere, in the past). We live out of our bodies when we are engaged in any of the aforementioned activities. We may be sitting at a desk, but we can go anywhere in an instant.

So I assume everything can exist together in exactly the same way, the living and the dead. Space as we know it in the physical world just doesn't have anything to do with it.

Once someone asked Meister Eckhart, a Dominican friar who lived many centuries ago, "Where does the soul go when we die?" Eckhart is said to have replied, "Nowhere."

By the same token, I've never been persuaded about the impossibility of space travel by the "scientific" argument that it would take "too much time" for those visitors to get here—you know, light years. Our earthly version of time would make that true, but I also know I can "go" anywhere in the time it takes me to think about it, and I assume that's the next step in the future of human travel. It's a whole different concept, but as it works mentally, well, I have no problem extending that to other travel as well. I also believe that "Inner Space" is more vast perhaps than Outer Space.

If our beliefs shape our world on this physical plane of existence, why should it not be the same in the world beyond this one? Do our diverse beliefs about the nature of the Afterlife shape what we will find after death, and affect events in that world as our beliefs do on earth? Will my dear Aunt Polly find the born-again Episcopal Heaven she believes in? Do American Indians find the Happy Hunting Ground? Do people with no belief in an Afterlife end up stuck and unable to move? Cultures ancient and modern have said yes.

And by the way, most ghost hunters, in my experience, strongly agree. I can't say "all," obviously, but everyone I've ever talked to agrees. Thus I conclude from years of reading, spirit-retrieval, collecting stories, and studying phenomenal events, that in general our beliefs define what is real for us, and influence how that reality works. It seems to be true for spirits we have contacted. When we die, we do not shed "ourselves."

Is this not also true of life on earth? If we expect people to act dishonestly, then we will focus on dishonest acts, recall them, and it will seem that we live in a dishonest world. If, on the other hand, we expect most people to act honestly and decently, then it will be our experience that most people do, and decency is what we will focus on and recall; and thus we will conclude that we live in a mostly decent world.

Some ghosts we have met don't want to move on, for fear that the drugs or alcohol they so crave will not be available to them on another plane of existence. It seems that the Afterlife is whatever you in this life imagine it to be. I here inject a question: *is that not true of this life?* If I *perceive* that I am having a good time at a party, I obviously am. If I perceive, on the other hand, on the same occasion, that everyone is staring at the pimple that has just popped out on my face, I obviously am *not*

Friends in High Places

having a good time. It's exactly the same time, the same event: only *perception*—ineffable, unmeasurable—makes the difference. The way you see the world does not merely affect what you think and feel about all that is going on. The way you see, or experience, the world determines how your world will be.

We've all entered into a social scene that seems dreary, boring. I have found it's amazingly easy to trump up energy and fun on such occasions, just *by acting as if* I am having the most wonderful time on earth. You can crack a joke, or tell an absurd story on yourself that makes people laugh. It's contagious, energizing, and before any time at all has passed, everyone in the vicinity is having fun, and I am too. It doesn't take much, just an absurd observation about the weather, for instance, which makes folks laugh and loosens up the social "tightness" most people experience. A famous distant relative of mine (his mother was a Letcher), General JEB Stuart, during the Civil War, expressed that sentiment once when he was reprimanded for enjoying too much foolishness and gaiety during such serious hard times. He explained that fun was like manure; you spread it around, and it made things grow. That makes a lot of sense to me. I like to think I inherited that from JEB.

It appears, from our spiritual work, that we get to choose what age we will be on the other side. Most of the spirits I've made contact with seem to be in their mid-thirties, which may actually be the epitome of human life on earth. Adult, yet still young. Mature, yet still youthful. Done with the awful insecurities of youth, and not yet burdened by the debilities of age.

❦

As I mentioned earlier, there may exist in some dimension we cannot even imagine what is often called the Akashic record, a sort of universal library of all libraries, a source of total information connecting everything in the universe. There, souls learn new things for service and pass them down to earth where people are still struggling to elevate themselves spiritually, improve, move upward. On an even higher level are those souls designated as personal guides, at least in part to help humanity progress. Many near-death experiencers have reported seeing cities of light where lofty ambitions are realized, and Master souls are happily at work. My own sense is that souls there are struggling to keep up with the technological advances we don't on this planet have the spiritual wisdom to use. The Internet allows us access to something like an earthly Akashic record, information about anything on the material plane; yet I've seen in print that its chief use is for pornography.

Following many recycled lives, the soul hopes eventually to reach pure Enlightenment. David McKnight has pointed out that this view of a many-leveled existence beyond this one, ever permitting growth, is not merely some quirky new-age notion, but has been and is attested to by psychically-sensitive individuals in all cultures throughout history, and lies at the heart of many religions. This multi-regioned Afterlife is also what has been gleaned from literally thousands of experiencers at the Monroe Institute, starting with Bob Monroe himself.

After ten years, what in general can I say about ghosts? I'm repeating, but ghosts seem always at least somewhat spacey. They are confused about time. Most of the ones we encountered were willing to go into the light, especially when they saw loved ones waiting in the light for them. Their clothing varies. Some ghosts are perceived in white nightgowns, some in period clothing. Sometimes we were not aware of clothing. This does not mean we perceived the ghosts as naked, only that clothing wasn't noticed. Strong emotions and violent deaths seemed to precede most of our ghosts. And our experience, over and over, has been that your loved ones wait to usher you joyfully into the lands beyond death. The people who have spoken to me of after-death apparitions have seen them fairly soon after a death, usually within a couple of weeks.

Friends in High Places

Some ghosts tap or walk or move objects. In the extreme, they are called poltergeists, or ghosts who throw things. Ghosts may appear by using whatever energy is available on the earth plane, including our energy. I was often exhausted after one of our sessions. And it's common to find cold spots where hauntings are happening, as if the ghost has snatched warmth right out of the air.

Ghosts seem pathetic. They are sad and lost, and they are *lost souls* if in fact we are not making them up. Sometimes they seem angry, but more often just frustrated, sometimes territorial (but mainly just confused) or eaten by guilt over something they did while living, occasionally defensive or bullying. They have been, without realizing it, separated from the homes they knew, the persons they depended on, the lives they understood while living.

I feel strongly that the good, the clear, action is to send spirits into the light. Intention is what counts, not knowing exactly what that light might mean. This world is for the living; that one beyond is theirs, though one group I know of merely communicates with the ghost and leaves things as they are. I've rarely seen a ghost refuse to go eventually; one I recall chose to stay where he felt comfortable but agreed to go to the light when he was ready. Many have been suspicious or reluctant at first, or afraid they're going to Hell instead of the other way.

So, the way I justify the long hours I spent for ten years retrieving spirits is that I believe those ghosts were souls in suspended animation, in darkness, and that our loving circle, in case after case, provided the love and spiritual nutrition that allowed those earthbound spirits, one by one, to end their torment and be free to go on.

There appear to be principles that govern the reality we are in.

One, everything in your life is a projection of what is in your mind. That is under your control. What happens is not, but how you react to it is your choice.

Two, whatever is going on is actually what you were trying to achieve in the first place. That includes the bad stuff: anger and alienation, addiction and alcoholism.

Three, God—whatever else he, she, or it—may be, does not interfere. You may ask to know God's will, but you have a radical freedom to live your own life.

We try to obtain whatever information we can from the ghosts, and are hoping always to validate our work.

You yourself could visit a haunted house, or maybe an abandoned house. But it works elsewhere, too. Many believe that the earth is full of earthbound spirits existing right here among us. In a meditative state of mind, pray for protection, then just ask in the quietness: is anyone here? would you tell me your name? would you like to ask me anything? Then just listen. You may be amazed.

Friends in High Places

Taken at Kerak Crusaders' Castle in Jordan in 2008, the scene of thousands of deaths over the centuries. Perhaps some of the spirits of those who died are still there. These orbs did not show until I took the picture with my digital camera.

This ghostly image in the snow in Stonewall Jackson cemetery one night with David McKnight in 2003 did not show until I snapped my digital camera.

This image alone among half a dozen others showed these odd lines of light. None of the others Nick took that day in 2006 showed anything unusual.

One of my fellow participants at the Monroe Institute took this group photo in 2008, which shows an orb smack in the middle of my forehead.

Friends in High Places

In Farmington, New Mexico, I was photographing an exotic ring-tailed cat. Right in the middle of about 15 photos of the cat appeared this strange apparition. My sister, and Nick, and I, discussing it, felt nothing strange. You can see the cat through the image. Nobody was smoking, and this strange horse-human appears in only one image.

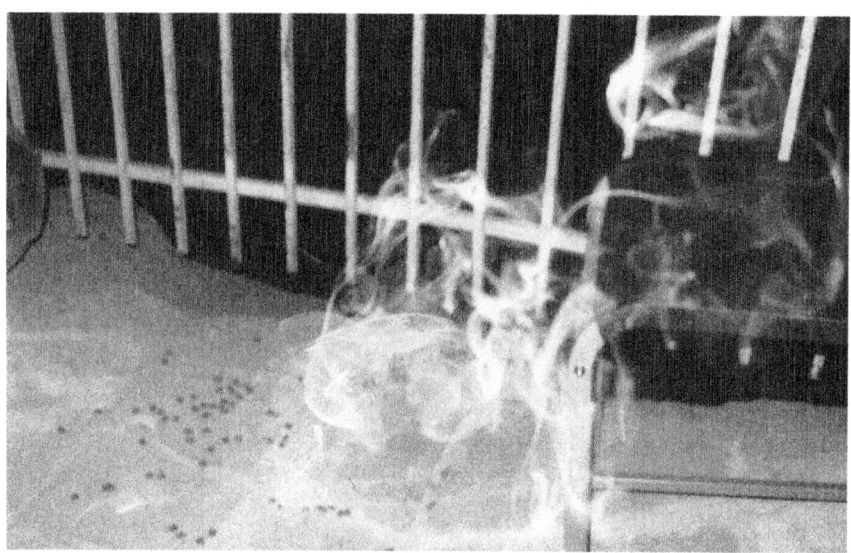

I took a picture of Jennie and Mary McKnight in 2003. At that moment, Mary said, "I think my mother just came." I took a second picture seconds later and an orb appeared.

Friends in High Places

An orb appears clearly in an empty storeroom at a local Domino's Pizza in 2002, where I was hunting for orbs. There was nothing visible until I snapped the picture.

The Ghost Busting Group 2002. Left to right: Tim, Bill, Katie, Rush and David

Photo of Madeline's ghost on the edge of the bed taken by Dick Halseth.

Modern man can't build walls like this one at Sacsayhuaman in Peru., with precisely cut stones often weighing tons and tons more than any stones we can move around today. What did ancient people know that we've forgotten?

Friends in High Places

6. Rockbridge Area Hospice

"Oh, look! There's Cassie! How far is it to Cassie?"
One of our patients, who died later that same day.
(Cassie, his wife, had been dead several years.)

I believed what I learned at TMI. But I was still scared of death. So I trained for, and volunteered for, hospice because I wanted to conquer that fear. I had no idea what amazing friends working with Rockbridge Area Hospice would bring me, what a privilege it is to be a part of the final leg of a human journey, or what grace accompanies a dying person and their families. I've been on the board of directors for fourteen years, and been a volunteer longer than that. Our mission is to nurture and support terminally ill patients and their families. It's only natural that we hear a lot of stories about death.

In the chapter called "Talking To The Dead in Church," I tell the story told by one of our nurses about the dying farmer whose brother came for him on the John Deere tractor. What can we make of this? Is it all just imagination, or could it be that the dead regularly cross back over to help the living across whatever line there is between life and death? Many books in the past few years detail similar stories by the dying, and our Hospice nurses tell many others.

A retarded black man we were serving told his Hospice volunteer that he saw God in his mirror, that God was a white man, long haired, and that he had "another guy" with him. He went on to say, "We visited, and I told him he's welcome here anytime." Two days later, the patient died.

One of my patients, George, as I walked into his house one day, told me his mentor (a man I knew too) had been standing in the door right where I was standing just before I arrived. Had I seen Keith? he wanted to know. I hadn't. Keith had been dead several years. George died the next morning, after telling me that at Keith's funeral, he had seen Keith dancing on top of the coffin. I have to add—though this was years before my ghost-busting experiences—that I "perceived" George clad in a khaki raincoat at his own funeral, up in front, interested in all that was going on, hymns and testimonials about his life.

Another of my patients told me just days before she died that her sister had been there earlier that day. She knew she was seeing an apparition, she calmly told me, because her sister was dead.

Ken Patrick, a friend of mine who is a Hospice chaplain in northern Virginia, told me of a patient whose whole dead family visited her in the

Friends in High Places

days before she died. She explained to Ken that between the living and the dead was something like a glass pane fogged over. She said that in her childhood, the glass had been clear, but that once she reached adolescence, it fogged over. She thought it was because we have to learn to focus singly on this life. Dying, she explained, was like the pane being gradually cleared again. She died soon after telling him this.

A police officer from Buena Vista, Virginia, edges up to chat with me at a bluegrass festival where I am manning the Rockbridge Area Hospice booth. We are raffling chances on a basket of bluegrass tapes each night, and the price of the raffle tickets supports the mission of Rockbridge Area Hospice, giving compassionate care to patients in the last days of their lives, and to their caregivers and families. The policeman wants to talk and circles around a bit, finally telling me he wants to thank me for what Hospice did last winter when his six-year-old grandson died. I thank him and ask the child's name. (I like to take good reports back to the office!) He's reluctant to say the name, he explains, as the child's death is still causing his daughter such grief.

As we chat, I dare to ask if he has had any sense of his grandson's presence since the death. This is my usual ghost question.

Immediately, he launches into stories about how the dog knew the child was going to die, how the boy himself reported that he frequently talked to "his angel," and that the angel told the child he was going to die.

Then he says, "It's going to be okay when I die, because Granny will take care of me."

The officer raked his hand back through his thin hair and said to me, "I wondered about that, because Granny, his grandmother on the other side of the family, wasn't old, or sick, and certainly not dead. But I didn't say anything. Then a couple of weeks later, she was diagnosed with a fatal illness, and went real quick."

The grandfather went on, wiping his eyes. "I remembered what the boy'd said. He died about ten days after his grandmother. There's no doubt in my mind that his angel was real, and that he and his Granny are together in Heaven."

Angela Gibson wanted to go and see her dying sister one last time, but the time was too short, and she was hundreds of miles away from where her sister lay dying of breast cancer. Her school-age son was sick with pneumonia, she had separated from her husband and had no one to leave the child with. She had to make a choice between her sister and her son. She prayed for guidance and went to bed, determined to decide the next day.

At 3:24 in pitch dark she was awakened by her sister's voice calling to her. She saw a brilliant light in the corner of the room which gradually melted (or formed) into the image of her sister, but not the thin, hairless, ill sister Angela had recently seen. Her sister, Angela tells me, was "absolutely gorgeous," had all her pretty hair back, and had both breasts back." Angela noted the time.

Angela reached for her sister, but her sister shook her head, and said, "Look at me. I'm whole again. But you can't touch me yet."

But the next day when Angela called the hospital where her sister was, she was puzzled and relieved to learn that her sister was still "alive," according to the hospital, but in a coma. By chance, at exactly 3:24 PM that day, they took the young woman off life support and she died immediately.

Angela is sure that her sister "left" this life twelve hours before she actually died, and that only the artificial life support kept her body going twelve hours beyond her spirit's departure.

A friend of mine and fellow Hospice volunteer, Raydot Swink, believes she had a visit late one night from her father in the form of an angel.

Friends in High Places

Her father Ray had died weeks before this happened, she was working near closing time at Kroger, when a young man bearing a startling resemblance to her dead father came in: same short build, same hair, same diffident sweet disposition, so she wasn't worried in the least by the appearance of this stranger. She was doing the books for the store, preparing to close up. The man asked to use a phone and stood making calls for half an hour, past closing time. She allowed him to stay because he so reminded her of her own dad.

She noticed he kept calling, apparently not finding what he was looking for, and eventually asked if she could help him.

He was trying to call a church, he explained, but couldn't find one open.

"But it's nearly midnight," Raydot pointed out, "And no church will be open this time of night. Can I help you with anything?"

"I just need something to eat," he said. "Just a candy bar and a drink would be all right. I haven't had anything to eat for two days."

Raydot found some leftover fried chicken in the deli, and got him a soft drink. He thanked her profusely, and when he walked out, she locked the door behind him, as it was now past closing time.

When she blinked, she says, he just vanished. He did not walk away. The still-lit parking lot was empty. He was just there one second, then the next, he wasn't.

Later it seemed to her that it had been a message that her dead father was all right. The man wasn't her father, she emphasizes, but he reminded her strongly of her father. The message dawned on her slowly. Because his appearance and disappearance were so startling, it was a long time before she told anyone.

∽

It is common, if not universal, for our Hospice patients to be visited by a dead relative within a day or two of dying. The patient clearly sees and interacts with someone unseen by the nurse or other family members.

Katie Letcher Lyle

Or the patient will report to a nurse or companion, "Henry was here last night," and upon questioning, Henry will turn out to be a long-dead brother, or other relative, or friend. No one of my patients has died while I was in attendance. But our nurses have some amazing tales. This appearance, or hallucination, is so frequent, that it appears on our Hospice list of the signs of imminent death. And what, exactly, is dying? You could define it as the irreversible nanosecond from which there is no return to the living. People as they die often utter final words that might give us a glimpse of what is coming, what they are "seeing." Admittedly, I chose these because I found them interesting. Stonewall Jackson is recorded as saying, "Let us cross over the river and rest in the shade of the trees." Max Baer, a famous boxer in the thirties and one-time heavyweight champion of the world, just as he died in 1959, uttered "Here I go!" Henry Ward Beecher, a nineteenth century evangelist, said as he died, "Now comes the mystery." Elizabeth Barrett Browning's last word was "Beautiful!" Emily Dickinson said just as she died, according to her family: "I must go in; the fog is rising." Thomas Edison said, "It is very beautiful over there." My own grandmother reported in a letter to her only living son, my father, that her other son, Greenlee "Gee" just as he died, at age sixteen, "turned his head from us and looked up with such wonder and love in his eyes seeing something or Someone wonderful and lovely beyond our knowing—and was gone, to be "this day in Paradise." My father chose to carry that one letter in his shaving case, folded underneath everything else, to and from World War II. I found it after he died.

My uncle Lamar Curry was in Hospice care at the time of his death. For many weeks previous to his death, as I sat with him, I noticed him taking what felt to me like trips away from his body. I say this because he could not be roused, appeared deeply asleep, and then suddenly he'd shudder awake. He never said where he'd been. (I asked, but he wouldn't say, or couldn't recall.) But his body during those times was as if dead. This too is common among our Hospice patients. It seems logical to me to suppose that they are, while still attached to life, going out and visiting the other side. We simply don't know. But when you deal with the dying, it becomes less and less possible to say death just happens and that it's the end of things. Although many believe that common experience cannot be necessarily equated with truth, it is persuasive.

*

A friend, Barney Brown, used to counsel dying AIDS patients in California. He says nearly every one of them, soon before death, would experience a dream about his own death. Though each was different, here are two examples. A dying man of 27 named Tony dreamed of being at a wonderful party, full of people he loved, including his mother and his favorite grandmother. It was warm, loving, in a beautiful setting, with fabulous food, and everyone having a good time. He loved being there, among so many people he loved and who loved him. Suddenly Tony realized that everyone at the party was dead, and awoke. Awaking from that dream, he was greatly comforted to think that party was waiting for him.

A month later, at the moment he was passing away, Barney had a sudden sense of Tony in the night, afraid, standing alone on a road with a big intimidating hill out in front of him. Barney tried with his mind to communicate with Tony, to remind him of the party where he was headed. He had a sense of Tony, stopping, listening, then running off happily towards the hill. Barney looked at his watch, and later confirmed that Tony had died just at the time of his "vision."

Bob, an Italian-American man who had never been to Italy, while still in his twenties was in the last stage of AIDS. His partner Ricky was also infected, but the disease was not as advanced as Bob's was. A week or so before Bob died, he related to Barney a dream he'd had. In the dream, he realized he was in Italy, walking along a pleasant road towards a beautiful hill town, its lights beckoning to him, one of those gorgeous, quaint medieval towns of northern Italy. He couldn't wait to get there, it appeared so wonderful. But then he came to a spa-like place by the road, with hot springs and places to rest, also beautiful and welcoming. It occurred to Bob that before he went to the hill town maybe he'd rest at this lovely spa for awhile, and wait for Ricky. Then he'd rejoin his partner and they would go on to the town together. He told Barney the dream, and was much comforted by it, and believed it to be "true" to the extent that he was no longer afraid of dying. He died a week after that dream.

I am also a bereavement volunteer, which means I visit monthly with the person left behind when a death occurs. We do this for a year following the death of one of our patients or any bereaved person who requests that service. One of my clients tells me that her [dead] husband talks to her all the time, and that he is especially useful at taxtime. Another has told me that her [dead] mother reminds her every day not to forget to feed the birds!

Jeanne Piersoll, one of my bereavement patients, a fascinating and loving woman, since moving into her house twelve years ago, has had two strange "dreams," if indeed they were dreams at all. Both times it seemed she woke up in her bed, in her house. Once it was to see three old men standing in her doorway. She said to them, "You look like something out of Dante's Inferno."

One of them snapped back, "Well, you would too if you'd been dead two hundred years." Jeanne has no interpretation for that dream, but agrees they could be ghosts haunting the land her "newish" house, built in the sixties, sits on.

Her second dream was in form much like the first; she felt that she "awoke" in her house, in her own bed, to see a "diminutive" woman standing in her doorway. She was dressed in a long, gray, nondescript dress. "Who are you?" Jeanne demanded.

"Your mother," the woman replied.

"You are *certainly* not my mother," Jeanne retorted.

"I am your mother's mother's mother's mother," the woman replied. Next day, Jeanne, herself a tiny person like the woman in the doorway, did some figuring. She had known her mother, and her grandmother, and had seen pictures of her great-grandmother. She realized that the woman who spoke to her was one generation beyond what she knew or had seen pictures of. Dream or a true visit from a remote ancestor?

So, through my experiences at Hospice and as a bereavement counselor I know that the dead are not dead, and that the dead are waiting to welcome the dying, and that they at least sometimes return to earth to lead their loved ones across death's barrier.

You can take Hospice training wherever you are, to become a part of this wonderful and compassionate organization. It will enrich your life as it has mine.

Katie Letcher Lyle

7. Imagination: The Eyes of the Soul

*A belief is a mental framework which organizes and
stores your experience in the world of events.*

A belief is a filter through which all incoming perceptual data flows.

*A belief allows connections to be made between objects and events,
organizing sense data into patterns and relationships.*

A belief structures your experience.

*A belief categorizes, labels, interprets, judges,
and defines your life's flow of events.*

~Ramon Stevens

Friends in High Places

I have made acquaintance with a group of spirits that I call my Upstairs Crew, or UC. They are guides, helpers, and friends on the imaginary level.

In 1993, when I was researching a book about wild berries, I decided I wanted to illustrate it with nineteenth century botanical illustrations of the berries in question: you've seen those glorious etchings, lithographs, and paintings of gorgeous flowers, bowls of perfect, lush, dewy fruits of America that graced our grandmothers' dining rooms. I believe that, consciously or unconsciously, the artists were intending to prove to the old world the amazing bounty of our new one. The old world of Europe was, and probably still is, a bit smug about their superior culture, cities, art. So Americans had to "show" them. Culturally, we lagged behind the old world, but "naturally," we were way out in front with our mighty rivers and endless forests and verdant growth. I think that was the impulse behind this school of painting, and of "Tole" decorations. Thomas Jefferson famously dug up a mastodon skeleton from Saltville, Virginia, then assembled it in Paris later to prove to Europeans that American dinosaurs were superior in size to those found in the old world! Early American theater featured the American "rube" always apparently inferior in dress, speech, and learning, coming out on top of the cultivated European fops—inheriting wealth, outwitting the dull English squire, and always (!) winning the luscious young lady's affections.

But I digress. I could find nothing about how those botanical illustrations were done, in a time before photography, before there was any printed form of color pictorial reproduction. I started at the beginning of the art books in the stacks of our three local libraries, trying vainly to find something about the artists or craftsmen who produced botanical illustrations.

One afternoon as I searched through yet more art books in the Washington and Lee University Library, a voice said in my head, "I am a colorist." There was no one else there in the stacks with me.

I said in my mind, "Who are you?" all the time "seeing" in my imagination a fellow who looked a lot like the guy on the Quaker Oats box. "Chuck," was the reply.

At once I shot back, scornfully, "Oh, give me a break. That's a modern nickname." It did not at all fit with the plump, short Quaker man I "saw," and I was irritated.

"Madame," the voice in my head said, clearly offended, "I am William Chuck. I am a colorist. I am the red man." I had a notebook with me, and started writing down his words. He went on to tell me he was the father of four, wife deceased, that he worked at 11 Greene Street in Philadelphia, and that the year (I asked this) was 1790. He knew of Benjamin Franklin but was not personally acquainted with him. He worked on the second floor of a large, cold building "while light prevails" to tint lithographs for a magazine out of Philadelphia called "The American Farmer" that had a quarterly run of about 250. He said he was the second most important. The "green man"—in charge of tinting leaves and other green parts of plants—was deemed the most important. The magazines, he informed me, were placed in frames to hold them open, and six people participated in tinting as close to identically as possible whatever fruit, flower, or vegetable was being illustrated. The green man had the most work, as green was the most frequent natural color. Red was next, followed by yellow, blue, and two other colors he did not specify. They worked quickly, as a team, passing the framed magazines around the table. He told me about his life away from work, and when I asked what his perception of me was, he replied that he'd come "in answer to my question" about how the lithographs were tinted, to tell me what I had been trying to find in all the art books. He seemed pleasant and eager to communicate. His wife had died of a chest complaint, and he was taking care of their four children. The two boys had been put out to work; the

Friends in High Places

two girls managed the home, a walkup fourth-floor flat, with no plumbing, no running water. All the children were between six and fifteen.

I relate this episode with some trepidation. Who really spoke to me? One reason I want to tell this story is that I have never found anything like the above description in any art books, so I have absolutely no idea if it's really the way illustrating work was done. Were there really people called colorists? I invite anyone who knows to contact me, for validation or refutation.

But I heard what I heard. It was my introduction to one of my spirit guides. William is with me, or available, any time I want to visit; he is knowledgeable about plants, especially herbs, and herbal medicine, and he likes to talk. William is the guide that David called upon on Sitlington Hill in the chapter on ghost-busting.

Being a lifelong skeptic, I fact-check everything I can. There are an intimidating forty people living in the USA today named William Chuck, so it's not realistic to check them all—not that I'd necessarily luck out if I contacted every one of them—to find someone who, at this late date, knows about my William. There is a Greene St in Philadelphia, and it was there in 1790. Franklin was alive then. There have been several publications in our nation's history called The American Farmer, at least one of which was being published in 1790. By 1810 there were three. I've never been to the city, or known of any way I could look up William Chuck himself. I checked the 1790 central Philadelphia census. There is no William Chuck in the twenty-four pages of the central city's census, and I "saw" him living in a downtown rowhouse near his work. What part of him could survive to communicate with me? I don't know.

༺༻

We are so aware of a general disbelief in spiritual matters that it may be useful to review what some writers have believed about the creative process (also called the imagination). Robert Louis Stevenson wrote, "My

Brownies are somewhat fantastic; they like their stories hot, full of passion and picturesque...." The brownies he claimed were a "team of little anonymous workers" that led him in his creative efforts. Samuel Taylor Coleridge wrote his famous "Kubla Khan" under the influence of some higher inspiration delivered, in his case, by drugs. William Butler Yeats delighted in phenomena that aided his writing, which he claimed were perfume, visions, and ethereal music.

I am sure that I live every moment with guidance from what I call my Upstairs Crew, or UC. I first met them in the aerobics class I've exercised in three times a week since 1983. In my class, while doing repetitive exercises, I began to imagine Roman soldiers marching throughout my blood system pouring fresh green olive oil wherever they found clumps of (high) cholesterol. My soldiers wore short, red uniforms with gold braid, and carried the green oil in blown glass pitchers. I envisioned them as they poured it along my veins, which were the roads they marched along. There were thousands of them: strong-calved, dark-haired, robust Roman soldiers. The olive oil I imagined melted away the bad cholesterol. The exercise might not be doing any good, but it certainly couldn't hurt me.

As an American woman who spent sixteen years on conjugated estrogens, I am somewhat nervous about breast cancer. Thus I soon added to my visualizations white-clad nuns who daily monitor my breasts for any cancer cells, picking them up like trash if they find any, and dumping them into yellow leather bags called macrophages, and disposing of them safely. Soon after, I noticed some small children dressed in blue. Some of them, shockingly, were the nuns' children! The children, closer to the ground than their mothers, find even the tiniest rogue cells.

I'm doing nothing but just "imagining" all this. Soon I invented a band of young, pretty girls whose job was to keep my outlook and body young; they scatter flowers everywhere and joke with anyone they meet. They laugh a lot, and walk a lot. I named them the Merrygolds. They are a

Friends in High Places

present and persistent part of me. When I developed bursitis on a hip in 1988, I imagined a blue wizard with a long white beard and a long pointy hat to take his magic wand and zap that hip whenever it hurt, which was often.

Whenever I would think of something I needed, I'd add it to my panoply of "helpers." A Mayan Dream-teller can often interpret my dreams for me when they make no sense to the here-and-now me. A Time-keeper wakes me when I need to get up at an odd time—without an alarm. No one had to know these things going on inside my body and mind while we danced, stretched, lifted weights, held yoga positions, did Pilates exercises.

Three times a week I still reconnect with some or all of these helpers. What's stopping you inventing your own?

Later, if I had trouble getting the right phrasing for something I was writing, or figuring out, I began to call upon a band of highly intelligent monks dressed in black or brown robes. They were medieval scholars and writers, thinkers and poets and philosophers, who could help with anything intellectual I needed. They informed me they'd been helping me all along, though I had not been conscious of them.

Soon I was "seeing" these characters in my imagination, and actually sitting down doing some "automatic writing." By that, I mean exactly, and just out of curiosity, sitting with a pen or pencil and a pad, going into an altered state by focusing on my breathing, and letting my hand write down whatever came to my head.

Automatic writing worked better if I had a question. I'd start by writing the question at the top of the page. Always, what I got was sensible—and sometimes astonishing—information.

I continued to envision them, the members of my Upstairs Crew. For instance, my blue wizard, a Disneylike creature with a perpetual frown and a spraying clean white beard, like hair that needs conditioning, could and can go anywhere in my body I direct him, to cure anything bothering me: a headache, an arthritic knee or thumb joint, a clogged sinus. Rubus and Ruby, who appear to me dressed in identical choir robes, he red-faced and bald with a big kind smile, she a homely serious woman with a big nose and brown hair that looks like a Prince Valiant wig, appeared. They seem parental and mildly cautious about my sometimes impulsive behavior. They help me avoid making decisions in anger or heat. All these "people" were at first just a "game" to me. I hadn't been to the Monroe yet. If my mood was low, I asked for help from my Merrygolds, who brought light, fragrant flowers, and lightness throughout my system, illuming any darkness, bringing joy in place of gloom or sorrow.

This kind of imaginative activity is within the reach of any person who desires it. At the Simonton Institute in Texas, cancer victims are taught to imagine away their cancers by various methods. My dear friend Jane Griffith Rushing Power beat cancer many years ago; she told me about the Simonton Institute, where she'd been for a time, and about the technique of imagining Pac-men eating up her cancer cells. The Simonton has an impressive record of success in curing cancer. So I think it is arguable that it's proven that visual imagining works.

This "game" accelerated when I began going to the Monroe Institute in 1991. I assume others have imaginary lives too, not necessarily anything like my own. Mine felt comforting and useful to me, didn't harm anyone, didn't add calories to my diet. My visualizations cost me nothing, and demanded no special equipment. It wasn't illegal. The imaginative life is free. And rich.

UC, how would you define imagination?
Imagination is the eyes of the soul.
Einstein and others have said that imagination is far more important than knowledge. How could that be true? Is it true? Think about it.

Friends in High Places

Imagination is the only faculty we have that can bridge time and space, visit the building of the pyramids or the other side of the moon. How do we express intention? With our imaginations. It's well-known that the greatest scientific discoveries are made by leaps of imagination, or in dreams. And how do we dream? With our imaginations, of course. Only our imaginations can take us to Mars, or allow us to have a conversation with Julius Caesar or Pocahontas or Robert E. Lee, all instantaneously. Imagination embraces everything there is to know and experience. When we exercise our imaginations, anything is possible.

With my imagination, I talk with dead friends and loved ones. I have learned things I had not known, could not have known, before. An important thing I've learned in writing this book is that imagination is far more important than I'd ever before considered, maybe the most important human ability of all. It's difficult, having been told dismissively all my childhood: "Oh, Honey, it's just your imagination."

Imagination has real effects on the physical plane. Athletes who rehearse their skills with their imaginations, who imagine winning, or running faster than they ever have before, do better than athletes who don't. Through visualization, or imagining, of a gorgeous natural setting, we can measurably lower stress reactions in our bodies. Visualization has effected many cures, and can be counted among the many forms of alternative medicine. Larry Dossey is the person to read on that subject.

Medically, western medicine imagines that illness attacks from without, and that to cure a person you must cut out, burn, or poison, to kill the illness. Orientals *imagine* something different: when illness occurs it is because your body and the spirit that inhabits it have become unbalanced, so you visit a physician for balancing, and he may give you a medicine concocted of ginseng, dried lizard, rhinoceros horn, and macerated sea sponge—and you are cured. We in the west do not understand how such a medicine can cure, but cure it does. As a Taiwanese physician named Paul Hsu asked me gently, as I years ago complained to him about the illogic of the Oriental way: "Are you going to argue with four thousand years of effective Chinese medicine?"

When my son spent a year in London, he visited a Chinese doctor recommended by someone he knew to try to deal with his psoriasis, which he got in a double-whammy genetic inheritance from one of my grandfathers and my husband's father, both of whom suffered terribly from it. He was given dried stuff in a bag, told to boil it for a certain amount of time, and take it as medicine. He said it was the worst-smelling, worst-tasting stuff he'd ever had. But his skin was beautiful the whole time he took it. It cured him absolutely, the first time in his life he'd been free of the embarrassing ailment.

One human *imagines* a solitary rainy day as a heavenly chance to stay indoors and read all day and breathe in the lovely scent of soaked earth, while the next-door neighbor *imagines* the day as dismal, claustrophobic, and depressing. They are both living the same day. Disagreement about what is true is what lawsuits are all about. If, say, the Nazis had won World War II, their war criminals would have been applauded as war heroes, while my father, a World War II general and hero, who killed as many Japanese as he possibly could, would probably have been considered a war criminal.

I am forced to conclude that there really is no such thing as truth—there is only what we imagine. Our culture dismisses imagination as being of little value, but if we do that, we cannot take advantage of its profound gifts.

The placebo effect in medicine is now unquestionable: in experiments, up to fifty percent of the time, non-medicinal substances (sugar pills, water injections) have been found to cure or remediate bodily illnesses—apparently because the patient *imagines* that he or she is receiving medication. People even experience side effects from placebos, a result which ought to be impossible.

Conversely, psychosomatic illnesses—ailments with no pathogenic basis—often make people ill and sometimes kill them. In some cultures "pointing bones" is enough to cause a cursed person to die, as the bewitched individual, *imagining* he is doomed, experiences a shut-down of his immune system and subsequent death. Thus imagination can radically alter our body functions, offering evidence of the power of mind over matter.

There is a woman at my daughter Jennie's home-school who is now around fifty, and has lived at the school since girlhood. When this mentally retarded woman was around fourteen, she menstruated for the first time, and was appalled. "What is it?" she asked, horrified. It was quickly explained to her that this was a natural event, no big deal, and that everyone female did this every so often.

"Not me," she said. "I'm not doing this anymore."

And to this day, she has never experienced another period. She, being mentally deficient, does not know the fact that women cannot control menstrual periods. So, how does she do it? She willed her periods to stop, another way of saying she changed matter by imagination.

When I was pregnant with my first child, I heard all the usual old wives' tales about the appalling pain of labor. My own mother had insisted on having "twilight sleep," and told me how the doctors said she screamed in pain, but the scopolamine made her forget the pain and screaming. I wanted my baby to be born without drugs, but I am physically a great sissy.

One day I went to a friend's house whose cat (Fred) was having kittens, because I thought it would be useful to see a birth, any birth, an event I'd never watched. While giving birth, Fred breathed hard, seemed focused, and pushed out of her womb five kittens, one by one. And as I watched, I thought, if this hurt, Fred would howl. If you closed Fred's tail in the door or stepped on her foot, she'd yowl. So why wasn't she crying if birth hurt so much? I decided then and there that natural childbirth ought not to hurt. And in consequence, I bore both my children amidst much sweating and panting and groaning, but I swear, though I felt labor was hard work, and aptly named, I never felt pain. It was more like heavy aerobic exercise—say, biking uphill—that continued to the point of exhaustion, yet you could not quit. You had to keep bicycling up the hill! I *imagined* that pain shouldn't be part of natural childbirth. And it truly for me was not.

A friend shared with me a similar experience. "I too watched my cat give birth and decided if she could do it without pain so could I. And I did. Like you, I worked and pushed, but the sensations I felt I would not call pain. Believe it or not, when my baby crowned I had an orgasm! I know pain; I've had a pinched nerve in my neck. This childbirth exertion was NOT pain."

I recall clearly the first time I was aware of getting direct help, an answer handed to me from Somewhere Else, literally words in my ear, when I said, *Help*! It was the mid-nineties, and my dear friend and the leader of our ghost-hunting band, David McKnight, was fighting cancer, having to go every day the more than 100 miles from his Highland County home to the University of Virginia for radiation treatments. I tried to help out when I could, and one day I offered to meet Mary and David in Waynesboro, let her drive on home to do necessary chores while I drove David to Charlottesville for his treatment, then back to Highland County.

It was summer, the day hideously hot, and David was feeling low. He would sip water, then have to stop and vomit by the side of the road. At one point, we stopped and got him a vanilla milkshake, but that didn't help much; he couldn't keep it down, and he was ill and depressed

He began doing a number on himself: as we wound around the curves of Route 33 back towards Monterey, he reviewed how he'd graduated from Harvard then obtained a ministerial degree from Union Theological Seminary, and still he felt he had always been a failure. He never believed what he'd studied. Could not stomach, he discovered too late, Christianity. He had been forced after he left the ministry to teach at community colleges, felt his head was full of cotton, and that he was stupid and... oh, on and on. He told me he had never been able to afford a house, or feel he could afford to have a child. He'd been married three times, he'd hurt the wives he'd left behind, he couldn't get it right, "it" being his life.

I had no idea how to respond, and felt his heart breaking along with his body, there beside me in the car in the heat of that summer day. I had no idea what to say, or how to comfort him. He was extremely popular among his host of friends for his kindness, modesty, humor, deep spirituality, and his intense interest in others. He was, and still is, my model for what a human being ought to be.

And the answer I gave him—absolutely true, and apparently comforting—was handed to me literally by a voice above my left ear. "David," I said, "the more successful you are on the spiritual level, the less likely, I'd think, that you'd be successful on the material level. And you are by far the most successful spiritual person I've ever known."

That voice was my Upstairs Crew at work. You want to argue that it's a mental trick? Okay. It still works. A few days later, when I told about this incident to my Methodist minister friend Ken Patrick, he quoted Matthew 10:20: "When they deliver you up, do not be anxious how you are to speak or what you are to say; for what you are to say will be given to you in that hour."

Soon David had whipped the cancer and was back to his wonderful, normal, upbeat self. I, on the other hand, floundering for something helpful to say to him, owe direct thanks to my Upstairs Crew.

There came a summer day in 2002 that I agreed to meet my husband to discuss the terms of our pending divorce. Lunch, at a local diner called the Redwood, my mouth dry as a desert as I walked in, sick at heart, feeling nauseated. I was hurting, bruised inside and out by the wrench of a divorce after forty years of marriage, the last seventeen tainted by his scary alcoholism. I was healing myself in Al-Anon, and in therapy for the first time in my life. I didn't want or need to have lawyers ripping our guts out, even though I had learned he was—in addition to being an alcoholic abuser—a philanderer, and I felt I had to divorce him. He was angry at me for separating, and depriving him of cooked meals, laundry, a clean house and so on, as well as for exposing his long-term affair. I wanted to avoid any confrontation with him, and thus had insisted we meet in a public place at a busy time of day, where I knew he wouldn't make a scene. (He, like most of the husbands I heard of in Al-Anon, was nasty to me only when no one else was around.) But, nonetheless, I desperately wanted to not be doing this. I do not believe in divorce, and divorced him only when he became helplessly and permanently alcoholic.

He was already there, sweating and trembling. As I reluctantly slid into the booth across from him, I heard a voice say as clearly as if a person had said it, "Mediation." It just came to me in that moment.

I said it, he looked amazed and said, "That's a great idea," and that's exactly what we did, saving money and more savagery. The mediator, his close friend Larry, charged each of us a thousand dollars for half a dozen sane and fair meetings where we negotiated our divorce. I expect any other lawyer would have charged more than that for each meeting!

Friends in High Places

In May 2009, I'd been hunting morels in the nearby mountains for ten days, looking two or three hours every day, and had found only a total of twenty-one. Pretty poor pay, I decided, for twenty-five or thirty hours' work. So there I was wondering why I wasn't finding any. I had snagged my son Cochran and his truck to take us into a particularly difficult area, where we broke through a fence (we had permission), rolled over a "road" that was all mud ruts and slippery slides, avoided a washed out bridge, tried to detour only to find ourselves stopped by a barb-wire fence. We got out and wandered around some, finding nothing. In the truck on the way home, I groused to my son that my Upstairs Crew wasn't doing its job, which was, at the moment, to help me find morels.

At my kitchen table at home we ate the Subway sandwiches I'd bought, and Cochran left to go home. Three hours later as I carried the garbage out, there was a little morel right in front of the garbage can. I thought that was cute, and curious, and then turned the corner to set down my bag of recycled plastics. There, before my eyes, was my lawn filled with morels, including a gigantic one right in front of me. It was like dreams I have had in which I find morels by the hundreds. In thirty seconds, I picked twenty-seven morels. That was more than I'd found all year long.

Talk about finding happiness in your own back yard! I apologized to my Upstairs Crew for doubting them, and thanked them humbly for such an amazing gift!

Others might call these voices God, or Jesus, or Higher Self, or Inner Self Helpers, or Allah, or Saints, or Yahweh, or Angels or Guides, but everyone has them and anyone can learn to pay attention to what they have to tell you, and to know astonishingly and absolutely that you are never alone.

How can you get in contact with these helpers? There's automatic writing, already described here. You can meditate, and ask for your guides to come and speak with you. I have never successfully been able to meditate, so I prefer to "wait." By that I mean I can get comfortable and have the intention of communicating with guides or a particular guide, or person. Then I wait until there's a response.

You can get past-life readings, and, even if you can't swallow the idea of actual past lives, you can consider the stories you come up with as metaphors for your studies of self. Why that particular story and not some other story? All you need do is ask and you will receive (just as Jesus promised). I've found it especially useful to ask how you died in any previous life you get in touch with. I have found that there is often a key there to things going on in your current life.

Whenever you have a question, the answer is always there if you will only pay attention. You are surrounded and protected at every instant of your life, whether you know it or not. But knowing it makes life easier; listening to your guides will help prevent errors large and small. I used to not listen to the little voices that said, "Be careful right here," because I didn't believe they were anything but my imagination. I am amazed to recall, as I am nursing some blow or fall, that, usually, just before the incident causing the injury or pain, I was aware that I'd had some sort of warning. I listen now, or at least I try to. If I get a "nudge" to call someone, or go check up on someone, I do it. And often, that call or visit turns out to be important.

It seems evident that we create our own realities. Two years ago, while I was reading *Cell-Level Healing*, by Joyce Whiteley Hawkes, I dropped a heavy vase on my toe while it was wet and slippery. I *heard* the crunch of bone as I *experienced* the horrible pain of the impact. At once I performed exercises in the book, and in a few hours my toe no longer hurt. I believe I healed it at a cellular level.

Friends in High Places

I now feel sure that those voices have always been there, as I feel sure that they are there for everyone. I (a slow learner or a late bloomer) have only gradually over the last quarter century met the cluster of angels and spirits and wise minds that lead me and sustain me—and always have—throughout this lifetime on earth. I think they are the eternal me, the higher elements of all that I am; they comprise my past and future lives, as well as my present one; they sometimes speak through the mouths of friends, children, pets, and even strangers, sometimes through my imagination. I feel most have lived on earth, and are, therefore, rightfully numbered among the "dead" I can talk to.[8]

U.C., *are all these lives I come up with in past-life readings really me?*

The stories, at least, really are you. Hey, here's a challenge you will learn to love. These could be real; they could be stories you make up about yourself. *Who cares?*

Who are you?

You created us; we create you. We are each other.

---

[8] One of them joined this troupe after death. Paul Shue, who helped me write two books, was a man I adored. Funny, smart, dramatic, with a wonderful voice, generous to a fault, he was my friend for only five years before he died. We shared many of the same passions: a glee at discovering errors in grammar and mispronounced words, country and bluegrass music, railroad lore, cooking, singing music together. Only Paul would call at eleven at night to report on a piece of news he'd just heard: that in a nearby city, there was a curfew, and that all children out after nine had to be in the care of an adult or an *adulteress!* In a restaurant, we'd overhear two people talking about the new "Medicure" program, and practically choke on our sandwiches and coffee. After Paul died, I was almost immediately aware that he was looking after me.

Katie Letcher Lyle

8. Weighing London Psychics

Psychics abilities are the powers of the unobstructed life.

~Shankara, c. 800 AD

On a trip to London with my husband in 1992, I *happened* (what a coincidence!) to be reading Michael Crichton's *Travels*. I'd chosen it because I like his work, and I thought his take on traveling would be interesting, especially while I was traveling. Well, it turned out to be about his *psychic* travels as well as his geographical meanderings.

I hereby change the term *coincidence* to *synchronicity*.

In the book I was reading, Crichton wrote about the Spiritualist Association of Great Britain and his adventures there. Maybe I could manage to find the SAGB and even go there! The day we got to London I learned that the Spiritualist Association of Great Britain was only two blocks away from our hotel, at 33 Belgrave Square.

For 150 years this London-based society, headed by eminent psychic researchers and scholars, has made scientific investigation of psychic claims. Their purpose is to solve that great mystery: can mind exist outside the body? If it *can*, there is the *possibility of immortality*. If mind exists outside of the body, that argues for a universe of "mind" that the living could share with the so-called dead. In the next several years, I went for "readings" probably a dozen times, and to free public sessions three times.

To each individual reader, I said, at the beginning, "I want to neither help nor hinder you, so I prefer to remain silent." Nonetheless, I'm sure my face betrayed eagerness when something sounded right, and the opposite when something did not. Most of the readings I have had are general, and seem to go like this, the first one, in 1992, by a woman whose name I didn't record:

"I see a big man..."

"Yes?" I ask.

"with a round face..."

"Yes?"

"blue eyes..." (I have blue eyes)

"Yes?" I swear I will not be led into betraying anything.

"in spirit..." (okay, someone who's dead)

"a business man..." (Who do I know? No one I can think of...)

"Is that your father?"

I was at that reading in my late fifties; so my father was likely to be dead; and he was a big-boned man, as I am a big-boned woman, and he had a round face like mine, and blue eyes.

"Probably not..." I say. Though clever at the stock market, he wasn't a businessman. Then, crash! "...who had a mustache...."

My father, a retired Marine Corps general, detested any form of facial hair.

Two of the psychics that first year, out of the blue, asked me if my husband had a drinking problem. He did, but I was still firmly in denial throughout the nineties. The first one I automatically told No, but several days later when a second one warned that my husband had a problem with his liver, adding some dire warnings about his drinking too much, I considered the possibility. But denial is a strong protector, and I decided not to believe it. My relationship with reality beyond the physical is a funny thing: I can easily dismiss anything I don't want to hear as irrational.

Often the readings were like this, and had me kicking myself for wasting the money to be there. But one woman, Elizabeth Hill, was uncannily accurate several times.

Before Ms. Hill enters the room, I try to envision her: she will be short, small, braids around head, I write. When she comes, she is prettier, younger, indeed petite. Plain hair in a tortoise shell headband. As I write this later, I recall that the second time I went to see her she wore a braided headband. This may be typical; a fleeting impression, and your brain rushes to make sense of it.

She started right off by telling me my husband drank too much. Much as I tried to deny it, I heard her.

Then she looked at me, said, "Do you know someone named Kate?" Immediately I became suspicious: they told her my name. I'd signed in using my real name. But they don't do that.

"Yes," I admitted, "it's my name."

Everything else she said seemed close to correct, though some comments were so general as to be fairly useless. "Expect special correspondence. I see paper work filled in and signed, forerunner of a change or takeover, but not until the New Year. I hear the ringing of a bell for something to happen. Are you going on a ferry?"

"Yes," I said, surprised. We were taking a ferry from Southhampton over to Brittany the next day.

"Your home office needs reorganizing, reordering. You are going to be successful, also successful in winning something. Are you a writer?"

I went back to her, and even today feel she read my future, or me, pretty accurately. How could she have "guessed" that I was a woman with a home office?

"There's a disturbing event you've been dealing with for some time." My husband's alcoholism? "There's a legal investment gathering around you." That was, I'm sure, my father's death and his Byzantine will, two years in the future.

"I see new bricks. Floor repaired in your house? We'd just refinished the floors of our house, but with no brick. "I see you talking to a priest or police." This remark didn't seem relevant at the time, but desperate about my husband's growing problem, a few years later I talked to both a priest and the police about what I might do to keep him from killing anyone driving while drunk.

She continued, "There are two Elizabeths here, and one Jack." My mother and grandmother were both Elizabeths, and my mother's brother was Jack, "Discussing of will or legacy, altering will, something to do with January."

My father altered his will frequently preceding his death in 1994.

"The name Ernest."

My husband's mother's father and brother were both named Ernest.

"I see antiques. Evaluation of antiques."

That happened with our antique family furniture after my father's death. Our own house, and those of all our relatives on both sides, are full of antiques.

"I see legal proceedings but not trouble."

That later proved to be correct; we were eventually able to sort out my father's difficult and complicated will.

She continued: "I see touring, hiking, a pleasant journey with someone else."

I do both, and love traveling.

"Sarah, Alice, are here."

I had an Aunt Alice, now long dead, and I have a niece Alice. Don't know who Sarah could be.

"Someone will apologize and wants to get together again."

I don't recall that happening.

"There's someone quick-tempered."

That might be anyone.

"I see you interested in music, play an instrument, playing for pleasure for someone."

Yes, I play guitar and sing.

"Have you ever worked in hospital?"

Not as nurse, but my first real job—when I was fifteen—was as a hospital ward receptionist and secretary,

"…but not with deaths or distress," she went on.

This seemed uncannily accurate.

"Concerning something you are wanting to undertake, some replies are not applicable to your needs. You are on the brink of a new condition here, new 'challenge.' Something will be settled for you, shortly. Not years, shortly. Settlement is important in your life."

Vague and I'd have to say inaccurate, but perhaps she foresaw my divorce in eight years, which I certainly never did.

She said, "It is as though you are in contact with two professions or occupations."

I am both a college English teacher, and a professional writer.

"There are lots of things you can do. Making a journey, trying to do something at the end of the trip, will keep you gone some longer."

No; we went back on time.

"You have a strong link with spirit contact. You can receive from the spirit world."

I was not yet doing spirit-retrieval, but I started soon.

"Do you actively do anything in that?"

I denied it.

"It is natural with you to have spirit contact. From your grandmother you got second sight."

If so, neither grandmother ever told me.

"Take note of your hunches. Are you discussing the welfare of children or a child?"

In fact, we naturally discussed for years what to do about our handicapped daughter as she grew up and needed friends of her own and a happy place to live, not with her parents and little other social support. We had just decided on a solution.

"Could she have an occupation like corrective training?"

She continued, with little or no help from me. "You change your mind when not to change would be in your favor. You are a bit stubborn."

Oh, yes, and I nodded to both observations!

"Spirit people around you are prodding you to act in your own favor. Don't be a doubting Thomas. Don't say, `I never win anything.'"

(I say that all the time!)

"You have a marvelous singing voice. Do you know someone near death? I hear `Nearer my God to Thee.'"

I was just then beginning Hospice training, and I was, in my much-younger years, a professional singer.

"Do you have discussion with property brokers? Know anyone buying or trying to buy property? You will make a change in the next year."

This did not happen, though it did several years later in 2005 when, after my divorce, I bought a house for a new start, changed my mind, and sold it only sixteen months afterward when the renter asked to buy it.

"You will remarry: there will be discussion about who will live where."

Though that startled me at the time, it's good to keep notes, because my new partner—though not husband—Nick, and I, talk constantly of moving somewhere to the beach! The reference to remarriage: I had never considered not ending my life as my husband's wife. I was concerned about him and tried for many years to change his drinking, and, as Ruth Graham once said about her marriage to Billy Graham, I had contemplated murder, but never divorce.

"The name Alma."

In 1992 we bought a rental house from a woman named Alta. Neutral on that one.

"Do you belong to a spiritualist church?"

No.

"Ever apply to have healing?"

No.

"Have someone nearby who needs healing? Just watch, when next you visit a church, and a discussion comes up, someone needs healing. Doesn't matter if they want it or not, it will still work. I see No. 26 on a door. Someone refers to Alice. I see study, reading of tarot and involvement with the spirit world. A letter coming from far away, making an appointment, it will be good. Something is very tragic—spirit people don't think it's complete, you will feel better about it, and get over your helpless feeling."

Was she seeing my ex-husband's devastating alcoholism, our divorce, and his tragic demise thirteen years down the road? Time often seems irrelevant in psychic readings.

"Is there an Irish link?"

No, but Scotch-Irish, yes.

"I see you vibrant, creative, lots of changes, expansion in spiritual awareness."

I think that's come to pass.

"Be careful who you get involved with—a lady, extreme... Do you know a Pat? Patty?"

Yes.

"She needs love. I see lots of tears. It will work itself out. Don't do anything to upset the daughter-in-law. Tell Pat to back off."

I do have a friend with that name in exactly the situation implied.

"I see a lady who died of heart problems. Lots of maternal love—your mother?"

Yes, she died of heart problems.

"She's saying life was difficult, and she wishes things could have been different. So unnecessary. Hard life. Worn out when she died. Did not achieve what she wished. Sad about that. Achieved a great deal with family, but that's not what she wanted."

And I have to say that was my mother to the core, who wanted many things she never got, but mainly to be an artist. Her first show was only months before her untimely death from what doctors said was only bronchitis. But she had a weak heart from rheumatic fever she suffered as a child, died at sixty-eight, suddenly, and there was no autopsy.

"You have a lot of help from spirit. Your energies are changing, and the next two years will be productive and changing. Some things are no longer appropriate in your life."

My husband?

"Some changes will be unwelcome."

My divorce, still years away?

"There are people and situations in life no longer appropriate. Within the next two years."

It actually took eight more years for me to divorce him and move on in life, but in the Beyond time seems to be fluid.

"Who drinks around you? Drinking holds you back. If you can do something, he will too."

I tried everything I knew to get him to stop drinking so much, but it didn't change anything. I told her my husband, and said I drink too. But not so much as he.

"Does he have problems with his chest? His nerves?"

Probably yes on both counts. I nodded then asked her to comment on my daughter.

"Daughter? She's confused. Frustrated. There's lots of love around her."

True; she is retarded, but had just been enrolled in a wonderful home-school in Kentucky where she is happy and much-loved.

"There's a child in spirit to help her. I see your daughter winning something, has lots of rosettes, laughing as well. She loves to be on horses."

Yes! This seemed spot-on. She wins medals all the time at Special Olympics. We must have fifty hanging on bulletin boards and vanities all over the house.

"Loves swimming and the water as well."

All true.

I visited Elizabeth Hill again. An example of Elizabeth Hill's specificity, which needs some background: my dear friend Paul Shue died in February 1987 of cancer that had invaded his brain, spine, and bladder. But, though he was a life-long heavy smoker, the cancer never went to his lungs. He went downhill fast, and spoke often of wishing the cancer would go into his lungs, for if it had, he'd have been eligible for some radical new drug or treatment. Having lost his wife only six months before his own death, he recalled that his first symptom (back pain) appeared on the day after his wife's funeral, when he went to retrieve a chair from home that they had taken to the nursing home when his wife went there.

Friends in High Places

He used to kid me all the time about being on a diet, for we traveled together doing research for two books, and his pleasure was to stop at every truck stop for a piece of pie and some coffee—and I would never have pie, afraid of gaining weight.

During the months leading up to, and following, his wife's death, I tried to spend as much time as I could spare with him, help him find a dog—he wanted a certain exotic breed, something called a Basenji. He also yearned to take a train trip through the Canadian Rockies, and talked about doing so up until he became ill. After he died, my car, already old, finally broke down in a major way, and I was able to buy his newer car. That all happened in 1987.

I got the following message from Elizabeth Hill, transcribed exactly as she gave it to me: *A gentleman, died with lung cancer, is here. I feel a great deal of love; he is a warm, affectionate man, has happy memories, personal memories. He's encouraging you. He's saying, "You're beautiful just the way you are," though he remembers your diet. He's often in the car with you. His car? Do you have his car? He had a dog? There's something about a dog. He appreciates what you did for him, and is not ashamed of what he did. Something about taking a trip to Canada?*

Our son graduated from Antioch in 1992, and spent the following year in London studying at the Chelsea Physic Gardens. I got my sister to go with me to visit him in London in January of 1993. While there, I saw a psychic named Amna Norman at the SAGB. We chatted about why I was in London. Here's what followed:

Norman asked, "Does your son live in a college town?"

Yes.

"Is it an old established college?"

Yes.

"With a lovely atmosphere?"

Yes.

"Does it have a statue of a southern general?"

Yes. Actually, we have several.

"Is your mother buried near the statue of the southern general?"

It could be a wild guess, as many, maybe even most, southern towns and southern cemeteries sport statues of southern generals, and my accent surely betrays me as southern. But in fact, my mother's remains lie less than one hundred feet from the famous grave and memorial statue of Thomas "Stonewall" Jackson, in the Lexington, Virginia, cemetery.

My sister is a determined skeptic. I dragged her along to the SAGB on that London trip. We each had a couple of half-hour sessions with psychics over several days.

One of those times, when Betsy asked that one medium see whether she could contact our mother, the medium suddenly looked up, surprised, and asked, "Why did I just see a butterfly come into the room?"

My sister says her hair stood on end, for she knows my idyll of Mama-the-Butterfly visiting me. As we discussed our separate sessions, my sister reasoned that, if there is any truth to my belief that Mama has in some way survived death (which my sister doesn't believe for an instant) if the psychic's message had come to ME instead of Betsy, I might have reasoned that the "psychic" was reading my thoughts. So is Betsy a believer now or not? No, and yes.

We sat in a dark pub after visiting the SAGB. "They all tell you the same thing," I groused to my sister, after a session in which I'd been told how spiritual I was, that my husband drank too much, etc. All the same stuff.

"No," she groused back, "they all tell YOU the same thing. They didn't tell me any of that. Maybe they all told it to you because it's the truth.

Friends in High Places

They never tell you your life is an emotional shambles, right?"

"Right."

"That's what they all told me," she said. She'd been married and divorced a lot, and still longed for a stable relationship.

The psychics almost always said I was a spiritual person, and that I was very creative. But I reasoned that I wouldn't have gone there if I weren't "spiritual," and doesn't everyone flatter themselves that they're creative? In 1994, several readings saw me moving "in the next two years." I did not. The other thing psychics tell me often is that I had a child who died. Absolutely untrue, unless I had an early miscarriage, which I thought I did early in my marriage but it was so early I couldn't be sure, and I never saw a doctor about it.

In 1996, as my marriage further deteriorated, a psychic named Eve Bennett seemed to get some accurate facts about me, two years after my father's death.

"Are you at a crossroads? Do you talk of spirit with friends? I sense a spirit: strong character, big man, gentle? wore blinkers on earth, wants to ask forgiveness for unfairness. He didn't give you credit. Was he a serviceman?"

Yes, Marine Corps general.

"He had a difficult upbringing and it stayed with him."

Absolutely true.

"By making things right for you, he can open doors. I feel you can get a piece of land you want. Your mother: she suffered a lot? Do you have a ring of hers?"

I do, though I don't think that was an unusual thing. Lucky guess?

"A young man in spirit: did you lose a son? Looks twenty-one or so, handsome, really blond, light blue eyes, long lean face, beautiful mouth, almost like a girl's."

Nope, but maybe....

"Your father's sternness came from discipline. He could talk to all nationalities and views. Very strong heart. Was he ever in England?"

No. South seas, New Zealand, China, Haiti, Nicaragua, Panama, Germany, but I think never England. I ask Eve Bennett about my father's surroundings in the spirit world.

"A field of corn, a path, poppies, a small house, a wood—not dark and old, but light, full of light, sunshine, trees, clear water, mountains. He's hand in hand with your mum."

Right up to then, she had me convinced. But he was deeply in love with my stepmother later in life, and she's the one he'd be with. Mama would choose to be with Stewart Granger in Heaven—at any rate, not my father.

When I say, "That was my stepmother, I think," she says,

"Your mum could have had her pick. Nice warm person, had a lot of children, I see her working with children. Mom had chest problems?"

Ms. Bennett coughs, holds her chest. Mama died of chronic bronchitis, and a weak heart from rheumatic fever.

"You are luckier than your mom?"

Yes.

"She's so pleased. Your husband, he pulls with you, not against you. He respects your views. Is he a professional man?"

Yes, I said.

"Takes all this [spiritualism] with a grain of salt, does he? But he has an open mind. He never speaks about the most important things, does he? We never speak of the most important trip we'll ever take, do we? You're going home tomorrow? I can see… that your mom had a lot to put up with; she'll help your dad if necessary. He's changed so much, he's really mellowed. Both your mom and dad send you lots of love."

"My daughter?" I asked her.

"Perhaps she's at a cross-road. Actually, I see her on a broad straight road, with many small roads off it. Does she get sidetracked? Lots of ability, does she not finish what she starts? I see many starts, not finished."

My darling daughter Jennie is indeed like that.

❧

It seems to me that nearly everything said to the group in the public demonstrations I attended (three of them, with twenty-five to fifty people at each) could relate to me and therefore probably to all the others there too, often even more than the content of the private sessions. Here are my notes from one in 1995:

"Don't discard any woman or man who comes to you in spirit. The name Gladys? Food catering, homemade jewelry, the printed word, writing, link with a legal document, you come often to places like this? I see a young female, changing schools for some special study. Richard, elderly, will be passing on soon; he has a connection with the Navy. Oh, I'm getting a warning about stairs, steps. Maud and Mabel? Some reorganization in a house? I see a futuristic connection with a marriage, someone linked with you. Comes from overseas. Auntie Bessie? Eva? Someone who has gone abroad concerns her. Expect some snapshots, photos, soon. Trouble with your back? Keep acupuncture in mind. The name Irene. Is that familiar to anyone?"

If I were a cynical sort, I'd have to notice that so many things were mentioned that it would be difficult not to connect to at least some of them. "Don't discard..." What does that mean? Ghosts? People who are spiritual? Who doesn't know an elderly fellow named Richard? A warning about steps or stairs touches us all. As does "reorganization in a house," a "futuristic connection with a marriage, someone linked with you," or "Expect some snapshots or photos soon." And which of us over fifty has not got some kind of back problem? Sure, I know two Irenes. Who doesn't?

Katie Letcher Lyle

At a public demonstration by Eve Bennett, the psychic, she points to people in the audience, and talks.

"Are you drained of energy? I'm hearing something about weight loss, mantelpiece with two vases, step into a room just from the outside, I feel children; you've been a fighter, haven't you? You are concerned about someone, a son? Just help when you can. We always hurt the people we love the most. Everything else fits? Then it has to be the son. Can't imagine that he'll ever ask forgiveness, but he will."

"Concern for your health?"

"Not really," the woman she has indicated says.

"Not a bit of heart trouble?" Eve persists.

The woman shakes her head stubbornly. Eve goes to someone else.

"Have you ever spoken publicly? sat on a committee? I see a tall, nice, casual, tweedy professional. Is there a problem with where you live?"

The man shakes his head No. She moves to the next person.

The lady with high cheekbones, a necklace, very dressy, expensive. "Is there a problem with your back?"

"Yes."

"Do you get Healing?"

"Yes."

"Enough?"

"Yes."

"You still drive, don't you?"

"No, I've never driven," replies the woman she's talking to.

"Who's the lady who drives you a lot?"

"No one drives me."

"Well, that's good because she's a bad driver. You have a friend who's a bad driver?"

"No," the woman says.

Friends in High Places

"Do you know someone in Parliament?"

"No," the woman says again.

"I see beautiful flowers, so well-arranged. Is there a birthday? Spirits are offering you beautiful flowers."

And the surprising answer from the No woman: "Yes, today is my birthday."

One reader, in 1996, said the following words to me: "Is your husband in spirit? I see him with a coughing condition, holding his hand up here [to his chest]. He has large hands, cross-footed, suffering with a head condition. Casual, relaxed, always looking around, with a stomach condition, long hands. Within three months, he will experience a problem on the material level. November is an anniversary month."

Long hands? Large hands? Which? My husband was alive until 2007, had none of this confusing array of conditions, and in fact had broad hands with short stubby fingers. No November anniversary; and we experienced no problem on the material level. Chest, head, stomach? Deep sigh… on my part, over wasted money….

In October of 1997, a woman psychic asked me: "Are you near an Indian reservation?"

No.

"I see feathers, tepees."

How ridiculous, I said to myself; to Europeans, America is still the wild west.

"Moonstone for your neck?"

No. I hardly ever wear necklaces.

"Are you a writer?"

"Yes."

"For children?"

No.... But I was in my first five books.

"Are you halfway through a book?"

What writer isn't? Yes

"Do you do translations?"

No.

"I see a house painted white, slanted roof, a farm but not a farm, around it a balcony. A chestnut horse with a stripe down its nose. Will you be home for Halloween?"

Yes.

"I'm seeing a celebration. What you want is for other people. Spirit will… see you get what you want."

Of all the above, most seem to me obvious: leading questions from the answers I gave, a conclusion so general as to apply to almost everyone. I am assuming if I'd said No to being a writer, she would have changed her tack. But since I admitted it, she went on. In most cases, however, her words could apply to anyone. I have a "fluffy" zaftig look that probably makes "writing for children" an obvious guess. I don't look much like a detective story writer—who I'd guess, now that you ask, might look like a lady lawyer, and perhaps I don't look serious enough to be what I am: a historian/nature writer, free-lance researcher. I have written five novels for young adults—still technically children, I suppose. The October thing didn't happen to be the case.

The last part about the house is mildly interesting: we had just bought a historic house on big acreage, in an attempt to save the entrance to a gorgeous mountain pass in our county. It is everything she said: painted white, with a big balcony; it had once been an old hotel in which our son took up residence in return for caretaking it, but not to farm (he is a landscape gardener). No chestnut horse. And she never saw me as anything but a writer, which I am, never asked me about city life (we are rural small town folks), never got far from the reality of our lives. So maybe she was on target.

However, Indians absolutely were not my thing at the time. But within the next year, I researched Pocahontas and her people, both in London and in Virginia, and became interested in the Eastern Algonquins. And a few years later, I was involved in a Mayan or Olmec dig (and, of course, those people were American Indians.) So I'll give her that one, too.

I read all the time of psychics—or often it is the psychics themselves who are tooting their own horns—who learn their clients' names, their dead mothers' names, specific minute indisputable facts about them. I have three times visited the famous spirit portraitist who works at the SAGB, Coral Polge, to sketch my spirit guides. She chats in sweet and vaguely motherly fashion as she sketches the spirits she "sees" around me, six or eight sketches in an hour. While sketching, she describes their connection to me. These drawings are supposed to be of spirits who are looking out for me.

But my mother, whom I feel I can talk to mentally whenever I want, and Paul, my friend that I still think of every day, are not among them. Nor are any of the three dead grandparents whom I adored. I took the portraits to my cousins on my father's side, and to Aunt Polly, my mother's sister, to see if they recognized anybody. Nothing. One portrait bears a similarity to a distant uncle of my grandmother's, but mostly because both had mutton-chops. Meanwhile, Coral Polge's autobiography recounts hit after hit: of dead relatives, children who died but are now grown up in Heaven, pets drawn so people recognize them at once, and unmistakably. The Unsolved Mysteries television segment on her is overflowing with weeping, grateful clients. My own experience is that she just likes to draw faces—and that they mean nothing.

I do believe some of the "warnings" I have received at the SAGB have been important in turning my attention more to my health as I've grown older, and in alerting me to my husband's worsening condition, which I resisted seeing for a long time. But warnings about health are also obvious: we all need to watch our health more carefully as we age.

Amna Norman was the psychic at the SAGB who said in the spring of 1998 she saw me "surrounded by Indian artifacts." Having never had any particular interest in Indians, I cynically rolled my eyes to myself, thinking of the British stereotype of all Americans as frontiersmen.

But on my return to Virginia from that trip, I had an invitation to go on a dig in Honduras a week later. Hastening to the travel clinic at the University of Virginia for malaria, typhoid, and hepatitis shots, I hardly had time to do laundry and repack before I was flying to Central America. On the dig, part of my job was sorting pottery shards, in the midst of Olmec Indian skeletons and pots.

When I arrived home after the Honduras trip, other demands awaited me. Thus a year passed before I got around to reading over my London notes from the previous year, and it was then I found the comment about being surrounded by Indian artifacts, which I had totally forgotten. If I hadn't written it down, I would never have recalled it.

In the autumn of 1999, on our last trip to the British Isles, I had some startling psychic readings. My husband and I went to London and Wales. I had warnings at every reading of dangerous times ahead for me, warnings about losing money, about unsavory and difficult business deals. It would still be nearly three years before my life fell apart. But R. lost over two hundred pounds of British currency somewhere, somehow, in London. It just vanished, along with his wallet. And in the airport, a change purse in which I had seventy pounds vanished from in front of

Friends in High Places

my eyes as I paid for something.

That was the last trip my husband and I took anywhere together (except for a dreadful week on Grand Cayman in January of 2002). I was growing increasingly desperate, and my life was careening out of control. I could not understand why R. was always, always angry at me. What had I done? I must have done something to deserve such scorn, sarcasm, disgust, abandonment. My life was unraveling fast. I had no idea what to do.

Katie Letcher Lyle

9. Hidden Help: My Upstairs Crew

I relax, pencil poised to take dictation, summoning my Upstairs Crew, my UC: "Can you help me organize my book? Also, I need to ask, what about those people whose lives don't seem to be under guidance, you know—those who seem just unlucky? People whose lives just don't seem to go well. You know what I mean. And finally, what may I call you?"

Back came the answer: *You know us already. We are you. We are your Upstairs Crew. You know some of us individually: Ish Male, the Merrygold girls, the Brothers, the Gatekeeper, the Timekeeper, the Dreamteller, Rubus and Ruby, Brother Basil, Paul Shue, William Chuck, Lord Norman (a British friend I'd made in 1970 on a trip to Greece with eighteen students from our college)—and many others. We have helped you know what foods to eat, what pills to take, how to keep your body strong and your spirit directed.*

You know how, sometimes when you're teaching, or writing, suddenly you know more than you know? That's us, Kiddo. Of course we ccan help you right, and write, the book; we've done it many times before. Some parts of every book you have written you've tuned in to us, even if you didn't know it. But you do know that now, don't you? We are from all disciplines.

Friends in High Places

Your second question: they are not listening, not hearing the guiding voices that are there for everyone. Unhappy folks create their reality just as happy people do. It serves them.

Your third question: You may call us your Upstairs Crew. Now: focus your intent and let go.

Is there a boss?

We are all you.

Is there a boss?

No more than your cat Lilly acknowledges one person or another as her "owner." She is equally friendly to all. All your guides are working together in your best interest.

Help me find an overview for the book.

No problem. Each chapter is another step in your psychic life. Choose carefully the stories you tell; there is evidence for all but the willfully blind.

Upstairs Crew, what is my life's purpose?

To teach, to learn tolerance, mutual support, yieldingness and openness to others in the fullness of human intercourse. If all mankind were to follow this model the earth could heal and realize its intended potential. The components are balance and humor, mutual help and acceptance of all cultures and races and faiths, seeing that all can be harmonious. This does not take advanced intellect, only emotional intelligence and a spirit of willing cooperation.

It was a Sunday morning, July 20, 2000, at Copan, Honduras. I was on a dig nearby, and the group had come to Copan for the weekend. By the swimming pool this morning I sought to draw to me the spirit of a Mayan who would come and talk to me. Just closed my eyes and invited anyone to talk.

The imagined entity I conjured up (or who agreed to converse with me. Or might have been an earlier Me) was an extremely thin girl of fourteen or so, with a pointed chin, slightly crossed eyes, bad and crooked teeth, long dirty hair, and roasted-almond eyes. Her head seemed slightly elongated at the top, not as flat as is usual today, but not with the typical Mayan pronounced slant either (the Mayans shaped babies' heads by binding with boards to conform to their sense of beauty). She seemed perfectly calm and happy, wondering expectantly what I wanted. She was barefoot, her garment appearing just a rectangle with a hole for the head, gathered around her middle by something like light rope or raffia. It was dingy and grayish, but had a slight design at the bottom edge of the weave. She wore nothing else. She seemed a commoner, not particularly pretty, and wore no jewelry but a string on her head (like vine) with three shells suspended from it like a crown. She was almost skeletal in her thinness. Her name was something like Mer-ah or Mee-rah.

I asked what she ate for breakfast. A thick tortilla, I think, was the answer, and a nasty greenish looking thick drink. I got that it was made from breadfruit, which I've never seen. John (Henderson, the leader of the archaeological dig) later said breadfruit grows there.

At my general question about what her life was like, I had a whole instant picture of it, from which many traits were clear: tribal, clannish, totemic (the Bat is the totem here at Copan, for it brings them intuition and stealth, and the ability to see in darkness and escape enemies, as it's small but fast). Leadership here is sometimes through blood, other times through conquest, but through the male line not the female. Women could adopt war prisoners and keep them from sacrifice, though it was usual to sacrifice prisoners. A confederacy (for strength and control) with a town I think was called Chirigua. They share a belief in the vitality of everything, even stones, and in the ability of everything alive—that is, everything—to shift shape, which they do often. A bat can become a man, and a man, a bat or a deer. The leader (king-like) frequently turns into a jaguar. The very rocks can change and water can rise up and become two-footed. This makes for a certain terror, because you too can change or be changed, and must constantly guard against it, with shells, blades, certain plant juices, even fire (hence the protective shells on string that she wears on her head). Blood is the greatest sacrifice to the universe, and always gets you what you want. Your name is secret, for protection, and you are named for protective spirits which are assigned you at birth. By whom? Magic men and women. Your day name is like a nickname. Mee-rah.

Sickness and death are caused by forgetting or ignoring your protective spirits. You may have many or few, and all have both useful and harmful faces. The jaguar is the strongest protector, but also the most evil and hardest to handle. The turtle is the longest-living, the least-changing, and thus wisest, but without any defense save his shell. Those guarded by the turtle have a heaviness of spirit. Spirits at death are sung, or chanted, out of their bodies. This must be done, or the soul gets trapped in the dead, decaying body. Children are raised communally by all the women and older girls together, and daily life consists of women and children, with men holding apart somehow, and only condescending to "visit" sometimes, but living elsewhere. They eat twice a day, morning and night, and the children, group-raised, are taught early to help. At puberty, boys are segregated for good, and from then on live largely separate lives; military, political, sporting, predatory. Mee-rah has two brothers already gone. She is not sure what the men do. There is no such thing as a man living with women and children. I see a happy world of chattering girls and women and children naked until puberty. I see most activities taking place out of doors, where the girls and women and even tiny children are weaving, grinding, scraping hide, butchering, filing or rubbing bark off limbs of trees with round stones, making thatch by lashing bundles of dried palm leaves together. Flies are everywhere, and the people look dirty. But they are happy, and quiet.

I then felt a need to get back out into the left part of my brain, except it isn't that exactly. What it is I have no words for. As usual, my brain suspects (my traditional training kicking in) that Mee-rah comes from early reading that I've forgotten, although it is lodged somewhere in my head; for if not that, then where does it come from? I don't know: Stephen Hawking says scornfully that mysticism is the final resort of someone who finds psychics too hard. Perhaps that's true, perhaps not. Physicists say instantaneous travel, and time travel, are not possible, but where is the proof of their claim that consistency governs the universe? And thoughts travel instantaneously; we can visit a past event or any person we've ever known instantaneously by only thinking of them—so why might that not be so on the other side of death?

What can I say to best convince readers that some part of us survives death?

I sigh deeply—to clear out my mind—close my eyes, get my pencil and yellow pad ready. A few deep breaths. Center. Place my intention.

Hey, Upstairs Crew! Am I at all on the right track?

What do you want to accomplish?

I want to explain about a "reasonable" process leading to belief in the so-called "unreasonable." I want to write a sane book on a subject so many people consider "insane." I want to show "the weight of evidence," as a reasonable basis for belief until the time comes that you arrive at "Knowing" for yourself.

Okay. Say what you will say. Then explain it in the book. And, at the end, tell them what you said. It's not that complicated. Guidance is what it's about. You are being led by guidance. Tell them how, all your life, you've been protected.

Yes, but I didn't know it.

No child does. You come to know it.

At sixty-something?

Friends in High Places

Well, better late than never. You're the one who taught the preacherly three rules for a quarter-century to college freshmen. Tell 'em what you plan to tell 'em, tell 'em, then tell 'em what you've told them. Oh, and try to stay under three hundred or so pages.

The Lifelines Program at the Monroe Institute is formulated on the idea that when people die, if they are unprepared to die, or have no pictures in their imaginations of the way the Afterlife works, or have no belief in any kind of afterlife, then their spirits may become stuck in a sort of limbo in which they may not realize they are dead. There are dead who move on, but they can still return to visit earth on occasion. David McKnight, our soul-rescue group leader, believed there were many levels after this life to which souls may go, and that our beliefs, or what we imagine, provide the deciding factor. If you die with only a notion of darkness, that may be what you will find. If you have no idea what happens after death, you may become a ghost. It may behoove us all to exercise the imagination, to get to know our guides, to think about possible past lives, even to visit some psychics.

You can start getting to know your own Upstairs Crew just by having a curiosity about them, inviting them to speak with you. You can tune in whenever you want, and if you will listen, they will talk to you. They will give you good advice, and open the door to things you didn't know you knew. With practice, it becomes automatic to converse with them. A pencil and paper will allow you to write down what comes to mind… anything you get.

Katie Letcher Lyle

10. Remote Viewing: The Proof

I saw the light, I saw the light,
No more darkness, no more night,
Now I'm so happy, no sorrows in sight,
Praise the Lord, I saw the light!

~Folk hymn, a k a spiritual

Oh, do not ask, what is it?
Let us go and make our visit.

~T.S. Eliot

The instant I heard about Remote Viewing, I knew I had to do it. One of the principles of scientific inquiry must be that a hypothesis must be abandoned when irrefutable evidence to the contrary appears. This chapter may be the most important section of this book. It refutes the erroneous notion that when you're dead you can't possibly be in communication with the living, because you're dead, your ears and eyes

Friends in High Places

are dead, your brain is dead, and *obviously* you need all those things to communicate with. Remote viewing comes close, in my opinion, to that elusive "unified theory" to explain psychic phenomena of all sorts.

Remote viewing is sending a part of one's conscious mind to a hidden "target" and returning with correct information. As with any new thing (new to me!) it's an erratic process not totally understood that, nonetheless, exceeds chance. It is real; to that I can attest. We have proven the non-locality of the human mind. Though it's done without mechanical intervention, such as electricity, it's the same on a personal level as dialing the correct phone number for your grandmother, and getting your grandmother every time. Anyone can learn to do it. It takes practice, and concentration, but that's all. You can learn to do it too.

I am the world's most anxiety-ridden pupil at anything I try to study. I think every teacher I've ever had has said in some way, at some time, "Just stop trying so hard. Just let go and let it happen." Well, I try to do that. Yes, try. If only I could let go and let it happen. I know that my eagerness gets in my way, but I seem unable to do much about it.

But in spite of myself, I have learned to remote view. I've taken three courses, and done a lot of practice with targets on the computer. Remote viewing is a perceptual skill enabling practically anyone to acquire information about people, objects, times, places, and events. During the Cold War years (1972 to 1995) the U.S. government had a secret Remote Viewing surveillance program to monitor foreign governments. More about that in a bit.

A quick story. One night, I realized I had lost my car keys, with all the other stuff on the ring. When I used the remote view technique to "see" where the keys were, I saw them fallen onto a dull carpet in darkness. I looked everywhere in my house and found nothing. I have no carpets. I went to bed and asked my guides to help me find them. At some point during aerobics the next morning, I knew where they were. We'd been to

Applebee's the night before, and that was the carpet where they were. I called, and they had been found, right by the bar stool I was sitting on. I believe I remotely viewed them right there, where I dropped them.

This is the absolute truth: there is a part of every human being that can leave the body and go somewhere else, complete with all our five ordinary senses, obtain information, and return to accurately give information about that "somewhere else." What this means, excitingly, is that a part of our consciousness or mind is certainly "nonlocal;" that is, it can travel anywhere, in no time, cover any amount of space, and return instantly to us—our brains?—to report accurately on whatever the "target" is. Thousands of experiments later, from many remote viewing schools, there is now overwhelming evidence for the truth of this, what Charles Tart in 1975, in *ESP,* called "statistical repeatability." He claimed, even back then, that overall, about one-third of psychic experiments get significant results. The estimate is higher now.

I wanted to learn how to remote view because therein lies the proof of the pudding. Being a slow learner, stumbling over my own enthusiasm, I have attended the Remote Viewing Practicum at The Monroe Institute three times: in 2002, the first time they offered the program, again in 2004, and the third time in 2007. The last time, I took my partner Nick Charles, along. He had been to only two programs at the Monroe, and is not the "junkie" that I am, having participated in about thirty programs in the last eighteen years.

Nick agreeably went to this program out of curiosity; and, because he didn't much care if he "got it" or not, he had almost a perfect record of hits. I know there's a lesson for me here, and I know my own performance anxiety inhibits my success, which has been and continues to be considerably less than his.

The boyish blond guy who heads up the program, F. Holmes "Skip"

Friends in High Places

Atwater, has been active in some capacity at the Monroe Institute ever since I began going there. He is a great friend and a great soul—and the unlikeliest Army officer I've ever known. Skip was the Operations and Training Officer for the U.S. Army Intelligence remote viewing program. He is assisted by Joseph McMoneagle, also of the government program. Using Hemi-Sync signals as aids (as described in a previous chapter), for a week each time at the Monroe Institute, we studied and practiced Remote Viewing (RV).

RV at the Monroe Institute is a protocol-driven, scientifically-designed course to learn to seemingly send part of one's consciousness somewhere else and return with correct information about the target location, picture, person, or time. It is an activity that the Monroe Institute, and other organizations, have proven without a doubt humans can do and can do consistently. Therefore, it is one of the few "paranormal" activities that can be proven and replicated.

Remote viewing proves that our consciousness can function away from our bodies. And so there is a part of us that *may* continue to function away from the body even after the event we call death. Think of all the near-death experiences reported in the last thirty years or so—when people have described leaving their bodies, viewing their bodies somewhere outside of the selves they were then. Not only was there no loss of the five senses that we have while in the body, but also people have described clearer vision, sharper hearing, while out of their bodies.

Back in the fifties, a gorgeous, suave French student came to Washington and Lee for a year. None of us had ever even met a Frenchman. In addition to being a celebrated exchange student, Phillipe Labro wrote a novel about his year here, and all my friends and I were gaga over this handsome foreign student we all sort of knew a little bit, wished we could go out with (but our parents said *over their dead bodies*) who had actually written a book about our little town. Labro, glamorous to this day, went on to become one of France's foremost journalists, as hard-nosed as they come. I have followed his career, which includes a book about a near-death experience while he was hospitalized for an unknown infection. He awoke to see his father standing there alive, telling him to come. He heard a voice say, "Don't go over there." He was suddenly aware of many many friends standing around his bed, all urging him to come over, come on, to where they were. But there was also something he didn't like about it all. He was gratified that they were there, *until he realized they were all dead.* His book, *Dark Tunnel, White Light,* details his "death" and his clawing his way back to life, refusing to go with the dead. My point is that Labro is no woozy romantic, but a smart and incisive international journalist and film-maker. Of course, this is just one story among, by now, millions by people who have left bodies behind, been conscious, and seen, heard, smelled, touched, while out of their bodies, and eventually returned to their bodies and lived to tell the tale.

In 1995, the American CIA released most of the documents about Remote Viewing, or "psychic espionage." Today, nonlocal awareness is used to locate archaeological sites make money in the stock market, solve crimes, win horse races, find new mineral deposits and locate lost people. The public apparently finds it unpalatable and frightening, not to mention unbelievable; thus rarely is it publicized.

Here is one example: *based on information obtained by several remote viewers,* President Carter and the National Security Council decided to send a recovery team to pick up Richard I. Queen, one of sixty-six hostages of Islamic militants. Queen, who had been captured 250 days before, was released on July 11, 1980, and was able to resume his diplomatic career.

And in a more recent case, it is now public knowledge that Saddam Hussein's hiding place was described accurately by a team of remote viewers in December of 2003, and this description definitively led to his capture six weeks later.

※

Let me describe how remote viewing works, and the way The Monroe Institute teaches it today. Three people are involved in the scientific protocol: the remote viewer, a monitor, and a judge. All three are "blind": that is, none knows the target. The remote viewer "goes" to the target, and reports what she or he senses, sees, smells, hears—giving whatever information comes to him. This includes information about time of day or night, slant of light, whether people are present, and so on. He always sketches what he thinks he sees.

The monitor prompts him: what do you smell? is the target hard or soft? is it indoors? what colors do you see? and so on. The RV-er is asked to sketch what he sees if he does not draw spontaneously. The monitor is the go-between, and takes the viewer's final report to the judge or judges.

Without the remote viewer present, the monitor and judges open the "target envelope," wherein are four target pictures, chosen randomly by a computer. The judge or judges then try to decide which of the four was the target. Nobody "knows," for the targets are randomly chosen, and sometimes are not even chosen until *after* the RV-er's reporting. Remote viewing is independent of time and space.

Here's how a discussion of the viewer's report might go: "Okay, she mentioned water and winter, and a lot of black—and her sketch shows this line across the middle clearly—so I think it's Picture Three."

"Well, but there's more green in Picture Four, and she said the primary color was green."

"But there's no clear middle line in this one."

"Picture One is definitely winter. None of the others are."

"But how can you tell the season? Two are indoors!"

And so the discussion proceeds until the judges agree on one picture as the probable target. The final act is the opening of the envelope or the computer screen that shows which randomly chosen target is the correct one. As you accustom yourself to this mysterious process, you get the right target more and more often. With correct responses, your confidence grows.

The best possible attitude is to have confidence that you can do this. When I asked the question of remote viewer Joe McMoneagle, "What is your secret?" he grinned and replied, "Only that I know I can do it." McMoneagle is Skip Atwater's Army buddy and another of our teachers, probably the world's most famous Remote Viewer, and winner of the Legion of Merit for his work.

You need, therefore, to desire to "visualize" the target and to *know* that you can do this.

The viewer's job is to make the team look good. The monitor's job is to make the viewer look good. The judges' jobs are to look so carefully that they choose the correct target, thus making the viewer and the monitor look good. The implicit expectation by all is that you will succeed. Your intention is to get the target (which can be geographical coordinates, hidden pictures, or a place—present, past or future, or even a person—present, past, or future.)

Yes, you can talk to the dead. You can visit Mars. There are many proven examples of psychic archaeology, which is not embraced by mainstream archaeology because those who can't do it don't want it to be true, or are threatened by it. I'd recommend that you read *One White Crow*, about the psychic archaeologist George McMullen.

So that's how it's done. This is not the only protocol possible. The course introduces us to five or six other schools of Remote Viewing. During the week of exploration, we learn how different protocols work, to enhance and further explain the process, and a participant gets many

Friends in High Places

chances to test himself.

It took me a long time. It's a delicate process, and undoubtedly too much eagerness, my typical "trying too hard," was my downfall from the beginning. The first time I took the course, I didn't hit the target many times. Oddly, what I did really well was hit *near* the target.

Here's what I mean: there'd be four pictures for the judges to consider: let's say they are a church, an aqueduct, a child playing with a puppy, a plate with a sandwich on it. One judge might point out that there's a rounded point in the R.V.er's drawing. But only one. So a vote for the church, shaped sort of like a rounded pyramid. Another judge might point out that the shape of the child's elbow as he plays with the puppy is a bit like gothic window shapes (pointed arch or rounded pyramid). A third judge might add that the aqueduct's shape is also rounded. The plate the sandwich is on is round. So the judges look to other hints in the R.V.er's description. The remote viewer may have described the main color as brown. (A vote for the brown puppy? The tannish-brown aqueduct?) Or he might have associated his target with music. (A vote for the church?) He wrote "Mainly white," so, a vote for the church or the white-bread sandwich? He might have said "running water." (A vote for the aqueduct?) In the end, the judge or judges must come to agreement on one of the four pictures as the target.

Then the computer randomly generates one of the four pictures as the intended target. You either got it or you didn't. The fact that it's generated after the fact doesn't change anything, because the human ability to remote view is independent of time and space.

The *intention* is what matters. Getting the picture next to it, complete with the three arches of the aqueduct in the same place as in the picture, doesn't count if it turns out that the aqueduct picture was not the target. That's what I kept doing, drawing near-perfect sketches of the picture right next to the target picture. When I asked Joe McMoneagle why I kept hitting near the target, but not the target, he responded in a way that helped me: "Because you just want to get *something*. You have to be extremely specific; intend to go to the target, and only the target."

After that, I took his advice and got more targets.

The remote viewer may find herself, as I did once, at an odd angle from the target. Behind it, or above it, say. I drew what looked like the back of an envelope, squarish with lines, and an open umbrella from above, with six segments. That's what I thought it was, an umbrella. I wrote "green, white, man-made, silence." The target was, in fact, a small church next to a covered, six-sided Greek-looking structure in a park, open to nature, nothing like what I thought I "saw." But the judges decided I'd been hovering over the structures, looking down on the roofs. My drawing matched a view of the scene as it might have been viewed from above, with the correct number of segments: six.

Joe McMoneagle also told us, "All your perceptions may be 100% correct. Maybe you just don't understand what you saw." So again, maybe you were *around the corner* from the target, or below it, or inside it when the picture showed the outside. Or on the lawn with your *back* to the target.

When reviewing an example of one of my early efforts, much of my reading was wrong. I wrote, "outdoors, wet, blue, children, laughing, a musty smell." But meanwhile I drew circles, flowing lines, round shapes, and spirals. I thought the target was a beach scene, with the water going in eddies, and I felt I was about thirty feet up in the air watching this.

Instead, the target was a picture of a plate of candies being coated, chocolate swirling and flowing around. I'd drawn a near-perfect rendition of the all-brown picture, and thus the judges deemed I'd hit the target. But I didn't realize in the least what I'd gotten, and had gone on to "fill in the blanks."

What about all the wrong stuff I got? That is the great bugaboo of

Friends in High Places

Remote Viewing, and it's called *"analytic overlay,"* or AOL. When you stop describing the shapes, colors, smells, etc, and start *Naming* what you get, thus analyzing and laying false (but to your left hemisphere maybe logical) details over your original perceptions, you swerve way off track. It's jumping to unwarranted conclusions. It's the left brain's logical, frantic effort to make sense of the target instead of just visiting it and sticking to the description, and describing what you saw.

As you work, and practice, you learn what you do best and what you do worst. I draw without thinking, and my drawings are usually the best parts of my viewing. I think sometimes I should stop there, go no further, for my left brain, in trying to make sense of what I've viewed, leads me astray.

Analytic overlay is the hardest thing NOT to do. So you try to avoid reporting or saying it's "like a lake," instead trying to stick to saying "flat, round, liquid." You should stick to "square shapes" instead of leaping to "buildings" or "boxes" or "blocks."

There is nothing "woo-woo" about remote viewing. It needs only clear, coherent attention. You, well, I, anyway, constantly battle the fear of failure. You need to relax, clear the mind, turn inward to where the inner eyes are. You make clear to yourself your intention to connect to the target and only the target. You need to listen, wait receptively for something without looking for anything—and this was, and is, difficult for me. Then you become aware of internal feelings and impressions, avoiding AOL. Finally, you need to report with words, feelings, smells, impressions, sketches. Research has also shown that "excited brains" have a detrimental effect on accurate performance, and I know full well that my brain is excited while I'm trying to remote view.

❧

One time I tried Remote Viewing while high on pot. After my split with my husband, I dated for a time a fellow, an old friend a decade younger than me, who smoked pot. So I tried it a few times, reverting pretty soon to my preferred drug, martinis. But this afternoon we were high, sitting on my screen porch. He wanted to test my Remote Viewing ability. "Do you have to know the target?" he asked. I said I didn't think so. Monitors and judges don't know the target the viewer is visiting. So he said, "Okay, go to the target I have in mind and describe it."

I set my intent easily, as I was relaxed to the point of wilt. At once I got a flash of red, a roundish square, and a lot of what looked like circle shapes. I wrote red, brown, a woodsy smell. I drew a squarish box hovering in the air, and to the right of the box, a bunch of circles overlapping each other.

Jay regarded the drawing, then said, "Let's go see." He led me across the street by a tall fence toward a neighbor's back yard. "Around here," he said. As we approached, we saw a red grill, a gate, and to the right, a pile of logs set against the garage, round ends out. I had drawn and seen, startlingly, the entrance to my neighbor's back yard. Jay had never been there and so had no knowledge of the target he had thought up. I was not reading his mind, which didn't even have the target in it. His target had been "whatever is over behind that fence." I had even gotten the box "floating" above ground, for it was, in fact, mounted on skinny legs that brought the grill up to a workable level. It was probably the best targeting I've ever done. Alas, I've never done remote viewing again while under the influence of any drug. But I think the drug relaxed me and took away my usual anxiety about performing.

People are quirky, and people I've done programs with have all manner of techniques for getting to the target. I think I must define "technique" as a story we tell ourselves to justify how it is we can do this! Some swear by wearing their striped socks or their diamond earrings; others, by imagining a blackboard or a whiteboard on which the target appears. Many admit they cannot hit the target when tired. One man, in fact, did tell me he could only hit the target when he was high on marijuana!

Friends in High Places

Another told me he asks his dead uncle to show him the target. Others imagine going to the Akashic records. Personally, I need to be in a darkened place to concentrate, with an eyemask over my eyes. I imagine a blank computer screen, and when I hit the ENTER button, the target will appear. Paul Elder, the best "lay" viewer I know, uses the image of a camera, with the lens opening several times, each time giving a clearer glimpse of the target. He is so good at Remote Viewing he has become the third member of the teaching team at TMI.

When we get discouraged the instructors remind us that if a baseball player can hit the ball thirty percent of the time, he gets paid a lot of money. So we are not to worry about our failures. For me, that is still the hardest thing. I know it and I fight it, but it's still hard not to berate myself.

When the Army took remote viewing seriously for a quarter of a century throughout the cold war, they estimated an eighty percent accuracy in the information they obtained when the viewer hit the target. They sought, tested, chose selectively, then highly trained their people, and some of their successes were remarkable. Though the Army reportedly dropped the program in the mid-nineties, Remote Viewing has flourished, and today professional remote viewers are often hired by police departments to target lost people.

The professional R.V.-ers I have gotten to know keep low profiles, so as not to be disturbed by the public and the press, but they are used in many "vanished people" cases. Often it is their under-cover work that leads to the arrests of perpetrators, and the locations of bodies. The public does not hear about this work, and this is how remote viewers like it. You can imagine how hounded they would be by people who have lost things, who want to find treasure, whose children have disappeared, or who want to know where Daddy's will is.

Theoretically, neither time nor distance nor any kind of shielding can interfere with hitting the target. Geographical coordinates are popular targets, along with pictures. But an event in the past, a person who has died, another planet, or some time in the future—all are just as possible targets as a neighbor's unseen back yard. There is no distance: you are just "there" as surely as you can "be" instantly in a memory. You don't know what you know until you know it; thus practice and success build your confidence.

So that you will understand what it's like—though I missed many targets—I had first-timer's luck, and here's how it went. My first effort.

"Going to the target," I immediately drew on the paper an upside down ice cream cone shape. It was as if my hand moved without my volition. By it I wrote, "concrete, white bricks, things laid out regularly. Military base? colorless water beyond. Little color, barren flat landscape. Something dead about the place, no greenery. 1950? Water beyond, not salty. Nothing on outside like fence. Abandoned site. Neat and clean but barren."

The target was the Great Pyramid at Giza—and I was thrilled beyond belief. A lot of AOL there, but a definite hit.

And one other time, I walked into the room where we were going to be working, and said out loud, "St. Louis Arch." I had no idea why I said it, but several others drifting into the room heard me. I'd not been there, didn't know anything about it. Written on the board were some geographical coordinates, but I hadn't even glanced at them, and certainly couldn't have told you what they meant. I don't know a thing about coordinates. I quickly shrugged off my odd "outburst," until, later in the hour, I learned the St. Louis Arch was indeed the target indicated by the coordinates.

I am no theorist; I only know that mind is nonlocal, at least sometimes. But it is a fair question to ask how the mind might be able to leave the body and take the senses along with it.

There are many theories about how psychic phenomena are real, and I feel the need to describe the ones I know about. One example is the theory

Friends in High Places

of David Chalmers, a cognitive scientist at University of Arizona, Tucson. He suggests that consciousness is an element of the universe, just like matter or energy, neither made by the brain nor dependent on the brain for its existence. He claims there is overwhelming evidence for his theory. Probably belief in, say, the ability to remote view, or the effectiveness of prayer, "oil" the hinges, so to speak, allowing the doors to open.

"Signal-transfer" suggests that waves analogous to radio or television waves transport information about the target.

"Field theories" suggest the existence of some "field" of nonlocal information permeating time and space that we can resonate with. Carl G. Jung's "collective unconscious," William James's "cosmic consciousness," and Rupert Sheldrake's "morphic fields" are well known examples of field theories.

"Multidimensional theories" posit multidimensional realities which exist but are invisible, and, in fact, such models are consistent with what is known of quantum physics and relativity. David Boehm, a protege of Einstein, spoke of an "implicate order," a source beyond space, time, matter, and energy, of which everything and everyone is a part—and therefore there is no separation between us: we are the implicate source, and can know ourselves.

"Mind" may be thought of as that portion of our brain that observes and directs the brain, which would have to be a nonlocal process. The mind would have to be outside the brain to think about the brain.

So what we call *attention* is the brain observing itself, but from where? What is that observer? What is it that is doing the watching?

And what we call *intention* is the act of directing that attention toward some goal.

The "matrix theory" also suggests a data base in the universe of all knowledge past, present, and future, popularly known as the "Akashic record," "The Mind of God," the universal library," or "the matrix" from which the remote viewing mind gets information. A famous remote viewer, Paul Smith, in *Reading the Enemy*, wrote about the government Remote Viewing program, "We learned that... the mind can roam virtually at will across the face of the planet."

Conscious awareness is thought to be maybe one percent of sensory input. The other ninety-nine percent lies beneath the threshold of consciousness. We may be eating dinner while a cat meows, the TV's on in the other room, twilight's falling, it's warm in the kitchen, your hair is in your eyes, you're thinking of the book you've been reading, you saw a friend at the grocery store who told you she's battling cancer, your spouse seems preoccupied, the refrigerator hums, birds call outdoors, and so on. But you consciously notice only tiny pieces of this, perhaps only the taste of the food you are chewing at the moment. But all that other input is coming in at the same time, including, if someone asked you, all your memories, hopes, anxieties, and on and on.

In order to Remote View, you have to find a way to clear your mind to allow some part of you to attach to the target. It takes no time; it is instantaneous. Not easy, but yes (!) possible.

ESP (extra-sensory perception) often seems to occur when the conscious part of the mind is diverted. One famous remote-viewer fiddles with a cloth and a spray bottle of water as he works, sketching then spraying and wiping away quickly what he's sketched or written. To keep from losing his written reports, his sessions are preserved via video. In the one I watched, the target was a man that had been influential in the Albuquerque Balloon Festival. The remote viewer saw desert, then various Indians, then round shapes in the air, and finally, finally, after fifteen minutes, zeroed in on the festival, the magazine with the festival write up, and on the man himself who was the target, whose picture graced the front of the magazine. Either it was a magnificent fraud, or it was truly a successful remote viewing.

Friends in High Places

Some Remote Viewing techniques stress exceedingly specific, numbered systems for reporting. The idea is that the left brain is kept busy with numbering and following intricate directions so as to free the right brain to do the global work of finding and reporting on the target.

Speaking of occupying the left brain, from time to time, needing a solution to a problem, I've opened any thick book at random—some Christians say it has to be the Bible—let my finger fall somewhere on the page, and trust that I come up with the answer I needed. The book itself seems to me not to matter; and the answer I need nearly always comes to me. I can almost feel what the mental process is: my finger lights upon a sentence that apparently has nothing to do with my problem, but thinking about the sentence distracts my conscious mind (or the left, logical part of my brain) long enough for my subconscious mind (or the right, intuitive, allusive, more-than-logical part of my brain) to push through the answer I've been seeking, getting me off dead-center, left-brained perseveration on the problem. Runes work the same way, as does the I Ching, the ancient and famously-accurate Chinese method of fortune-telling.

Even using plain rocks works. Try this. The rock exercise is simple; I do it often, and to great personal advantage. If I have a problem or a question, (1) I go outside and select a rock, any rock that I find appealing or interesting; (2) I pose my problem or question clearly, and it's a good idea to note the question on a piece of paper to remember it, and to phrase it the way I originally mean to; (3) now, I try to forget the question and turn my attention to the rock. I want to examine the rock carefully, turning it over, looking at it from different angles, and jotting down on paper all my impressions of the rock. (4) At the end of five minutes of doing this—observing, phrasing, looking, jotting any impressions—I usually have the answer to my question—surprising and original—yet with the feeling, "Of course!"

Don't expect to intellectually understand this. You will not understand it until you try it; then you will see how it works.

I learned this technique at my Gateway program, the first Monroe Institute program I attended, found how well it worked, and kept doing it. When I think about it, it seems that focusing on the rock distracts the conscious, earth-bound mind to enable the subconscious knowledge, which is always available to us, to rise to the top. It's the same process that you go through in remote viewing. The process itself seems to open one's conscious mind telepathically or clairvoyantly to the source of wisdom.

Remember Moses' burning bush story in the Bible? The bush, always a mystery to me, may have been a distraction, to get Moses' logical left brain occupied (and thus out of the way) so that God could reveal Himself to Moses, so Moses could hear in a new way through the global, illogical, intuitive right, or subconscious, brain. At any rate, that's what my friend Ken Patrick believes may have happened.

Remote viewing seems to work the same way: it may let you quiet the logical, jump-to-conclusions brain—which tells you, you "can't" do this, so we have to overlay what you're perceiving to make some sense of all this—and concentrate on what images arise in your mind and report them, without letting the logical mind lay logical data on top of your impressions.

There is no doubt that many, perhaps all, humans can accurately describe elements of a situation far beyond our visual, aural, tactile field. I recommend the book, *Miracles of Mind*, by Russell Targ and Jane Katra, as the most interesting I have read on the subject.

More to the point, I've done it myself. I don't know how I've traveled to locations that don't even yet exist as targets when I go to them, but I know I can do it because I've done it. My feeling is that anyone can if I can. I'm not psychic, and only average in intelligence. The lesson is that intention is the key. Intention is what makes the difference. What we intend comes to pass. Not what we wish, or want, or whine for, but what we *intend*.

Friends in High Places

People have long argued with survivalists that it is our bodies that possess our sense organs, our bodies only that can see, hear, smell, touch, sense—so how can there be survival of some form of spirit without a body to exist in? Now we know, know, that some part of the consciousness can still smell, taste, see, without the presence of flesh, eyes, ears. It is proven. Many many times.

Four times I know of, I have left my body behind and gone somewhere else in my sleep, and retrieved information. Once when I was still with my husband, and he claimed not to be drinking, though he was obviously drunk, I had a strange dream: that I'd gone into his bathroom and found, in his undersink cabinet, three of those giant bottles of gin or vodka. As soon as he left for the day to go to our country house, I looked under his sink, and there they were, exactly as in my dream. I conclude that some part of me actually went there, saw the bottles, earlier—and it wasn't my body, which lay sleeping in bed.

I found a lost gold earring in a muddy parking lot a year after I'd lost it. I just woke up early one morning knowing where it was, and could hardly wait for daylight to go directly to the parking lot, get out of my car and find it, crushed but malleable, and repairable. I once walked directly to the spot on the beach in Mexico where our lost room key had washed up, right where I "knew" it would be. Once I "woke up" mid-aerobics to know where my car keys had been lost. I'd say I was spontaneously remote viewing in all those events.

Further, this nonlocal perception correlates with the information given us by thousands of near-death experiencers as they leave their bodies. They find their eyesight clear, their poor hearing restored to perfection, their bodies without pain. The only way remote viewing can be true—and it is true!—is that there is no time or space, that we are all connected, and that we know everything all the time, at some level.

Try this on your own. You may be in for a surprise. Search for "remote viewing targets" on the Internet and try some. What have you got to lose? They are free.

And here's another version of the "rock" exercise. Look around you and choose some object that attracts you. On paper, *describe it*. Tell *why* you chose it. What's its *greatest trait or asset?* What most *limits it?*

Now think: your answers are really not about the object, but about you. What insights does this bring you? Note: it's not important *WHAT* you chose, but *WHY* you chose it.

Remote viewing may be the most valuable thing I have ever done.

Friends in High Places

11. Way-Out Stuff: Talking to Other Species

Student: "How did you get those big trees from the woods
to the ocean to build the whaling boats?"

Old man: "We just picked the tree and it came with us...
You go into the forest and you walk around and you find a tree
that's fitting, and you say to the tree, 'Would you like to be a canoe?'
Then you sing the tree a song. If the tree sings back,
it wants to be a canoe... you keep walking around
until you find the tree that wants to be a canoe.
It just gets up and goes with you,
lays itself down, and you build a canoe....
You've lost the ability to see the trees walk."

**~George White Wolf Branham, Monacan Indian,
to Ruth Huffman, for the Rockbridge Advocate, October 2008**

Katie Letcher Lyle

You already know what your dog is saying, what your cat wants. Remind yourself of what you know: communicating with different species is possible, maybe even easy.

Then, consider this June 2007 story from Rosemont, Illinois: its longtime mayor (for fifty-one years), Donald Stephens, died recently, and within weeks many local folks began to see his face in the peeling bark of a fifty-foot sycamore he had twice saved from being destroyed. Before his death, he told his son Bradley, who was appointed to take his place, "You screw things up, I'm gonna haunt you." How better to keep an eye on his beloved town?

Druids, priests of the original Celtic inhabitants of the British Isles, believed that after death souls went into plants: the process is called metempsychosis. The famous ballad of Barbara Allen, dating perhaps to the time of the Druids, has a curious ending suggesting just that. Jemmie loved Barbry, and dying, asked to see her. She came, he announced he was dying of love for her, but she spurned his love. He turned his face to the wall and died. Barbry Allen immediately began to rue her haughty dismissal of him, and she died shortly thereafter of a broken heart. They buried him in the old churchyard, and laid Barbry close by, just over the wall, in the new churchyard. The song ends, "From Jemmie's grave there grew a rose, and from Barbry's a green brier. They grew and grew to the old church wall, 'Til they could grow no higher, And there they tied in a true love knot, the rose bush and the brier."

I love the symbolism, the sharpness of her, the sweetness of him, truly as though their souls went into the plants.

My friend Beth Ford's mother was buried on a calm, sunny June day. When the family returned to the house from the funeral, they were flabbergasted to see that her favorite maple tree, over forty feet high, one she'd loved, one she'd planted before her children were born, had just toppled over in the yard. Though the children soon planted another maple tree, Beth believes its falling when it did was just too close to her mother's burial to be a coincidence.

Messages are often so subtle that they may escape notice, or leave the observer puzzled. My friend, Nancy V.R., had a younger brother who died at twenty-three, a victim of drugs and alcohol, probably a suicide, at the least an overdose, perhaps accidental, perhaps not. On the day he died, a huge willow tree he'd loved and climbed on blew over in a sudden fierce wind. This was Nancy's first death of someone close to her, and she was devastated. Three days after the funeral, on her twenty-sixth birthday, Nancy went to the old historic cemetery near Fairfax, Virginia, for a quiet solo visit. It was a beautiful July day. She was sitting in her jeans near her brother's grave, crying, when to her right she saw a grackle. It flew down to a tombstone within a yard of her, and stared at her. She decided to quietly stretch out on the ground. The bird then landed on her stomach and walked up her body and looked in her face. Why? she felt herself demanding of the bird. Where is he? Is he at peace? She felt she was getting an answer, that the bird was telling her something, and she felt that she had to accept her brother's death. Her grief lightened. In about three minutes, the bird flew off. She's not willing to say the bird was her brother—she still feels it's a mystery—but sums up her experience thusly: "Contemporary man is cut off from aspects of his own mind, so when these things happen, we don't know how to think about them."

You can converse with parts of your body to great advantage. On my right hand, at the base of my thumb, is a hard painful lump that X-ray informed me is arthritis, not the earlier diagnosis, deQuervain's Tendinitis. It swells up angrily and hurts every so often; other times it's acceptable to live with. One day, I decided to ask my painful thumb joint what was going on, and listen to the answer. It responded to me thusly: "You are impatient. You need to slow down. In your life, you've tried opening too many doors roughly, too many mayonnaise jars impatiently. You barge ahead as if you were a teenager. Slow down, be careful, or I will flare up to remind you." Nothing could have been more helpful or more specific or more true. The result? It is much better, and when it flares up I know exactly why, and I know what to do. No doctor told me, just my body itself.

Try this yourself. It works.

I taught a creative writing course at a local nursing home, and one day asked the class to do an exercise like the one above: to contact a part of the body that might benefit from some help, and converse with it. All of us over about fifty probably have something that doesn't work quite right. All but one of my fifteen or so students tackled the work with enthusiasm, and as we discussed the exercise, they said they'd learned a lot and enjoyed doing it. One woman, however, wrote only about how much she hated her legs. She had a circulation problem and experienced pain constantly. I could not convince her to listen to her legs, or in any way try to solve the problem; she just wrote a stubborn and angry rant about how she hated her legs, and how they'd betrayed her. She couldn't enter our discussion about it, either; her anger was too great. I didn't have a chance to ever discuss it further with her. It was near the end of the class meetings. Life went on. About two years later I learned that she had died. Her sister told me her death was related to the circulation in her legs. One had been removed and the other was gangrenous. I wasn't surprised. I only wonder if, had she been able to dialogue with her legs, she might have lived longer.

My cousin Posey Neidigh, a Christian counselor, suggested that we might look at how our illnesses serve us. What does this cancer give you

Friends in High Places

that you need? She told me the story of one of her patients who was just naturally quiet, shy, and loved being alone. But her husband, whom she'd been drawn to because he was extroverted and sociable, demanded that she keep up with his social schedule. She developed migraines, which allowed her two or three days, alone, withdrawn, and quiet. Posey saw the pattern, and tried to persuade her to confront her husband gently about their different needs. When she did, and he accepted her need for solitude, he backed off and her migraines disappeared. Presumably you can communicate with anything you want, even your own illnesses. Heck, it's worth a try! You just might learn something. A woman might choose cancer over an abusive husband, or a domineering sister. I believe I've seen those "choices" more than once among my hospice patients.

George Washington Carver, born in the last year of the Civil War, talked with peanuts. "Anything, if you love it enough, will converse with you," he wrote once. Carver discovered over *three hundred uses* for the ground nuts, including instant coffee, ink, shoe polish, wood stain, talcum powder, axle grease, and face cream. When asked why he didn't apply for patents and grow rich on the cheap edibles he so loved, he replied that God had given him the ideas, and that it would be wrong to sell them to other people. He told people he was happy just to serve mankind.

How do you think he did all that? I think it's because he *communicated with the peanuts,* just as he said.

Meryl Ann Butler, a quilter and fiber artist I was briefly friends with, moved to Virginia Beach in the spring of 1994 with her unemployed husband, five children, and no job. It became her habit in those early weeks to walk out every morning from their tiny place on 66th Street, onto Virginia Beach, to meditate, and ask the universe, "What am I supposed to be doing? Why am I here?"

Soon they found an apartment to sublet for the summer; but what would they do after the owners came back on the first of September? They desperately needed an inexpensive apartment. Her quilts had always brought in plenty of money. But here she was not known, and commissions and sales were so slow at first that some days she didn't know where the next meal was coming from. Her husband looked and looked for jobs, but with no success.

One brisk June morning as her daily meditation on the beach drew to a close , she sighed and got up to go. But as she did, something in the ocean caught her eye: a dolphin, far out in the water. For some reason, she was drawn to it, and mentally "called out" to it. To her delighted surprise, the dolphin swam in closer, staying in view.

Meryl Ann decided to walk along with it, as it was swimming south, and she loved watching it. She admired the animal's grace and soon felt that they were walking together, the dolphin close to shore, Meryl's feet making imprints in the wet sand just at the water's edge. The wind was blowing and it was a fine day for a stroll. Pretty soon they had gone ten blocks south, into the fifties. She began to play a game. What would the dolphin do if she slowed down? If she ran? The dolphin kept pace with her exactly, and she felt it was enjoying the game as much as she. Time and the city blocks passed easily.

In the forties, she suddenly heard excited voices, and a noisy tourist couple rushed down the beach, nearly knocking her over. "Oh, look!" they both shrieked, "a dolphin!" "Oh, Harry," shouted the woman, "get a picture!"

Meryl Ann kept walking, and the dolphin kept swimming. The rambunctious couple fell in with Meryl Ann, and soon seemed to notice that the dolphin was staying near. The husband kept pointing his camera, but whenever the dolphin appeared, Harry was always pointing the

Friends in High Places

wrong way.

The man and woman chattered incessantly, while Meryl Ann continued her quiet conversation with the sea mammal, whom she was now convinced really was pacing her. But she didn't know how to get rid of them. It was a public beach, and there was no law against running around shouting, "Look here! No, there! Harry! You're too slow!" No law against Harry yelling, "I almost got it!" as he pointed his camera towards the ocean.

Then Meryl Ann got an idea: Dolphin, she thought, why don't you come up where this guy's pointing? All he wants is a picture, and then we can be rid of him.

To her surprise, the dolphin made a graceful leap precisely where the man was pointing the camera, and the man snapped it and exclaimed in excitement. Sure enough, immediately the couple left the beach.

Meryl Ann and the dolphin continued on their "walk." At some point, she told it, If you're leading me anywhere, change your direction so I'll know. Give me a sign.

At 34th street, the dolphin made an abrupt turn out to sea, for all the world as if its tail were waving goodbye, letting her know she'd been delivered to her destination. The dolphin disappeared among the white caps the wind whipped up.

Before Meryl Ann could even look around, an expensive man's hat rolled off the highway towards her and hit her in the leg. She grabbed it and looked around for an owner. No one appeared. It was too good a hat to just leave on the beach.

There was nothing but a little bar close by. Meryl thought perhaps the hat belonged to someone there, so she walked up to the back where several people were having coffee out of doors in the lee of the building. When she got up close, she saw it was called The Dolphin Watch Cafe.

After she had left the hat at lost-and-found and returned to the beach, she stood wondering why the dolphin had led her there. As she glanced up the street, Meryl saw what was clearly a nice apartment building. We couldn't afford to rent here, she told herself. But before she began her long walk home, she went in and got an application anyway.

Sure enough, it was expensive, and the application asked pointed questions about one's finances, bank accounts, savings. Still, she kept it. She thought about it, and a week later, took the portfolio of her work and her scrapbook of news stories, and went in person to see the manager. He looked at her work, smiled up at her and said, "I may have something for you. But the catch is that it won't be available until September the first."

Meryl and her family moved into a small apartment there on September 1. The owner decided that her quilts were perfect to adorn the lobby, and they began to sell. Soon a larger apartment became vacant, and so her family got more room.

Her husband found a job, the family thrived, and only months later she was amused to find herself the star renter and in line for the big penthouse apartment. For one day shortly after they had squeezed all seven of them into a two-bedroom apartment, a newsvan had pulled up to interview Meryl Ann. Not only was the apartment manager impressed, but the other residents were too. The news visibility attracted business and notice.

Meryl Ann attributes her good fortune to the dolphin who led her there.

There is much anecdotal evidence that dolphins talk to humans. Once again, I have to argue for the mere weight of evidence! Dolphins communicate with people, nearly all the communication is beneficial, and it's been going on for at least as long as man has kept records. Dolphins seem to be devoted to helping human beings in spiritual ways. In the presence of dolphins, it is now known, human brains begin to produce alpha waves, brainwaves associated with relaxation and openness.

Friends in High Places

Dolphins and the handicapped interact in mysterious ways. This interaction definitely enhances the progress made by people with learning disabilities.

❦

"Congratulations!" shouted the trainer at the Dolphin Research Center on Marathon Key, Florida. She grinned at the young woman she was helping back onto the dock.

"For what?" the dripping woman asked.

"The dolphins say you're pregnant!" the trainer said.

"Oh, no way!" the young woman protested. Blushing, she nodded shyly over at her husband, who had just gotten out on the other side of the dock. "We've only been married two weeks."

But a month later, the Dolphin Research Center on Grassy Key, Florida, where this happened, got a letter confirming the news. It has happened so often that the trainers who facilitate dolphin encounters now understand from certain actions of the dolphins that they can detect new life before doctors can, before women themselves have any idea they're expecting. When the fetus is still smaller than the human eye can detect.

And dolphins can apparently "diagnose" as well as cure diseases. They can also spot invisible anomalies in humans. The training staff at DRC, where I've twice spent time as a volunteer, love to tell Amazing Dolphin Stories. Like the time one of the swimmers was an elderly man; the dolphins kept coming up to investigate him. Finally one of the trainers commented, "The dolphins seem interested in your head."

The man laughed up from the water. "I've had a steel plate in it since Guadalcanal!"

A woman with liver cancer once visited, having heard that swimming with dolphins often soothes ill people; in the water the dolphins seemed to echo-locate for a long time on her body. She left feeling better, though the next scan was distressing: the one tumor had suddenly become seven.

But the woman kept feeling better and better, and another scan a month later showed the disappearance of all tumors. The working theory at the DRC is that the dolphins used some form of energy to break up her tumor into smaller ones that her body could dissolve. At the report a year later, the woman was still alive.

They tell the story at the DRC of the dolphin Bea and the autistic child who at six had never spoken. *The Reader's Digest* has recounted this story. While a patient at the Dolphin/Child Program, Deane-Paul made dramatic advances out of the isolation of autism. His first word ever was Bea's name, and many other words followed during the exciting week he spent at the DRC.

More than a year later, Bea, though apparently healthy, died; the morning staff at the DRC were shocked to discover her body. That same day, Deane-Paul's mother called the Center from their home in Oklahoma, worried. "Is Bea all right?" she asked. "Deane-Paul was agitated all night, and kept calling out Bea's name...." Everyone at the DRC believes that Bea and the child were in communication.

While at the Dolphin Research Center, I had two of my own dolphin experiences.

The first, waiting in line one day to go into the fish house to "make bucket" to feed the dolphin I was taking care of, I projected a wish to Santini, a young dolphin who was curiously eyeing me, and that I'd felt a special affection for: *If you can really tell what I'm thinking, go out and do a flip.* Immediately, and to my surprise, the dolphin did exactly that, then swam back, rolled over on her back, and grinned. Of course the thought that crossed my mind was, *What a coincidence!*

Wow! I "thought," that was great! In my mind then, I said, *Now go get some seaweed, and let's play catch.* But no. The dolphin seemed to laugh, and rolled lazily about the shallow water, for all the world as if to say,

Friends in High Places

What do you think I am, a dog? No seaweed was forthcoming.

Then it was my turn to go into the fish house. I weighed Theresa's fish, tucking her despised vitamin pills into the gills, as Theresa objected to taking them straight—well, I should say refused, as she just spit them out. Then I walked out to her dock and fed the grumpy Theresa, who knew there were vitamin pills hidden in her food and didn't like it, which made the whole process a rather complicated and lengthy operation. Then I returned to the fish house to wash out and sterilize the feed bucket.

After I'd washed up and recorded Theresa's feeding, I headed back out of the fish house the way I'd come in over an hour before. I wasn't thinking about much of anything, when out of the blue a piece of seaweed hit me on the cheek. There, laughing at my startled reaction, was Santini. (Dolphins definitely laugh.) The action seemed to me the clear answer to my request, which had also included some questioning of the real intelligence of the animals. *You thought I'd forget? You think I'm a dog?*

My second experience was that, while watching "my" assigned dolphin Theresa, who was old and not in great health, swimming circles one afternoon and coughing, I became worried about her, and as I did I got the clear message, *This water's bad. You have hands; you can do something about this. I can't.* About then, another volunteer came up and stood next to me silently. We'd been instructed to remain quiet while observing the animals. After a while Valerie, the other volunteer, wandered off.

But that night at dinner, Val asked me, "Did you get that message from Theresa about the water being polluted?" thus validating my communication.

༄

There are several places in the world (Stradbroke Island, Australia; Mauritania; and two places in Brazil, are among them) where men and dolphins cooperate even in modern times; the dolphins drive fish towards shore so both men and dolphins can feed. There is a bay in New Guinea where dolphins have cooperated with men in fishing efforts for at least 350 years. When the men want to fish, they "call" the dolphins from the shore. The dolphins come and hang around several hundred yards offshore. When a school of fish arrives, the dolphins signal the fishermen, who wade into the water with long, heavy nets. The dolphins drive the fish towards shallow water and the nets; both men and dolphins benefit. Nobody knows how long it's really gone on; three and a half centuries have passed since the first westerner observed and recorded the phenomenon.

There is no doubt whatever that dolphins communicate with, and choose to help, humans. If they can communicate mentally with us, and we with them, does that not prove that at least some part of our minds are nonlocal?

What's the connection between you, UC, and aliens?
Those who are psychically open perceive many realities not available to those who aren't.
Yes, but…are aliens real?
In what sense?
Physical reality, I mean.
Sometimes they manifest physically. There are more than a few types. They manifest differently. There's more than just time and space, you know.

In his amazing book, *Passport to the Cosmos,* author and Harvard Professor John Mack remarks, "I am not skilled in disciplines necessary to argue effectively for or against the reality of a divine presence immanent in nature. My sense is that the kinds of evidence that people find relevant are more likely subjective and experiential than objective and empirical."

Friends in High Places

And it is impossible to prove a negative proposition, such as: There are no such things as aliens.

The difficulty with UFO's is not lack of evidence but rather the impossibility of consistent explanations. As any reader knows, many trained police and military observers, and airline pilots, have reported anomalous flying objects in the years since World War II. As Ash and Hewitt suggest in *Science of the Gods*, the inexplicability of the sudden appearance and disappearance of anomalous craft suggests that they interact with space and time by moving in and out of it instead of through it.

Many, probably most, of my friends consider the subject of alien abductions so far out in left field that they dismiss the possibility with that exasperation: "Oh, for God's sakes, Katie!" that we reserve for only the most absurd, ridiculous, puerile speculations. Yet several other of my friends have seen UFO's, and others still claim to have *dreamed* of being on space ships. One friend actually claims she was abducted from age three to thirty-three, when she felt she had abruptly been "kicked out of the program." For myself, (deep sigh), I've never even seen a UFO.

My friend Jeanne Tracy Eichelburger and her first husband twice watched UFO's, once high over the California desert, zig-zagging without slowing down at the sharp turns. On the second occasion, on a May night in 1973, in Indiana, they walked out of their house with their baby and saw a low-flying double-saucer, with lights around the edges and a scalloped shape to the bottom half, coming towards them. It was absolutely silent, swooped right over their heads, and over the hill behind their house, and down too low to see.

The next day, they headed through the woods in the direction in which it had gone, and came upon the next open field, where, in the center, was a huge flattened circle of grass about thirty feet across, appearing blown outward from the center, as if the centrifugal force of a landing of something huge had flattened it out in all directions. Jeanne has all her life been a sane, centered, extremely rational librarian.

Some friends named Gwen and Dick living in the sparsely-populated mountains of southwest Virginia in rural Patrick County watched one night an overhead display of bright lights that made sharp turns without slowing, criss-crossed, and appeared to be "playing tag" in the heavens. In the next days, local newspapers reported many light sightings in the neighborhood. Again, sane, sober, rational folks, I swear it.

John Mack, a professor at Harvard, risked his job and his reputation when he decided to specialize in patients who believed they had experienced alien abductions. His book *Abduction* consists of interviews with self-proclaimed alien abductees. He died an untimely death in London, hit by a taxicab while crossing a street. He was a rationalist, a skeptic, and never himself saw a UFO, but he became convinced that something real, and extremely odd, was happening with his patients. He has written that abductees come forth reluctantly, knowing as well as their critics how crazy they sound. They are often terrified, experiencing symptoms that appear to be similar or identical to Post Traumatic Stress Disorder. After testing many, he believed they were ordinary, non-neurotic people who wish fervently that these abductions were not happening to them. They often come to accept these experiences they cannot prevent, and some go beyond acceptance to active involvement, to something akin to the Stockholm Syndrome, in which unwilling victims eventually begin to empathize with their captors.

At the time of his death, Mack believed their experiences were "neither totally subjective nor totally objective."

☙❧

In conclusion, communication isn't just for human beings to each other. You can speak to any physical problem you have. Dialogue with it. You might be surprised at what you get. Also, you can open your mind and

Friends in High Places

enter into a dialogue with one of your pets. It, too, can be eye-opening. Or you can try talking with a wild animal, say a squirrel or a bluejay. You can also do an exercise that Avatar teaches, in which you imagine merging with another person, creature, or thing. It's very enlightening. Try this: for fifteen minutes, allow yourself to feel what it's like to be a tree, a kitten, an orange, a crystal, or anything you want. Write down what happens. Just use your imagination!

Katie Letcher Lyle

12. Talking to the Dead in Church

Old friend Horace Douty, a minister I several times double-dated with when we all were young, has returned to Lexington, Virginia, where I have always lived. Delighted to have him back on the scene, I've enjoyed chatting with him several times since his return with his new wife. I count him among my local fans. He has read some of my books, and knew I had a book looking for a publisher on the subject of whether anything of us survives when we die. This book. As a Christian and a believer, he's intensely interested in such matters. We're both retired now, but he offers his services to a country church.

One day in 2009 he called me and said he wanted me to come and speak at his (country Presbyterian) church. "You don't know what you're asking," I told him. "They'll tar and feather me. And maybe you."

"No," he said, "I think you'll find there's a lot of interest."

" How big is the congregation?"

"About 200."

I envision, with luck, eight or ten wary but curious folks who *might* be interested in my subject. I've never seen the church. "Let me think," I stall.

Friends in High Places

A couple of weeks later, he called a second time to urge me to come and do this. Specifically, he wanted me to talk about communicating with the dead. So I said, "Maybe. I might. I've thought a lot about this. I need to run my plan by you."

We met in town one day for lunch. I described the plan I devised to talk to his congregation, the way I felt I could comfortably introduce strangers to the fact that I do indeed talk to dead people, sometimes, under some circumstances. He liked my plan, and repeated that he believed a lot of his congregation would too.

Lexington, Virginia, where I have lived for most of my seventy-two years, is a small college town in the Shenandoah Valley. It's got around 6000 inhabitants, 8000 when the students are here. Pretty much everyone knows everyone. The next day, at lunch with several friends, I met a new person who said she was in Horace's congregation, and that he'd told them I was coming, and she couldn't wait to hear me! This made me nervous. Trouble is, it wasn't a book yet. It was still just a manuscript I was hoping to sell. This book is way out there, this talking to dead people. It's such a conversation stopper I've quit talking about it when folks ask me what my next book is about. "But it has not even been accepted for publication yet," I protested.

On the September Sunday as I entered the lower level of the lovely little brick eighteenth-century church, I was amazed to count sixty-six people at the crowded tables in the Sunday school room where someone brought me a cup of tepid coffee. Did they have a Xerox machine? Yes, so I sent back for more handouts. I'd optimistically brought twenty-five.

Horace introduced me so I sounded like some kind of mystic, scholar, prolific author, angel, and rock star all rolled into one. I knew half a dozen of the folks there, and I rolled my eyes at them. I cracked a couple jokes about preacherly exaggeration, and emphasized that this book I have written, about talking to the dead, had not yet found a publisher.

Then I said, "First I have a question to ask each of you, and then I have two things to tell you. Then we'll try an experiment."

So I launched my presentation: "Is there anyone here who has ever felt, seen, heard, or in any way had experience with a ghost?"

Three hands went up. I nodded. "Okay, great. Out of sixty-six people in this room, three were already admitting to having a ghostly experience." A fourth hand went up, rather tentatively. "Oh, four," I amended. I did some quick math. "That's maybe six percent of you. Six out of a hundred. In polls, among the general population, a much higher percentage professes to believe in ghosts. Depending upon the poll, forty-four to eighty-eight percent."

"You didn't ask if we believed," offered a woman near the front.

I nodded. "Good point. How many of you believe in ghosts?" This time maybe fifteen hands went up.

"Now we're getting somewhere!"

I let that sit a second. Then, "The first thing I want to tell you is that Albert Einstein himself wrote once that *imagination is more important than knowledge*. That is because imagination, when you think about it, is the only vehicle that can take us to the past, to a childhood birthday party, to Mars, to San Francisco where we visited a year ago, to the future. Knowledge, Einstein went on, is limited to what we know now and understand, but imagination embraces all there will ever be. Jamie Paolinetti, the famous American bicycle racer and film-maker has written, 'Limitations exist only in our minds. But when we use imagination, our possibilities become limitless.' Robert Monroe has insisted that we are limited only by our imagining that we are limited.

"We are all taught to denigrate or ignore our imaginations," I told them. "Right?" Nods. So I added, "But Einstein may have been right."

Then after I've let that settle for a few seconds, I said, "I have just one more thing to tell you. It's a true story that happened here last summer

Friends in High Places

with one of our Hospice patients." (Horace had told them I've been on the board of our Hospice for over a dozen years, and an active patient care volunteer—the angel part of his introduction.)

"One of our patients, an old man, a farmer, was dying, and this story happened during the final week of his life. One of our nurses was checking on him daily. He announced one day that his brother was coming to see him.

"At Hospice, we are big on reconciliation before death if it's at all possible. So the nurse asked, 'Has it been long since you saw your brother?'

"'Oh, a long time,' the old fellow replied. He couldn't tell her exactly how long.

"The Hospice nurse was happy that the two brothers were going to get together. But the next day, the old fellow told her he guessed his brother wasn't coming now, as his car had broken down. The nurse said she was sorry.

"So, on the way out, the nurse spoke to his grand-daughter, who was his caretaker. 'Is there anything Hospice can do to help get the brothers together?'

"The young woman looked baffled. 'What brother? He doesn't have a brother!'

"When the nurse looked puzzled, she frowned. 'Well, he did have a brother, who was killed in a farm accident, way back in the sixties.' The grand-daughter obviously had momentarily forgotten about the uncle she'd never known.

"Next day when the nurse returned for her now-daily stops, the patient said, 'My brother's coming! He's got him a new tractor since his car broke down.' The nurse wasn't sure how to respond to that, so she murmured that was good. Pre-death visits from dead relatives are common among our patients.

"And on the day the patient finally did succumb, the nurse knew he was near the end. Suddenly, after a long silence, when he seemed to be comatose, he roused, pointed towards the corner of the room, became restless, and said, 'Look! It's a new John Deere! There's my brother! Lookathere, it's got two seats! Look at that green color!' The dying man struggled to lift his arm towards the corner of the room, saying, 'I can't reach. He wants me to come.'

"The nurse, obeying an instinct, lifted the weak arm of the dying man towards the totally empty corner of the bedroom, and he took his last breath and died."

There was silence in the Sunday School room as they took this in. Hospice is one of the most respected organizations in Rockbridge County.

"Any questions?" There were none.

"And now," I went on, "I have an exercise I'd like you to do. While I pass out these handouts and pencils, be thinking of someone who's dead that you'd like to talk with, or wish you could've known. It could be Napoleon, or your grandmother who died when you were three, or Jesus, or a relative you never knew but wished you had. Be thinking, and choose anyone you wish. Don't start till I tell you. You have some questions to think about on the handout. You'll have five minutes once we start."[9]

When the papers were all distributed and everyone had a pencil, I invited them to close their eyes so they could see better on their inner screens, to take three breaths, center their attention, and invite their person to come chat.

What happened made me shiver. Within a minute, I could hear sniffles, see the tissues begin to come out, and most of the people in the room wrote feverishly until I stopped them. Only one or two sat silently and did not write. Later, the participants wanted to share their conversations. One woman "saw" her dead husband, who assured her he was fine. Another saw her sister, dead many years, who told her she was waiting for her. One man was overcome by the strong emotion of having been in

---

[9] The questions were: Where are you? What details do you notice? Record your conversation.

Friends in High Places

touch with his beloved daughter, who had died young. All felt the validity of the visits. They invited me back the next week. They asked questions, commented to each other, affirmed each other's experiences. We had to break then; it was time for church.

I'm sure the experiment wasn't successful for every one of them, but it certainly seemed to be for a vast majority. I've now spoken at a second church, and at a library, to much the same responses. I've heard later by email or phone from five or six people. For me, this is an exciting and heartening validation that I'm not alone in this. And so far, I haven't been tarred and feathered. Neither, as far as I know, has Horace.

Katie Letcher Lyle

13. Just Remember: A Message from the Dead

> ...To die, to sleep:
> To sleep: perchance to dream: ay, there's the rub:
> For in that sleep of death what dreams may come,
> When we have shuffled off this mortal coil,
> Must give us pause.
>
> **~Hamlet, (contemplating suicide)
> Act III, Sc.1**

Forty years to the day after our first date, I told my husband I wanted a divorce. I'm a record-keeper. He was an alcoholic, had been for seventeen years. I'd tried an intervention with his two friends Otis and Larry, which failed miserably, as he later told me it was "a little meeting to get Otis to stop drinking so much."

By then, I'd spent two decades trying to prove to myself that I am more than my physical body, by studying at the Monroe Institute, retrieving earthbound spirits, recording automatic writing, visiting psychics in

Friends in High Places

London, participating in spiritual healings, becoming friends with over fifty dying patients through Hospice, getting to know my Upstairs Crew, taking Remote Viewing three times. Could I sustain my still-developing faith? The moment I told him to leave, crying, frustrated, I was in the back yard on my knees with a hose and soap, scrubbing stinky rugs. I'd been scrubbing brown streaks off the bedroom *walls* all morning.

I had believed my husband a decent and loyal man until alcoholism overtook him, and as it increased over seventeen years there were moments when I suspected that he loved this other woman-friend of his more than he loved me. He yelled at me a lot, lied about everything, said terrible things about our good and upright son (whose worst sin was some tattoos), tracked shitty footprints to the bathroom and back, and absolutely refused to see a doctor. He hated all my friends and was rude to them. His driving drunk caused me sleepless nights. The police would not set a trap; his doctor would not return my calls.

On June 4, 2002, a Saturday, I was scheduled to meet with a Richmond book club at a downtown restaurant, and for the first time in my life, I nearly forgot to go to an agreed-on presentation. (The fourteen women thankfully didn't seem to realize what a basket case I was when I arrived dirty and fifteen minutes late.)

That morning, I had had no idea where R. was; there was more shit on the rugs; when he staggered into the yard drunk at around eleven, hardly glancing down at what I was doing, I exploded. And sent him off to our "Country Estate" twelve miles away, where his office was, the farmhouse we nicknamed the "CE." I told him not to come home until he saw a doctor. He called an hour later, saying meanly, "I guess this means divorce. There are eight among your siblings already. Guess that's how your family deals with things. There's never been a divorce in my family." I was amazed how he could have thought that up so fast, drunk as he was. No wonder I nearly forgot the book club.

Katie Letcher Lyle

Five days later, he jumped (or fell: his stories changed hourly) off a bridge, barely survived, was helicoptered to a hospital. His friend Otis and I raced down the Interstate to Roanoke, where I saw bone sticking out of his leg, a sickening bloody upjutting. A fortnight, a horrendous detox, and two surgeries later, he ended up in a wheel chair in a nursing home nearby. The eerie x-ray of his lower leg showed that every bony thing had been replaced by a skeleton of metal rods and nails.

Two weeks later, I suddenly realized unpaid bills were piling up, while he, who had always controlled our finances, was now crippled and unable. His hospitalization and surgeries cost a quarter of a million dollars, as he had quit paying bills, and we were without insurance. To his credit, he had been a wise investor. I paid the bills in cash from our joint account, which, at the beginning of the end, was comfortably large.

I didn't want him back as he was: addicted, angry, and abusive. Yet how could I abandon my ill, now disabled, husband of forty years?

The answer lay in a curious occurrence, without which I'd have undoubtedly taken him back, and continued trying to control his drinking.

At the CE, the kitchen table was mounded with unopened bills and mail, envelopes with neon labels screaming *Last Notice! Final Warning!* dating back a year. The house reeked of vodka. There were orders for porn films and numerous beginnings of manuscripts about his mother, most trailing off after only one or two pages. The weird message was: *she was perfect and I loved only her, and so did my father and so did her father.*

I set to work to pay bills, spent phone hours getting us re-insured. Days into the process, I followed my nose into his office at the front of the house, where sat the glass of straight vodka I'd been smelling. The shades were lowered. In the dimness, his answering machine blinked. I returned to the kitchen for a pencil, to write down messages to take to the nursing home, where I went every day with sox, new pajamas, and Hershey Bars. I'd read that chocolate candy eases the discomfort of detox. I jotted down names and numbers for him to call, some dating back three weeks.

Suddenly I was hearing a conversation between him and his close woman-friend. He'd picked up the phone *after* the answering machine cut on, and accidently recorded a four-minute discussion between him and *her*, on the day I'd gone to ask her (and she'd refused) to participate in the Intervention. She was afraid I'd found out *Something*. Their chat referred to their twenty-year affair, and included a bit of sexy talk. I couldn't believe my ears in that dark room, as he trashed me and lied, as she oozed sympathy and agreement with him. It confirmed something I'd feared, intuited, recorded in my dream journal—seven dreams in twenty-five years. Friends had even hinted, but I had never let myself believe, that he and the other woman had been having an affair for half our marriage. I'd always tried to like her but never felt quite comfortable. She was not a "girlfriend" type.

Deeply shocked at first, I took a police officer friend out to his house with me to look for evidence, or something. I didn't know what other snakes lay in wait to bite me. I took the tape out of the phone, and made copies of that conversation. The nearest neighbor said to me later, "Oh, the woman in the green truck? She was out here all the time."

I confronted them both, her at home, then him in the nursing home a half hour later. Both repeated the same sentence: "The tape is misleading."

"How so?" I asked. "Misleading in what way?" Neither would say.

Angry and drunk, he later railed, "I could have committed adultery any time I wanted. I had plenty of chances, especially with your so-called friends!" Misdirection, that trick of magicians.

I soon realized, however, that hearing the truth about the affair in their own words was a gift, and the only way I could have accepted the reality of their affair. I was on the verge of inviting him back home as soon as he could leave the nursing home. But hearing this conversation gave me the steel I needed to free myself. The infidelity did not strike me as so bad; I myself had three times not been faithful, but I had never spoken disloyally of him, nor lied about him. We had not had a very satisfactory sex life. But his betrayal, and lying! And her collusion, her pretense at being my friend! I got a legal separation that day, then took half the money that we had left in our joint account, which was by then pretty skimpy, and put it into an account with only my name on it. My hearing that phone conversation was the first "coincidence." If I'd not heard it, I might still be struggling with him and his addiction.

Another striking coincidence occurred a month later. Almost at once, I began dating a once-famous jazz musician who *came the day after our separation* to interview me for a magazine article—a sympathetic stranger to whom I could vomit out the whole story! But in a matter of only a few weeks, things were not going well. It would have been okay that he was impotent—I'd have been glad for a male friend—but it was not okay that he blamed my neediness for his disappointing condition, while promising great things "tomorrow," which never came.

On the phone I explained to the man that "I wanted a relationship in which I could freely give and freely get affection." He coldly reiterated that I was too "needy." I stood outside in my hedged-in backyard, phone in hand, fighting tears of disappointment and the awful knowledge that I was alone again.

At that moment, I heard an excited voice out in the driveway call my name. I stepped out to meet a darling man I'd known forty years before. A decade younger, he had been a student with whom I acted in four plays when he was an undergraduate and I was a young college professor. He'd kept up with me, observed from a visit the previous Christmas that R. was drunk the entire three days he was here, even early in the morning.

The previous night he'd been on business in Greensboro where he saw a sign saying 88 miles to Roanoke. He knew I was an hour beyond. He also knew I was already dating someone else. (This is a small town!) Yet

Friends in High Places

he drove here the next day, arriving *at the very instant* I was making my farewell speech to another man. "Not dating anyone anymore," I told him. He told me that day that he'd always waited for me.

For nearly a year we enjoyed a juicy affair which made me feel beautiful and cherished. We consummated our early crush, as entwined as a cornstalk and bean vine. He'd appeared like a Prince Charming *exactly at the moment* I was expressing a need for a relationship just like the one we had.

Here were two *apparently chance* events that precisely met my needs of the moment: the accidentally overheard phone call, the arrival of my old crush. Events like those in our lives often go unnoticed because we don't believe they're anything but coincidence.

I'd never lived alone, had moved from my parents' house to living with R. In our last seventeen years together, he'd quit his job and become depressed. Or, he became depressed, then began to drink too much—who knows which came first? I'd tried to stop his drinking, which is what wives of alcoholics do: tried to reason, even that old chestnut, hidden his booze. I didn't know about Al-Anon then. A friend told me he'd been fired, had not quit of his own accord. He lied about everything conceivable, told me I was unbalanced and crazy, and I kept falling for it, kept believing him. This is all my fault, I thought, for years and years. I didn't understand how, but accepted that it must be my fault.

I continued to say publically (and actually believe) that he "drank a bit too much, but that everything was fine." Denial, as I learned in Al-Anon, is a strongly self-protective trait. One late night I became terrified as I perceived that some monstrous spirit had slipped into and inhabited the body of my husband. His face became red-eyed, twisted, and downright evil. It was so chillingly awful that I had to leave the house. The hair on my neck literally tensed and stood erect.

But that June day when I told him to leave, I was shocked to hear myself say, "I'm through dealing with your shit. You go live at the CE and deal with your own shit!" I meant it on so many levels. I was sure I'd never have dinner with a man again, much less ever find someone else to love. You couldn't start over at sixty-four!

In the weeks following, I filed for divorce, found a wonderful counselor, and began what would be many grateful years as a member of Al-Anon, missing only four weekly meetings in the next five years –all for programs at the Monroe. Somehow I learned to be comfortable in my skin, in my house, in my dependence on myself. I took strict care of my health, fearing that under the distress that kept my mouth dry and my stomach upset for months, I might develop shingles or cancer or trip myself up with an accident. I worked on a collection of poems about my divorce and the year following it. Many were published. For the first time in my life I made a budget, met with financial planners and a lawyer, bought a life insurance policy to care for our handicapped daughter. We divorced with the help of a mediator which my Upstairs Crew nudged me to: R.'s friend Larry.

Within a year I had to break up with that wonderfully generous, funny, sexy—but, tragically, bipolar—man. Eventually I found a new life with a wonderful partner, but that's another story.

On my 69th birthday, in May of 2007, my husband, by then my ex-husband for four years, blew his brains out. To clean his office where he did it cost ten thousand dollars; you dial 1-800-TRAGEDY.

In Al-Anon, I learned that when gratitude becomes the atmosphere you live in, resentment and anger are nearly impossible. After a while, I overcame my anger at my husband's girlfriend and my strong urge to somehow retaliate—surprisingly by praying for both of them, which I did only reluctantly at first, when my fellow Al-Anon members suggested that prayer was a good method of forgiveness. Al-Anon helped my frustration at his refusal to even try to get well, and my rage that flared

Friends in High Places

at his frequent drunken rants at me over the phone. "My father told me forty years ago you were no good, and that I shouldn't have married you!" "You took presents that my parents' friends gave us back to stores when we got married!" "I'm going to make (her, the Other Woman) my executor because she knows more about my books than anyone else." "You let Cochran get tattoos! Everyone in the penitentiary has tattoos! Tattoos are the first step to life in prison!" And his favorite, "You've ruined (her) life!" as though he and she had had no hand in that.

I went to programs at the Monroe Institute as often as I could afford to in the next few years, and am forever grateful to that amazing place. I eventually forgave my husband and his mistress, realizing that they had unwittingly done me a huge favor. I finally understood that alcoholism is a disease, and really and truly beyond his control, at which point I stopped attending meetings. But for five years I did daily readings, attended weekly meetings, examined my own thoughts and motives, supported my fellow travelers, and came to understand that fault really cannot be assigned. Our failure wasn't my fault, nor was it his. If he could have quit drinking, he would have. If I *could* have stuck it out, I would have. In the remaining five years of his life, he was frequently in the emergency room, and once spent a night in jail, picked up near her house for public drunkenness, truculent behavior, and refusing to leave. He was an intensely private man, and I know these events would have withered the soul of the person I married. I was sorry for our son, who once said to me, "When you dumped Dad, you dumped him on me."

I replied, "You didn't have to go to his rescue. You could have called 911 when he called you instead of taking him to the hospital."

"I couldn't," he said. "He's my father."

Peter Russell once said in a workshop at The Monroe something like, "Every human wants warmth, sustenance, safety, acceptance, love. All of

us—even mass murderers and child-molesters—want those things." In alcoholics, that search can become twisted and unhealthy. My ex-husband was terrified of his weaknesses becoming known. In realizing this, I found the beginning of compassion.

My husband was once a good man, gentle and scholarly, lofty of character, and a good provider. He wouldn't have taken a nickel that wasn't his. He was a kindly if remote father (the norm for my lifetime, and for the South). Alcoholism is a disease so horrible it defeats the strongest among us—with wives nearly always the primary casualties. Looking back, I understand that we had a Victorian marriage, mutually respectful and productive of two wonderful children and twenty-three books between us. We welcomed friends and strangers, had a genial union, and cherished each other's accomplishments for many years. I married him because he was, I now think in my therapy-enlightened years, the *approving father* I'd always longed for. As for his expectations, I was supposed to be a good Southern wife (he once expressed disappointment that I wasn't interested in teaching Sunday school as his mother had.) But it doesn't feel right to sleep with your father. We married as virgins, which I would counsel anyone is a bad idea. Sex didn't work out well for us. Certainly that was the reason he took a mistress. As he absolutely rejected religion, I understand how my dawning spirituality was as threatening to him as though I had become a born-again Christian, a Muslim, or a witch. I no longer blame him more than myself. It was a marriage well-intentioned, and for two decades anyway we were good mates.

In the months following his suicide, I worried a lot about his soul. Believing as I do, I feared that R. would be, like many of the ghosts I met in my ten years of spirit retrievals with David McKnight's group, confused and stuck. I feared this because I knew R. had no belief in an

Friends in High Places

Afterlife, and therefore no map to make his way through whatever process takes us from this world to the next.

I couldn't seem to contact him. I tried a few times, assuming he did not want to "talk" to me. When I finally did see him (while listening to a Monroe tape), I felt I was forcing him to talk. I saw him looking about the same as when he died, but his crippled leg no longer looked swollen and grotesque. He had his back to me, and when I spoke, glanced over his shoulder and said, "Uh, hi."

He was (we were) in a colorless depression that felt to me hellish, a place like a smoggy, smoky gulch a disagreeable hue of olive-beige. We seemed to be standing on a small earthen rise below which tires were burning in a greasy pit, sending off a putrid black smoke that obscured the distance. There was no greenery or living thing as far as I could see. Just looking at him, I "got" that he didn't intend to hurt anyone, that alcohol was the only medicine he knew, that he was anguished, and that his suicide was a rational decision to be done with life. He impressed me as "stuck."

Me: Hi, how are you?

R: (nervous? embarrassed? both?) I don't know exactly how I got here.

K: Are you glad to be here?

R: I guess so. I don't… know what's happening.

K: You remember killing yourself?

R: But I'm not dead.

K: Oh, yes. You are dead.

R: I sort of remember; I was… um… finished.

K: I know.

R: (dully) What are you doing here?

K: Just visiting. I'm at the Monroe Institute.

R: The Monroe. Oh, I remember.

K: So… what are *you* doing?

Katie Letcher Lyle

R: I'm not sure.

K: Is it a good or a bad place?

R: Neither. Just boring.

K: Have you seen anyone you know?

R: Seems like I saw Miss Betts. (His step-grandmother, dead since 1966, and one of his favorite people in his life.)

K: So that proves you're dead. She's dead, you know.

R: Oh, she's not dead. But I couldn't get close enough to talk. She was way over there.

K: You sleep a lot here?

R: I'm not sure. (He kept his back to me, which I read as symbolic of his not wanting to "face" me.)

K: Can you see a light anywhere?

R: No.

K: Well, R, look around you. I'm not dead. I'm visiting.

R: I'll be okay.

K: Of course you will. You accomplished a lot in life. Where do you think you are now?

R: It's a funny thing. I can't seem to wake up.

K: You're in a space where hearts can talk to each other.

R: Yeah... (without enthusiasm.)

K: You can know more. You can keep going. You seem kind of stuck. Kind of out of it.

R: Well, I don't... know about that.

K: You can move on.

R: To where?

K: I don't know exactly, but into the Light. Look for a light, follow it. If you can accept you're dead—to earth life, I mean...

R: How's Jennie?

K: She fine. But you should contact Cochran in his dreams and tell

Friends in High Places

him how to proceed.

R: Aw, I can't do that.

K: Yes, you can. I'm here, and we're talking. You can get in touch with Cochran. You can contact anyone you want. Yeah, her too. Come with me to the Garden, the Park...

R: No.

K: Can I come back sometime and see how you're doing?

R: Sure, just call before you come.

K: What, you have a phone here?

R: Oh, I guess I don't.

K: Do you remember how you got here?

R: I don't want to think about that right now.

K: You can talk to Otis and Larry.

R: I'm tired. I don't want to talk to anybody.

We were in the murky smog of 23, the Monroe-named area of the unsettled, troubled, new-dead, I'm pretty sure. Most of the spirits I've met while ghost-busting went rather quickly and easily into the Light, but others had a harder time getting there. It didn't seem a terrible place, just tedious, dead, with those hills of sand or dirt, nobody else I could see, the burning garbage. He didn't seem especially unhappy, and not afraid, mostly just irritated at my being there.

Now he resolutely faced away from me, and his body language said that the conversation was over. There seemed to be no movement, not in him, not in this landscape.

About "calling first": he'd had a rule, which I observed, that if I came out to the CE, I was to call first. Until hearing the tape between them, I'd assumed he just didn't like being dropped in on. (And I understood that: I prefer to *choose* when to put down my projects and do something else, to plan to see friends rather than be jarred by an interruption.)

Katie Letcher Lyle

The second time I contacted him, I wasn't trying. I was on an airplane, flying to visit my sister in Albuquerque, several months after his suicide. The plane's engine noise lulled me into an altered state, and suddenly there he was: behind a green chain-link fence, in front of an advancing flaming wall at his back. The vividly colored and fast-moving scene was almost a comic book stereotype of Hell. I could see that R. was terrified because he couldn't escape the fire behind him, which seemed to loom and gust closer and closer to him. He was stuck between the fire and the chain-link fence. He gave me a desperate look, but said nothing. As I approached, closer, I realized that the crossed-wire fence up close was nothing more than his hands in front of his face, creating what looked like an impenetrable fence.

"There are no bars," I said. "You put them there. You can take them away. You can come out." Then I said, "Look for Miss Betts. Look for the light. She's there. Follow the Light. I really don't want you to suffer." He glared at me, but terror was in his eyes.

I said, "Look, you made that fence yourself. You can take your hands away. It's an illusion. It's not a real fence." He stood there in his prison that *he had made*, his hands still in front of his face. It made sense metaphorically; he was *always* in a prison of his own making, and frightened by a lot of things that weren't real, like his fear of anyone learning that he wasn't perfect. Something woke me then.

That episode distressed me so that later that night, in my sister's guestroom bed, I sought to communicate with my old friend David McKnight, dead for a few years by then. He had, of course, known my husband. I encountered him on a wintry road, walking. "Why is it winter?" I asked. "I thought this was Summerland."

"Oh, it's not winter," David replied cheerfully. "It's a crisp fall day, just the way I like it." (We create our own reality!)

Friends in High Places

"What are you doing these days?" I asked.

"Me? Serving. I'm just serving."

"Can you help R.?"

"I can't do that," he said immediately. "I never resonated with him." (It was true; my husband thought David was crazy, a person of no consequence—an opinion he held, at least in later years, about most of my friends. In Al-Anon I learned how common it is for alcoholics to dismiss earlier friends.)

"He wouldn't listen to me," David went on. "This place is no different from earth life. He can only be helped by someone who resonated with him in life. You and I were on the same frequency, we resonated; but he and I never did. It would be jarring for both of us, and he wouldn't listen to anything I said."

There was more. David went on: "We all need our similar resonances. You two never really resonated with each other. He and (she) resonated. He resonated with Otis, Larry and others. You, on the other hand, resonate with hundreds of people. Others will eventually take care of him. You don't have to be concerned. You spread sunshine and fun around like manure. That wasn't his thing."

Which leads me to the uncomfortable conclusion that my husband and I, though peaceably married until he was overcome by another woman and alcoholism, never really resonated at the same frequency. We weren't often drawn to the same people. He was a mystery to me, and I gave him all the private space he asked for and created a life for myself. Nick, my current mate, and I are in total resonance; we think each other's thoughts, and often express thoughts at the same moment. We wake, sleep, exercise, eat at similar rates. We travel harmoniously through life together. Though we differ in many ways, and can make each other very mad, we are most definitely on the same frequency.

We sometimes speak of being "in tune" with the people we love.

Emotion has been called "energy+motion." With some people we have it; with others we obviously don't. In the liminal first stage of love, humans can often feel the vibrational change, colors are brighter, arthritis may disappear, a woman of sixty-four may experience again the hot flashes she left behind fifteen years before, a man may experience again the orgasms of a younger man. Love, that undeniable energy, has coordinated the vibrations of two people.

I asked my Upstairs Crew about vibration, and here is what I transcribed from them: *there is a unifying principle: energy. South Americans like Luis (a Colombian friend) know it better than North Americans. Things vibrate in ways not yet understood by physicists. In altered states, we vibrate at different rates.*

(Often in UFO encounters, one person sees the UFO, and the other doesn't. This was true of our ghost-busting circle; some actually saw the spirits; I never did.) *If a part of your vibration happens to match the vibration of, say, a UFO, or an earthbound spirit, you perceive the visit. Events leave their vibrational patterns on landscapes, in houses, on people, on the very DNA. Thus we are forever vibrating, changed by a vast multitudes of events, such as divorce, death of a loved one, sudden fame, falling in love, becoming a parent.*

A third contact with my ex-husband was in a dream. I dreamed I called his phone number from my bedroom. He answered, and I thought, *Oh, that's how we can talk!* "Are you okay?" I asked. "No!" he shouted, "I'm not!" His anger was clearly still about the other woman.

In Al-Anon, we practice tolerating what we cannot change, changing what we can, and being wise enough to perceive the difference. His not even trying to explain about the phone message is a thing I couldn't change, and I felt it as a painfully sharp detail about where his loyalties lay.

Friends in High Places

A fourth attempt to contact R., after our son's 2008 wedding, brought a surprise. R. was standing quite a distance away, in a cold light the color and feel of a wan sunset after a stormy day. Though he was this time facing me, he was still keeping his distance. He seemed thin, tired, and very young: "How are you?" I asked.

"Okay. You?"

"Did you see Cochran get married?" I asked.

"I looked in on it," he said.

"Did you see Jennie reading her poem?"

"She's her mother's daughter."

"Can we talk?"

"I really don't want to."

"Why not?"

"We never—as you say—*resonated.*" (Sarcasm was his favorite weapon.)

"But I understand now. It's okay. We loved each other once. We both did the best we could," I said.

"You've ruined (her) life."

"That was her doing—and yours. I just exposed it."

When he didn't reply, I said, "What do you expect me to do?"

"Give her back her painting," he said. I was surprised, but at once knew which one he was talking about.

"The water lilies?" I had liked the painting, and I like to support local artists and friends. It had cost a thousand dollars. But in my house, even in a little-used room, it was a constant reminder I didn't need. I'd already thought about donating it to a local charity.

"Give it back."

"But if I give it to Habitat or Hospice, people without means will benefit."

"They'd sell it for nothing. Give it back."

He looks thinner, but his leg seems healed. He's in a white shirt, khakis, his hands folded in front of his groin, sneakers, very young, maybe younger than when I met him. I didn't quite understand the implication of that, but later it occurred to me that maybe he needed to somehow return to a purer, younger state to be rid of the layers of protection, deceit, and fear he'd piled on throughout life. That may be part of his process.

I didn't think it a fair request. I came to a compromise. I didn't feel I owed him—or her—any favors. But I respect messages from the dead. So I called her, on my cell phone, figuring she wouldn't answer if my name appeared. I told her I was thinking of donating the painting to a charity, but had decided to ask her first if she'd care to buy it back. She said no, it was mine, and to do anything I wanted with it, thanked me for the offer and quickly hung up.

Time passed. I consigned my unhappy dead ex-husband to the care of others: like his mother, our dogs, General George C. Marshall, whom he'd hugely admired, his step-grandmother (with whom he requested his ashes buried)—in the excruciating, shaky-handed, skritchy suicide note he'd left our son in May.

In November of 2008, I had another "visit." We seemed to be on the porch of the CE where there are rocking chairs. He was in one, and I in another.

K: I see you're better now. You seem relaxed.

R: I'm okay.

K: Not happy?

R: Well, funny, but I'm a dog most of the time. Dogs aren't happy or unhappy. They just *are*.

K: Are you well-treated?

R: Can't say. Dogs don't know that.

K: Do you remember your life?

Friends in High Places

R: Oh, sure. There are things to contemplate, it's… like a book I once read.

K: Was it a good life?

R: Not particularly. I was lonely my whole life.

K: You can ask for friends to come be with you, I think.

R: Don't be telling me what I can do.

K: How do you read the world now?

R: A sad place. You were always so happy. (sarcastic, resentful)

K: I'd hoped to find you better.

R: I might be.

K: Do you still want to drink?

R: Sometimes… none of your business.

K: But we were married forty years.

R: Not like my mother and father.

K: No, but I know that your mother always thought that she might have done better.

R: My father thought I might have too.

K: Do you wish for (Her)?

R: Emotion fades here.

We are relaxed during this conversation, but our chairs are turned away from each other.

And then Christmas of 2008 came. A year and a half had gone by since his death. There's a folder in which, for years, I've kept leftover, or extra, Christmas cards to send at the last minute to people who send me a card, or whom I've forgotten. That's most people. I'm what you'd call a *defensive* Christmas card-writer.

On Christmas Eve I got out the folder to find a card for someone I'd gotten a card from. My eye hit on one we had made years before from a photo R. had taken of a fiery sunset over our back yard of winter-bare trees, and I chose it out of the folder.

Katie Letcher Lyle

I opened the card to write a message—and there, unmistakably, in my ex-husband's handwriting, were the words…

Just remember that I still

No punctuation, just those words, written large in a stronger version of his handwriting than I recall ever having seen. I turned to my handicapped daughter, who was home for Christmas. "Jennie, whose handwriting is this?"

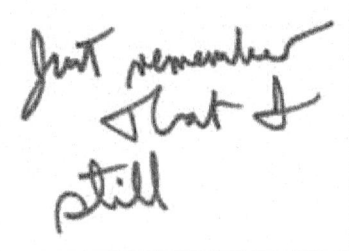

"Dad's," she replied, grinning.

The vigor of the handwriting was the first thing I noticed. It was clear, firm, steady, alive—dare I say happy?—and it almost vibrated off the page, in stark contrast to the trembly chicken-scratch of the suicide note.

But he didn't write it years ago. There was nothing in that folder but blank cards. I swear it.

And the words! An exhortation to remember him, as though I could ever forget—remember that he is *still*, but also that he *still*—I took it, and take it, to be a confirmation of his persistence, his survival—I Still—enjoining me to Remember—a Christmas present, a message that he has somehow gone beyond the suffering, the self-hatred and despair, in short, a sign that he had triumphed over the horror of suicide, gone beyond to a peaceful place where he can gather his wits, and that he persists, as I believe we all do, and that I am just to remember that, not all the sad things.

It isn't a love letter—and I didn't expect one—love fled a long time ago. I love someone else now—and I'd like to think he's able to be honest, finally, as I hope I am, but I think it's a thank you for my obvious concern, and a reassurance that he *still is. Somewhere. Nearby.* Near enough, in fact, to give me (and Jennie) a present to find on Christmas Eve.

A year or so later, I asked Barney Brown, a recent friend, to read this

Friends in High Places

chapter I had written, and comment. Barney had been an AIDS counselor in California. We'd talked a few times, though I didn't know him well. Why I asked him to look at this manuscript I can't say, perhaps casual conversation at a dinner party. I think the operant word here is *synchronicity*.

It turned out that Barney is a loyal AA member, sober for years, which I didn't know. After he'd read the manuscript, he came down with flu, and our intended conference was postponed for a week. When we finally got together, he said he liked this, but found parts of it "toxic." He opined gently that I shouldn't write about my divorce yet, because I hadn't gone beyond history to wisdom—which he defined as a "state of having no emotional charge on a thing."

I realized that writing this had stirred it all up again. I knew he was right.

It has since been rewritten.

Barney then casually remarked that he'd met R. once—when Otis and Larry brought him to an AA meeting. I was surprised, as R. constantly disparaged AA, calling it a "cult." I didn't know he'd ever been to a meeting. "I never saw anyone less interested in rehab," Barney commented.

Then Barney told me that, after reading the manuscript, in the throes of fever, tossing wakefully one night, he'd contacted R., and perceived that he was still struggling, pieces of his "toxicity and anger and remorse and humiliation spattered across the landscape."

Barney went on. "I tried to gather up the pieces and send him to rest. I suggested to him that he try his next life as a dog."

"Why?" I asked, the hair rising on my arms.

"Because he liked dogs, and he was so damaged I thought he'd need another lifetime to be rid of the poison of his last life. A loyal dog. Clean, brave, reverent."

"Wait!" I said. "R. said those words all the time! Clean, brave, reverent! They were like a mantra. You really were in touch with him!"

Katie Letcher Lyle

Final Comment

What do our little human dramas mean? Are they even real? Those are the questions that led to this book. I went from vague "intimations of immortality" to being challenged to see "reality" differently. I was obstructed often on the pathway by many near and dear to me, most notably my husband. At the time I was living that miserable dream of life with a depressed alcoholic, I didn't think I was dreaming. Until I did it, I didn't know I could wake up to a different reality.

But here I am, beyond the storm, resting on a lovely shore. From ghosts, I learned that beyond this life, the norm is, or appears to be, something like a dream. Is that the same with life? Wherever we are seems real at the time—dreams or real life. But are they? Can we wake up now and change? Is death a waking up from the dream of life? Near-death experiencers come back to report time and time again that beyond this life, in the presence of the Light, the only questions asked of us are, *Did you love? Did you serve? Were you generous and kind?*

The message brought back again and again is that nobody else judges us—just we ourselves, who are obviously our harshest judges. Our lives are given back to us as in a mirror, so that we can see clearly what we did right and wrong. Presumably, we learn so as to do better the next go-round. Another thing we learn over and over is that we chose whatever life we are leading.

Does that seem surprising? We have that choice right now, it seems to me, to love or not, to serve or not, to change or not. We are not pawns of fate. We make what we make of our lives. Guidance is there for us, if only we will listen for it, and have the grace to trust it.

For myself, I know that some essential part of us continues after earthly death. It's my hope that readers can reach the same happy conclusion. I've said all along, you do this with your imagination. Honor that in yourself. Talk to your dear dead. I am sure that they in turn will talk to you.

Katie Letcher Lyle

End Note

If you are interested in how I personally experience some of the focus levels, then you are welcome to read the next paragraphs. (But remember what I said about Mexico! Your definitions and experiences will not be the same as mine.) You might be better off to skip to the next few paragraphs, or, best of all, to go to TMI and experience the focal levels for yourself. If you can't do that, you can listen to some of their tapes.

F10 is described by Monroe as "body asleep, mind awake": it feels to me as though I am half-in, half-out of water at a warm, safe, shallow beach, getting ready to take off for deeper water. Halfway out, between straight ahead and directly to the right, lies F12, (the state of "expanded awareness") with an air of expectancy, a floaty medium like saltwater or "heavy air" you can breathe in or air you can swim in. There I have created an imaginary "office" for working, receiving messages and information.

F15 (described as the "edge of here and now") is beyond that, dark but friendly, a cliff or breaking-off place, the edge of mystery, of possibility, with a sense of expansiveness; it's where (in my view) artists, friends, and lovers dwell when hours go by without their notice.

F21 is left and forward, sunny and bright, a fairyland of locales where I can find the answer to anything I am looking for if I can accept flexibility and newness. It's where all that the human imagination is capable of is possible. I think maybe the Akashic Record is there. It is the beginning of the planes of the Afterlife.

For instance, F23 I sense as a band surrounding earth, full of the unresolved souls of humans who have died. I perceive a dirty smog of zonked-out people, with the unpleasant oniony smell of nervous and unwashed bodies. I think it's where people who have died but don't realize it often go, and it has an unpleasant reek of earthly filth.

F24 and 25 (which Monroe defined as "belief-systems areas") feels to me like a vast movie set in a flat desert where you can move from one set to the next: Presbyterians "cold as dogs' noses," in the words of one author, a sacred grove, a shrine where a red-lipped virgin weeps from blue eyes, Baptists loose-lipped and drunk on Jesus, a formal, quiet Shinto temple, a Buddhist monastery, a cut-rock cave, the entrance a skull shape, mouth gaping open. Over all of area 24-25, I find a pall of falseness, as a movie set is merely a fool-the-eye imitation of reality, as I feel all religions are false.

Focus 27 (which Bob Monroe calls the Park) seems to be where souls can reside—forever or for awhile. To me it is an endless, glorious, lush summer landscape as far as the eye can see, which I approach by zooming in. It's known in esoteric literature as "Summerland," and is comparable to Heaven, Valhalla, the happy hunting grounds, etc. Up in the nearby hills away from the Park is the dwelling place I have "built" for myself; a beach house on a rocky prominence, with a natural pool between the house and ocean which refills and cleans itself with every high tide, a natural gathering place of friends I can no longer visit with in the flesh.

All of these are non-physical locales, so presumably they could all exist in the same non-space.

I've been beyond there, too. At F35, which has no description, I found utter stillness, the sense of another medium neither air nor water, a mist hard to see through, a sense of expectation such as you might feel while waiting for muddy water to clear so that you might see what's in the bottom. I have a sense of an aura of being watched with curiosity. And finally, I have perceived other levels, such as one where the souls of beloved pets who've died are hanging out, waiting. Perhaps when owners die, those pets can go with their owners.

Once again, I remind you that others naturally perceive the levels differently, according to their own imaginations.

Friends in High Places

Grateful Thanks

This book is dedicated to the memory of my dear friend, mentor, and supporter, David McKnight, 1938 -2005.

I am grateful for the support of my amazing writers' group, now over twenty years old: The Good Old Girls. They are Janet Lembke, Patty Pullen, Amanda Cockrell, Judy Ayyildiz, Lisa Tracy, Charlotte Morgan, Jeri Watts, Molly Odell, and Nancy Johnston. All have weighed in with suggestions for this book. Past members of the Good Old Girls include Anne McCaig, Mary McKnight, Toni Williams, Nancy Venable Raine, Mary Bishop, Anne Goethe, and Miriam Rogin, now deceased. Twice a year, we meet, read aloud to each other, and discuss our writing. At the beginning, I was the only one who'd had a book published. Now many of these women have.

Louis Rubin will always be the reason I've persisted as a writer. If I hadn't met him at Hollins College, where he came to teach in 1957, I might never have become one. To him I am entirely and forever grateful.

High-spirited thanks to my ghost-busting group for ten years of serious fun, fellowship and insight: David and Mary McKnight, Bill Walls (now deceased), Tim Ogden, and Rush and Susan Earman.

Eternal gratitude to The Monroe Institute for its constant support, and especially to Darlene Miller and Skip Atwater for their warm responses of friendship in my worst times of need.

Warmest gratitude to my agents Carole J. Greene and Jacqueline Simenauer for their equal parts of wisdom, support, and persistence in my behalf, and to my patient and talented editor, Jeff Schlesinger.

Warmest thanks to Barney Brown for his incisive and wise comments on this book.

And special love and thanks to my "other," George Roland ("Nick") Charles, for his support in the eight years we have resonated together!

Friends in High Places

Bibliography

This is a special kind of bibliography, one that supports this book. The books listed here are carefully chosen out of a mountain of books (about 1000) that I own on various subjects touched on, with a brief description of their contents. These books are on subjects most often regarded as "flaky"—but they are books by unflaky people. They are all well-written. These particular criteria required that I leave out some other fascinating books which may also be in their own ways true and even outstanding.

Allen, Mary. *The Rooms of Heaven,* Knopf, 1999. A non-believer psychically seeks her dead lover. Beautifully written, a model for any average person seeking to communicate with the dead.

Beck, Martha. *Expecting Adam,* 1999. A woman professor at Harvard, highly skeptical, is bombarded with psychic events while awaiting the birth of a Down syndrome child.

Borgia, Anthony. *Life in the World Unseen,* M.A.P., Midway, Utah, 1993. A channeled description of life after death by a Christian clergyman who, after his death, dictated corrections to all he had written during his life.

Chopra, Deepak, M.D. *Quantum Healing*, Bantam, 1987. America's current most popular proponent of mind-body health. Chopra is an Indian-American physician trained in eastern ayurvedic medicine and western medicine.

Cott, Jonathan, *Search for Om Sety*, Warner Books, 1987. True story, with scholarly documentation and testimony of eminent Egyptologists, of a British woman, Dorothy Eady, who after a fall as a child was "changed" into an ancient Egyptian.

Cremo, Michael, and Richard L. Thompson. *Forbidden Archaeology*, Bhaktivedanta Books, 1998. A critical review of suppressed evidence related to human evolution on earth, and an argument for reinvestigation of outdated scientific paradigms.

Crichton, Michael. *Travels*, Ballantine Books, 1990. Physician and popular novelist (Jurassic Park, etc.) details his personal journey from rationality to spirituality.

Dossey, Larry, M.D. *Healing Words*, Harper Collins, 1993. A medical doctor investigates the possibility that conscious intent has helpful effects even at a distance, even if the sufferer does not know he is being prayed for.

_____*Meaning and Medicine*, Bantam, 1996. Carefully controlled studies by the Chief of Staff of Medical City Dallas Hospital prove that prayer hastens healing, that illness has meaning far beyond the conventional explanations of bacteria or viruses, and that mind, meaning, and illness are connected.

Doyle, A. Conan. *The Edge Of The Unknown*, Putnam, 1930. Classic investigation of paranormal events, concluding "That they still lived and still loved was the constant message from the beyond, accompanied by many material proofs."

Dunne, JW. *An Experiment With Time*, Faber and Faber, 1927. A classic that appears to prove the reality of seeing the future, thereby demolishing our concept of time.

Fowler, Raymond. *The Allagash Abductions*. Wildflower Press, 1993. One of the two most convincing abduction accounts.

Fuller, John G. *The Interrupted Journey*, Dell Books, 1966. The famous first, convincing, account of a couple abducted by aliens in 1963.

Green, Celia, and Charles McCreery. *Apparitions*, Oxford, 1975. Excellent documentation of English ghost stories, divided by type, by two university researchers.

Greene, Marilyn. *Finder*, Crown, 1988. Fascinating and impressive account of a combined intuitive/intellectual approach for finding lost persons.

Huxley, Aldous. *The Doors Of Perception, and Heaven And Hell*, Penguin, 1963. Famous essays on altered states of consciousness, discussing some drugs that have been among man's doorways to paranormal experiences.

Friends in High Places

James, William. *The Varieties Of Religious Experience,* Penguin, 1982. First published in 1902. Has among other discussions the classic one on types of mysticism.

Liverziano, Filippo. *Life, Death, And Consciousness,* Prism, 1991. Investigating these three things, he concludes that those who have visited the beyond universally experience difficulty in expressing the experience in human language, a sense of peace, an abandonment of the physical body, and autoscopic experiences.

Mack, John E., M.D. *Abduction,* Ballantine, 1994. This Harvard professor and psychiatrist has risked his reputation reporting on his clients who claim to be abductees by UFOs. Fascinating, terrifying, and sad accounts.

_____*Passport To The Cosmos,* Crown, 1999. This book studies the meaning of the alien abduction experience. "Crossover of the unseen world into the material world is a regular occurrence in indigenous cultures." Mack argues that something real is going on.

Mackenzie, Andrew. *Hauntings And Apparitions,* Granada Publishing, 1983. Report of carefully investigated hauntings by the British Society of Psychical Research.

_____*Adventures In Time,* Athlone, 1997. Reports by people who have found themselves suddenly in another time and place. Carefully researched, proof of Haldane's statement, "The world is not only queerer than anyone has imagined but queerer than anyone can imagine." MacKenzie states, "The task of the psychical researcher is, as a rule, beset by disappointments as case after case collapses for lack of supporting evidence...," and goes on to report some that do not collapse.

McMullen, George. *One White Crow,* Hampton Roads, 1994. An amazing account of intuitive archaeology with Canada's leading archaeologist Dr. J. Norman Emerson, who confirms the accuracy of McMullen's intuition time and time again regarding achaeological sites. McMullen was able to psychically view with great accuracy previous sites where archaeological remains were, and lead diggers specifically to important locations—not once, but over and over.

Monroe, Robert. *Journeys Out Of The Body,* Doubleday, 1971. Report of a remarkable man's unbidden out-of-body experiences, and his subsequent adventures while out of the body. His further books are also interesting.

Moody, Raymond, M.D. *Coming Back,* Bantam, 1991. This physician and psychiatrist is the foremost authority on near-death experiences by patients brought back from death by state-of-the-art technology. He held a post at the University of Virginia Hospital in Charlottesville for many years, and now lives and practices in Georgia.

_____*Life After Life,* Mockingbird Books, 1975. The first, and still classic, best-seller on near-death experiences.

Osis, Karlis, Ph.D, and Erlendur Haraldsson, Ph.D. *At The Hour Of Death,* Hastings House, 1997. Careful and thorough treatment of the near-death experience.

Rico, Gabriele Lusser. *Writing The Natural Way*, Tarcher, 1983. An effective method for opening creative channels for writing or problem-solving by a simple technique called clustering.

Ring, Kenneth, Ph.D. *Heading Toward Omega*, Morrow, 1989. A discussion of the meaning of the near-death experience.

Ritchie, George G. Jr., M.D., PhD. *Return From Tomorrow*, Chosen Books Publishing, 1978. A near-death experience in 1943 changed this highly-regarded psychiatrist's life forever. This story was the inspiration for Dr. Raymond Moody's work.

Rogo, D. Scott. *The Infinite Boundary*. Dodd, Mead & Company, 1987. Can modern mental illness be the result of spirit possession? Can spirits of the dead influence the living? A discussion of the possibility of spirit possession in modern madness.

Rohr, Richard. *Discovering The Enneagram*, Crossroad, 1992. An ancient and remarkable Sufi method of understanding human personality—both the self and others.

Russell, Peter. *From Science To God*. New World Library, Novato, CA, 2002, 2003. The famous author of *The Global Brain, White Hole in Time*, and The *TM Technique*, details his journey from being a "convinced atheist" to a convinced believer in God.

Sabom, Michael. *Recollections Of Death*, Harper and Row, 1982. A rational physician investigates the near-death experience.

Scott, Cyril, Editor. *The Boy Who Saw True*, C. W. Daniel Co., Ltd, Essex, England, 1953. A convincing Victorian diary (edited by Cyril Scott and in print ever since) by a psychic child who didn't understand that the rest of the world was not. I have no way to judge its truthfulness, but it's a wonderful book to read.

Sheldrake, Rupert. *Seven Experiments That Could Change The World*, Riverhead Books, 1995. How does your pet know you are coming home? Can people tell when they're being stared at from behind? How do termites build two towers that meet exactly in the middle? And more. An invitation to explore the unknown and create new science.

Shroder, Tom. *Old Souls*. Simon and Schuster, 1999. A skeptical journalist is made a believer as he follows Ian Stevenson on his investigations of children who remember past lives. (Includes a brief retelling of Joseph's story.)

Siegel, Bernie, M.D. *Love, Medicine, & Miracles*, Harper and Row, 1986. A classic about how to be pro-active in self-healing.

Snow, Robert. *Looking For Carroll Beckwith*, Daybreak Books, 1999. An astonishing document by a skeptical and hard-headed police captain who found a past life he had lived or somehow remembered, to his astonishment.

Sylvia, Claire. *A Change Of Heart*, Warner Books, 1997. A woman who receives a donor heart communicates with the previous owner of the heart. The book details other examples of this new phenomenon.

Friends in High Places

Stevenson, Ian, M.D. *Twentycases Suggestive Of Reincarnation*, University Press of Virginia, 1974. Stevenson is a physician, a psychiatrist, an excruciatingly painstaking researcher who has become the world authority on reincarnation. He held until his death an honored post at the University of Virginia in Charlottesville.

_____*Children Who Remember Previous Lives*, University Press of Virginia, 1987. The weight of evidence is strong in this book.

Vallee, Jacques. *Passport To Magonia*, Contemporary Books, 1969. An account by a world authority of 100 years of UFO sightings worldwide, and a persuasive argument that fairy tales, monster stories, elves and gnomes represent ancient human encounters with alien entities.

Wakefield, Dan. *Expect A Miracle*, Harper Collins, 1995. An account by a skeptical writer of the "miracles" that occur to ordinary people. Interesting, as it sensitizes us to the fact that extraordinary things occur often in the ordinary world.

Watson, Lyall. *The Secret Life Of Inanimate Objects*, Destiny Books, 1992. Thousands of documented anecdotes of the strange behavior of things. The weight of evidence is particularly strong.

Wickland, Carl. *Thirty Years Among The Dead*. An out-of-print book from about 1930 detailing a psychiatrist's effort to aid the mentally ill by using his wife as a channel. His conclusion: that mentally ill patients are suffering from soul-possession by people who are dead and unaware or resentful of having passed out of life.

Zaleski, Carol. *Otherworld Journeys*, Oxford, 1987. Historical examination of near-death and other out-of-body experiences over 500 years, by a Harvard professor.

Zukav, Gary. *The Seat Of The Soul*, Simon and Schuster, 1989. Premise: man is evolving from a five-sense animal to a multisense animal. "...just as there came a time when the use of candles became inappropriate because of the discovery of electricity," a Newtonian view of the world is no longer tenable in light of what mankind is learning from quantum physics.

And finally, touches of the so-called paranormal occur without apology in more and more modern books: Bill Bryson's *A Walk in the Woods*, and John Berendt's *Midnight in the Garden of Good and Evil* are two best-sellers that come to mind immediately. Sylvia Fraser's *The Fourth Monkey*, Walter Edmond's *Tales My Father Never Told*, Derek Tangye's *Somewhere a Cat is Waiting* Paul Broks' *Into the Silent Land*, and my own *When the Fighting is all Over*, and *All Time is Now*, all contain anecdotes by skeptical people who have experienced remarkable and (rationally) unexplainable events.

Katie Letcher Lyle

About the Author

Katie Letcher Lyle is the author of 20 books and many articles. Her short fiction has appeared in many magazines, including Viva, Shenandoah, and The Virginia Quarterly Review .A writer, teacher, folksinger, and speaker, she taught for twenty-five years at Southern Seminary College, has taught in the graduate Writing Program at Hollins U, and has been visiting professor at Washington and Lee U, Mary Baldwin College, and Randolph-Macon Woman's College. Since 1983 she has taught over 250 Elderhostels at several Virginia colleges, including Virginia folklore and folk life, History of the English language, Virginia history and pre-history, and creative writing. She holds the world record for three "My Turns" in Newsweek. She has been active in organizations that serve the handicapped, and serves currently on the Rockbridge Area Hospice Board, where she is also a volunteer. She has chapters in several books, including *Field Guide to the Chessie Nature Trail,* Rockbridge Area Conservation Council, 1988; *Uncommon Wealth,* The Nature Conservancy, 1999; *The American South,* Louisiana State University Press, 1980; and *I Thought My Father was God,* Henry Holt and Company, 2001. She lives in Lexington, Virginia, and has two grown children. All Books Available Through Any

Friends in High Places

Bookstore or Out-of-Print Book Search, or on Amazon. Google-search her by name, or visit katieletcherlyle.com

1. *Lyrics of Three Women* (Linden Press, 1964) Katie Letcher Lyle, Maude Rubin, May Miller.
2. *I Will Go Barefoot All Summer for You* (Lippincott, 1973; Dell, 1974) Novel. Newbery finalist.
3. *Fair Day, And Another Step Begun* (Lippincott, 1974; Dell, 1975) Novel. Newbery finalist.
4. *Footsteps* (I wrote four of sixteen half-hour PBS television programs for OEO in 1977.)
5. *The Golden Shores of Heaven* (Lippincott, 1976, Bantam, 1978) Novel.
6. *Dark But Full of Diamonds* (Coward McCann and Geoghegan, 1981; Bantam 1982) Novel (Made into TV movie, *My Father, My Rival*, aired on HBO over 100 times since May 1985. Won Bronze Medal in 1985 New York Film Festival.)
7. *Finders Weepers* (Coward McCann and Geoghegan, 1982; Scholastic, 1984) Novel.
8. *Scalded to Death By the Steam* (Algonquin Books of Chapel Hill, 1984; W. H. Allen Company, 1985) Historical nonfiction, sold over 100,000 copies. In thirteenth printing.
9. *The Man Who Wanted Seven Wives* (Algonquin Books of Chapel Hill, 1986) Historical non-fiction. (Second edition with additional material, Quarrier Books of Charleston, WV, 1999.)
10. *The Wild Berry Book: Romance, Recipes, Remedies* (NorthWord Press, 1994)
11. *The Foraging Gourmet* Nonfiction. (Lyons and Burford, 1997)
12. *When the Fighting is All Over:* a memoir (Longstreet, 1997) (Ingram Pick of the Season, 1997; short-listed by The Virginia Center for the Book for best non-fiction book in Va., 1998)

13. *Goodbye to Old Peking,* ed. with Roger Jeans (Ohio U Press, 1997). American United States Marine Corps letters to Virginia from China, 1936-1939
14. *Free Mel Greenburg* (a musical comedy) with Richard B. Sessoms. ©1996. New York preview November 1999. Professional productions, 2001, 2005, 2006, Greenbrier Valley Theater, 1998 and 2005; Firelands, Ohio, College Theater, 1998; Don't Tell Mama Cabaret Bar, NYC, 2000; Flushing Town Hall,Flushing, NY, 2000; Stonewall Jackson Theater, Covington, Va., 1998.
15. *My Dearest Angel: Lives and letters of Katie Paul Letcher and Greenlee Davidson Letcher,* 1895-1954. (Ohio U Press, 2002) Short-listed for Best Non-fiction book in Va, 2002)
16. *Complete Guide to Edible Wild Plants, Mushrooms, Fruits, and Nuts* (Lyons Press, 2004.) (Pequot Globe, 2010, second edition.)
17. *All Time is Now: Adventures with Jenny:* Memoir about handicapped daughter (Infinity Press, 2005) (Mariner, 2007 reprint)
18. *Archeology:* a novel --still seeking a publisher.
19. *My Neighbor's Ghosts.* Nonfiction (Mariner, 2007)
20. *Friends in High Places* (Barringer Publishing 2011)
21. *Hoping for Grace:* divorce poems, 2002-5. (Many published individually. In progress.)
22. *My Appalachia* (in progress.)

CPSIA information can be obtained at www.ICGtesting.com
Printed in the USA
BVOW08s2127190115

383946BV00007B/52/P

9 780983 308881